Bonded to the Abuser

Bonded to the Abuser

*How Victims Make Sense of
Childhood Abuse*

Amy J. L. Baker and Mel Schneiderman

ROWMAN & LITTLEFIELD
Lanham • Boulder • New York • London

Published by Rowman & Littlefield
A wholly owned subsidary of The Rowman & Littlefield Publishing Group, Inc.
4501 Forbes Boulevard, Suite 200, Lanham, Maryland 20706
www.rowman.com

Unit A, Whitacre Mews, 26-34 Stannary Street, London SE11 4AB

British Library Cataloguing in Publication Information Available

Library of Congress Cataloging-in-Publication Data

Baker, Amy J. L.
Bonded to the abuser : how victims make sense of childhood abuse / Amy J. L. Baker and Mel
Schneiderman.
pages cm.
Includes bibliographical references and index.
ISBN 978-1-4422-3690-5 (cloth : alk. paper) -- ISBN 978-1-4422-3688-2 (electronic)
1. Adult child abuse victims--Case studies. 2. Adult child abuse victims--Rehabilitation. I. Schneiderman, Mel. II. Title.
RC569.5.C55B25 2015
362.76--dc23
2014042698

∞™ The paper used in this publication meets the minimum requirements of American
National Standard for Information Sciences Permanence of Paper for Printed Library
Materials, ANSI/NISO Z39.48-1992.

Printed in the United States of America

We dedicate this book to the authors of the memoirs for their courage and grace in putting into such beautiful words the pain and sorrow of childhood abuse and neglect. We also dedicate the book to victims of childhood maltreatment everywhere—may they each write their own story in their own way.

Contents

Acknowledgments

We gratefully acknowledge our appreciation for the team at Rowman & Littlefield for overseeing this project and providing helpful feedback along the way. We also acknowledge the very able assistance of our interns Courtney Dimick, Rachel Middleton, and Deidra O'Loughlin.

Introduction

Stories make us more alive, more human, more courageous, more loving.
—Madeleine L'Engle

This is a book about child abuse and neglect. It is also a book about stories and the power of stories—especially memoirs of childhood maltreatment—to help both the author and the reader to understand and heal from the trauma of maltreatment.

According to the Federal Child Abuse Prevention and Treatment Act, child abuse and neglect are defined as "any recent act or failure to act on the part of a parent or caretaker which results in death, serious physical or emotional harm, sexual abuse or exploitation"; or "an act or failure to act which presents an imminent risk of serious harm."[1] It then falls to the states to determine how child abuse and neglect will be defined within their jurisdiction. In none of the definitions is every specific maltreating act delineated. There are simply too many to catalog. Child maltreatment is also far too common. In fact, child maltreatment is considered a public health crisis. According to the U.S. Department of Health and Human Services,[2] over three million child maltreatment reports were made in 2012, about two-thirds of which were deemed worthy of an investigation based on the initial screening. Roughly 17 percent of the investigations were "founded," meaning that child protection services decided that the child was in fact a victim of maltreatment. About one-fourth of the child victims were under two years of age, and parents were the perpetrators in 80 percent of the cases. Among all founded cases, about 70 percent were for neglect/medical neglect, about 20 percent were for physical abuse, and fewer than 10 percent were for sexual abuse and psychological maltreatment. These numbers reflect the fact that certain types of maltreatment are more common and that some are easier to

1

substantiate than others, and also that certain types are more likely to be deemed serious enough to warrant action. For example, psychological mal-treatment has been found to be quite harmful, but few children are removed from their homes due to psychological maltreatment alone.[3]

Not only is childhood maltreatment widespread, but it is also associated with serious long-term consequences for the child's emotional and physical well-being, and by extension, for society as well. Child maltreatment, for example, is considered one of the ten primary adverse childhood experiences (ACE) studied longitudinally. The ACE study, a joint project of the Centers for Disease Control and Prevention and Kaiser Permanente in San Diego, is the largest ongoing examination of the association between childhood mal-treatment and adult health and well-being, with data collected from more than seventeen thousand participants. Findings demonstrate that certain early childhood experiences (such as maltreatment) function as risk factors for a variety of medical illnesses and poor health later in life. ACE researchers have found that the greater number of adverse childhood events, the greater the likelihood of physical and emotional impairment in the individual. For example, those with four of the ten adverse childhood experiences were twelve times more likely to attempt suicide than individuals with no ACEs.[4]

The ACE studies do not identify the impact of specific types of maltreat-ment, which reflects a trend in the field away from "abuse-specific" concep-tualizations to an understanding that all types of child maltreatment may represent a trauma for the child. The concept of trauma—originally defined as a "wound, injury, or shock" to the psychological integrity of an individu-al,[5] has been expanded to include a pattern of failures in the caregiving environment, referred to as "complex trauma"[6] because of the ongoing na-ture of the maltreatment, which is now conceptualized as "developmental trauma"[7] in recognition of the unique impact of trauma experienced early in life. Developmental trauma, however, is not a diagnosis recognized by the American Psychiatric Association in its *Diagnostic and Statistical Manual*, despite being advocated for by some trauma specialists in the field.

The trauma-informed perspective emerged in recognition of the fact that many children experience more than one type of maltreatment and that there is not necessarily a one-to-one correspondence between the type of maltreat-ment and negative outcome.[8] Accordingly, all victims of childhood maltreat-ment are likely to be impacted in various domains of functioning such as cognition (distorted ideas about the value of the self and the safety of the world), emotion regulation (hyperarousal and/or numbing), physical health (stress level, illness), and social relationships (social withdrawal and/or ag-gression). What appears to matter in terms of impact of maltreatment on a child is how the child perceives and constructs meaning of the maltreatment experience.

PURPOSE AND STRUCTURE OF THIS BOOK

The purpose of this book is to examine that meaning-making process, to hear the voices of adult survivors of different types of maltreatment experiences so that adult survivors, their friends and family, as well as mental health professionals and the lay public can have a firsthand perspective in a way that might not otherwise be possible. We want to honor the voices and the stories of adult victims of childhood maltreatment in order to deepen the reader's empathy for and understanding of the experience. Because people still think of themselves as being victims of one type of maltreatment or another (i.e., "I am a survivor of sexual abuse"), we chose to organize the stories we read and analyzed into broad categories based on the primary type of maltreatment experienced. Thus, we were able to explore the themes and issues that appear to accompany different types of maltreatment.

Five types of maltreatment are the focus of this book: physical abuse, sexual abuse, emotional abuse, emotional neglect, and physical neglect. All available memoirs written and published by adults about their firsthand experiences with at least one of these forms of childhood maltreatment by a parent were read and reviewed (although admittedly we may have missed some). For each of the five types we begin with a set of three in-depth narratives, which is followed by an analysis of the major themes that arose from all of the narratives read about that specific type of maltreatment. For example, nine narratives about physical abuse were read, three of which are summarized in chapter 1, all of which are analyzed in chapter 2. Likewise, six narratives about sexual abuse were read, three of which are summarized in chapter 3, all of which are reviewed in chapter 4.

The most common themes are discussed in each chapter, although others were present as well. The themes presented in each chapter are for the most part documented in the academic and clinical literature but are described here from the victim's point of view, thus adding a new dimension to the knowledge base. It is important to bear in mind that the memoirs were written by abuse survivors when they were adults. Therefore, it is not always possible to determine at what point in the life of the victim certain experiences first occurred, as the stories are told with the benefit of both psychological distance and hindsight.

Each story is a poignant account of a young child being raised by a parent who is unable or unwilling to provide him with consistent, loving attention; by a caregiver who puts his or her own needs above those of the child. The child then is placed in an untenable position of seeking comfort and nurturance from the very person who is the source of his pain. The lack of early appropriate parental care (i.e., not enough or the wrong kind of caregiving) is experienced as a "stressful environmental event"[9] that disrupts the child's physical and emotional well-being both in the short and long term. These negative effects reverberate throughout the lives and the stories of the authors as they struggle to make meaning of the incomprehensible. In discussing maltreatment, we are talking about legal definitions of abuse/neglect and not poor or bad parenting (although bad parenting can impact the child in similar ways that abuse and neglect do). [10]

One of the themes that appears to be relevant for several types of maltreatment is the experience of being invisible, of having the maltreatment be a secret and the consequent feelings of shame. Writing their memoirs can then be viewed as an act of becoming visible, of being seen and understood. In the same light, the act of reading the memoirs becomes part of the healing process for both the author and the reader, who engage in a joint storytelling venture of spinning straw into gold, pain into healing. This book was written with the desire and intention of continuing that healing process for victims of childhood maltreatment and those who care about and want to understand them.

Chapter One

Stories of Physical Abuse

In this chapter, three of the memoirs about physical abuse are summarized. In the first memoir, *Unloved*,[1] Peter Roche tells of his harrowing upbringing in South London in the early 1970s.

UNLOVED BY PETER ROCHE

The ninth child of poor parents, Peter had a harder childhood than most. By the time he was just a toddler, he was roaming the neighborhood unsupervised, unloved. "There was nothing out of the ordinary about wandering the streets to me. I was more comfortable in the alleys and walkways around the flats where I lived than I ever was in my home . . . I was pushed out of the flat every day for hours on end by my mother and left to go where I wanted."[2] In his home, boys were expected to raise themselves and stay out of the way. "It was out of nappies and out the door . . . It was as if I was a dog being let out to pee."[3] It seems, however, that a dog might have gotten better treatment. There were few, if any, moments in which Peter received positive regard from either parent. "Love and affection were not emotions I could ever have associated with either my mother or father."[4] His father had cruel nicknames for all of the boys, such as Deafy for the son with hearing difficulties, Dunce for the academically challenged son, and Dwarf for Peter, the smallest son in the family. When they weren't ignoring or taunting him, his parents beat him, hard. "She wasn't the kind of mother who only used the flat of her hand. It was fists, feet, everything,"[5] often using hard objects to make her point when her hands and feet were not sufficient to discharge her rage. Peter's father was worse, especially when he was drunk or angry, which was often. "'Crying, are you? I'll give you something to cry about' he roared, and he gripped my hair tighter and laid into me. . . . With each lash of the belt, my body

5

swung and juddered as if I was a rag doll being flung about by a rabid dog."[6] The household was violent, chaotic, every man for himself, which left Peter at a distinct disadvantage being the youngest boy. "Violence of this kind seemed normal to me. It was what parents were for, what they did to you."[7] Hypervigilant to his father's moods and presence, Peter anticipated violence by the sound of his footsteps, "the sound of hate and cruelty on legs."[8] For Peter, attacks were regular, relentless, and usually unprovoked.

The abject poverty they lived in coupled with his parents' inability or unwillingness to emotionally nurture any of their children resulted in Peter (and his siblings) being in a constant state of hunger, cold, exhaustion, and fear. They were the kind of kids who became targets in the neighborhood and at school. Wearing dirty and smelly clothes, jittery and untrusting, Peter was perpetually bullied and humiliated at school. "With skinhead haircuts and Charlie Chaplin clothes, we might as well have had the word 'victim' painted on our backs."[9]

For Peter, every day was filled with impossible choices between "one horrible thing and another that was just as horrible."[10] For example, if he took off his pants at night before bed he avoided wetting them but they might be appropriated by an older brother, leaving him nothing to wear. If he participated in gym at school he would have to take his pants off and reveal that he had no underwear, or he could refuse to participate and be scolded and labeled as difficult by his teachers. If he went to school he would be bullied, but if he didn't go his parents would beat him for risking inviting the truant officer to the door. He would be sent by his mother to fetch something from his father with the threat of a beating for not obeying while fearing that his father would beat him for annoying him. Every day involved navigating land mines and making difficult if not impossible choices. In response, Peter learned to turn off his feelings and emotions and endure the beatings and humiliations. "The whipping continued until every part of me was numb. I guess I stopped being able to process any emotion, any feeling. Whatever kicked in, I was grateful."[11]

Although the family was marked by cruelty, hunger, and lack of nurturance, Peter bore the brunt of it as the youngest. The home environment fostered aggression and cruelty among the brothers who competed for scarce resources such as clothes, food, and rags to use as blankets at night. Peter was the runt and was therefore the object of scorn among his siblings as well as his parents. He often found himself wondering what he did to deserve his parents' treatment of him. He shamefully covered the bruises and marks of his abuse, not just to protect his parents, but also to hide the proof that he had been bad. The marks were evidence of the "shame and punishment" he had brought on himself. "If I thought about it at all, I believed it was no more than I deserved and that it was my fault I brought this kind of punishment on myself. I often thought that if only I was not so bad, I would get affection and sympathy. I was beginning to ask myself why I was always in trouble."[12]

Despite the abuse, Peter still longed for love and acceptance from his parents. "There had never been a moment when being good got any reward, but I still tried hard to do what they wanted. Especially for my father. I wanted to be loved, but most of all even from a young age, I wanted to make my dad happy."[13] As a young boy Peter would stand by the window waiting for his father to return home. "Stupidly, I looked forward to seeing him. He was my dad and I wanted him to be pleased to see me. The hopefulness that very young children have hadn't quite been bashed out of me. I don't know what I expected but I would run to meet him when he came in."[14] Sadly, Peter's father did not return the affection his hopeful son had for him. "Every single time he'd walk in and lash out at me for being too near the door. 'Get out of the way you little bastard.' He'd yell, hitting me and often sending me sprawling."[15]

Not surprisingly given the lack of parental supervision and affection, Peter became a troubled teenager and ended up in detention for a period of time. As a teen he found a mattress but no love in his mother's home, and he set off—rudderless—to make his way in the world. Riddled with anxiety, highly distrustful of other people, and undereducated, he struggled to find a place for himself and to find a way to leave his past behind. Part of that process for him involved tracking down a social worker who had come to his home when he was a baby. He found a picture of himself hanging on her wall. "I try to think of that as proof that although she could do nothing for me, she really did care and didn't forget me."[16] Knowing that this woman had his picture for thirty-seven years helped him to feel seen and held by a caring adult in a way that his parents had never been able to. Peter had a rocky start into adulthood, marrying a woman and having three children with her while they were both young and immature, but eventually he developed into a loving parent and worked through his early traumas. "Like all children who have known themselves to be unwanted and unloved, even now I find myself wishing that I could talk to my own parents and get them to talk to me, explain it all,"[17] but then he reminds himself that there is no explanation that could ever justify their behavior.

THAT MEAN OLD YESTERDAY BY STACEY PATTON

In this next memoir, *That Mean Old Yesterday*,[18] Stacey Patton shares her experience growing up in New Jersey in the 1980s, having been first raised by a kind but elderly foster parent and then adopted by a strict, domineering woman, Myrtle, and her passive husband, Mr. G.

As a young child, Stacey's elderly foster mother shocked her one day with the news that she wasn't Stacey's "real mother." She sadly informed her that she was "gittin' a new mommy and daddy"[19] who would be able to provide a better life for her. What is a better life, Stacey wondered, having nothing to compare her life to. Too soon Stacey learned that her old life was the better one. Her adoptive parents, Myrtle and Mr. G, behaved kindly toward her in the car with the social worker but turned out to be anything but, especially Myrtle. As she stood on the porch of her new home, Stacey observed Myrtle take all of her possessions and toss them in the trash. "You need to leave your foster home, that garbage on the curb, and your foster mother behind. Forget about it all. Thank God for what you have now."[20] The next morning Stacey tried to reclaim her possessions, only to be slapped across the face by Myrtle. "The back of her hand stopped the rest of the words from coming out my mouth. When I snapped back to my senses, the mean look on her face along with her hand moving away from my mouth confirmed for me that she had slapped me."[21] And then came the rules Stacey was to follow, including "Don't get out of bed in the morning until she tells me, don't let her have to tell me to get out of bed twice, don't question her, don't come downstairs in my pajamas, don't roll my eyes, no whining, and don't ever talk about my foster mother or foster home again."[22] Myrtle assured Stacey that "a good butt whupping"[23] would follow any infraction. And the beatings came. "That day would begin a pattern of searching for her lurking around every door and shadowy corner in every room. Although the initial slap shocked and hurt me, I could never be prepared for what followed: beatings for any small infraction. I had to make sure I knew where her weapons were at all times. Of all of them, those pretty latte-colored adorned hands became the worst weapons."[24] That was Stacey's introduction to her new life, one in which Myrtle was the master and she the slave. Her father's role was ambiguous. "Sometimes I wondered if G was really a grown man or just a big boy because Myrtle relegated him to the same child status that I had held in our house. . . . Myrtle called us both 'triflin' backward niggas.'"[25] Through the force of her personality, Myrtle loomed large for Stacey. "I believed there was no person or force bigger, stronger, or meaner that Myrtle Jenkins."[26]

Getting whipped was nothing new for Stacey. In fact, most black children she knew were beaten, "whenever, wherever, and with whatever. This was part of our identity as black children. I didn't think there was another way except for the way that white parents raised their kids. But, of course, that way was white."[27] And so, for a while Stacey believed that Myrtle beat her because she loved her. "She had to yell at me. She had to call me names. She had to whip me. She had to put scars on me to toughen my skin. It was all for my own good. She had to prepare me for a life and a world that cared nothing about me because I am black and female."[28] Myrtle would explain that the white man didn't care about her and would not want her to have a good life, only Myrtle cared about her; that was why she beat her, to help her be a good girl. "Resisting Myrtle was not something that crossed my mind. I believed her treatment of me was normal. . . . Everyone called it love and God's will. Pain and whippings were for my own good and would make me stronger."[29]

Stacey tried hard to please Myrtle, especially by studying diligently in her religious lessons. She had to memorize extensive sections of the Bible and be prepared at a moment's notice to perform pop quizzes. "When the drill was over, Myrtle never gave me an approving look or complimented me. She just sat there reeking of misery."[30] Stacey recalled, "On a good night, when I hadn't gotten hit with the Bible or yelled at, I felt proud that I had recited perfectly. I lived for Myrtle's approval, for her to say, 'Well done.' The smile would always fade from my lips when she said, 'You can do even better next time.' I just wanted her to like me."[31] Then Myrtle would command Stacey to kiss her good night, a terrifying proposition.

Approaching Myrtle was treacherous and frightening. "I couldn't let her see me shuddering. I didn't want to get slapped for acting like an imbecile, so I inched closer to her face. I searched for a pleasant aroma but smelled nothing but anger and bitterness mixed with Lifebouy soap. I wished for warmth but instead felt cold and tension. I hoped for a positive vibe to settle my fear. Instead I grew more terrified as I heard her take a deep swallow."[32] A chilly reception awaited Stacey in response to her kiss.

The fear and loathing Stacey lived with night and day kept her anxious, afraid, and tense. Everything was a potential battle, including food. "I wasn't hungry. But I couldn't tell Myrtle. I never had the choice to eat or not. I ate when I wasn't hungry. I ate when she was hungry. And I most certainly never dared tell Myrtle when I was hungry because she made me feel guilty about the most primal feeling, 'I'm hungry too' she'd say sarcastically and then continue on doing her own thing."[33] Although Stacey did not experience hunger for food, she did have a hunger for love and nurturance. "My yearning for love, affection, attention, trust, and safety wouldn't let me breathe right or sleep peacefully. The kind of hunger I had made me so wary at the dinner table that I couldn't digest my food right. Everything went right through me. Fear kept me skinny. Fear kept me hungry."[34]

Although there were times when Stacey would imagine a life away from Myrtle and G, she was nonetheless shocked and terrified when Myrtle threw her out of the house, at age ten. She stripped Stacey of all the clothes that Myrtle had bought for her (basically everything) and screamed, "Get out of my house, you little heathen."[35] Stacey begged for Myrtle to take her back, "Please Mommy, don't make me go."[36] Standing on the freezing porch in nothing but underwear, Stacey feared being sent to a place worse than this, a dreaded place for "bad girls," and she was flooded with relief when the front door slowly opened and she was allowed back in the house.

The beatings continued. "I often touched my scars, even named them. I dabbed my blood with cotton balls, sucked it off my lips and cuts. I lifted my bandages and checked the scabbing process. Sometimes I tuned out some of Myrtle's lies about me being stupid and useless, and sometimes I believed her when she said I was unattractive and unwanted. I felt a deep deep gash in my soul that I couldn't touch or adequately describe."[37]

To her surprise, on a family visit Stacey learned that Myrtle was in fact capable of being loving and affectionate, toward someone else. Myrtle's goddaughter Tera was the child Myrtle really wanted. "She was a fat child and extremely attractive . . . she got every bit of affection and attention that I craved. I watched Myrtle as she kissed the little girl, stroked her hair, hugged her, and told her how beautiful she was while I sat on the couch, quiet and envious."[38]

It was not just her home life that was painful and demoralizing. School, too, held its terrors. Her classmates had their way of reminding her that she was different, didn't belong. "At least I ain't adopted" was the familiar retort, the trump card that ended any volley of insults. Also isolating for Stacey was the fact that she was not allowed to socialize or involve herself in after-school activities and events. She didn't play sports, talk on the phone with friends, go to the movies, attend birthday parties, or join clubs or teams. Myrtle exercised complete control over her. Other children didn't see her scars and her fears, and she didn't see how other parents raised their children. Sometimes at bedtime Stacey would wish for a sibling, a compatriot, someone to plot her escape with, someone to cuddle with at night, someone to bear witness to her pain. Instead, alone, she hugged a pillow, pretending it was a nurturing mother, warm and safe.

One day Stacey overheard Myrtle telling her own mother that she needed to have a hysterectomy. Her voice quivered and broke when she shared the news with her mother, losing the fight to hold back the tears. Brimming with sympathy, Stacey felt a desire to love Myrtle. Then she overheard Myrtle tell G that she could never have children of her own, confusing and then confirming for Stacey that her being adopted mattered to Myrtle. "There I was again reminded of my inauthenticity."[39] That still didn't stop Stacey from wanting to make herself perfect for Myrtle, to finally capture Myrtle's love and approval. "I wanted to lighten my complexion to high yellow. I hated my brown skin because I believed she hated it. If I looked more like her then she wouldn't beat me so much. . . . If only I could roll myself as small as I could and push myself between Myrtle's legs, and snuggle back into pregnancy, that floating bubble under her belly button."[40]

Absent a rebirth as the biological child of Myrtle, Stacey continued to be on the receiving end of her mother's scorn and anger. A new element was introduced into their relationship when Stacey began to develop physically. Myrtle would subject Stacey to physical inspections and then pronounce her inadequate. "You ain't got nothing," she said, turning her head. "You ain't got no titties."[41] Then Stacey was ordered to drop her panties so that Myrtle could inspect between Stacey's legs, fascinated with her body. She would then triumphantly declare, "I got the biggest titties in the house. And don't you ever forget it!"[42]

By age twelve, Stacey was highly attuned to the moods and activities of Myrtle. "I hated being scared and walking on egg shells around Myrtle all the time. Listening to the night air to see if her waking breath turned into sleepy snores so I could finally shut my eyes in peace."[43] She was tired of being reminded by Myrtle that no one wanted her, loved her, took care of her, that she had nothing, that she would be nowhere without Myrtle and G. Stacey did in fact love G, despite his inability or unwillingness to stand up for her. At least he was able to show her some love and affection. One day he made her ice cream and said that she would be able to taste his love in it. "It was the smartest and warmest and most meaningful thing I ever heard G say to me. . . . He was making his love visible for me. It was moments like this when I felt I mattered, like I was somebody's little girl."[44]

Myrtle, too, had moments of affection, especially after the beatings when she was feeling contrite. Myrtle would tend to Stacey's pain with cocoa butter, peroxide, ice cream. Stacey soaked up the affection, "like an abused puppy that never learned from the smacks and kicks."[45] Myrtle would be contrite, apologize, buy her treats, promise she'd change. "Her promises seemed to convince me that things would be different. Her good nature would last a few days before a slap in the face or a whipping crashed my hopes."[46] But like a slave, Stacey stayed out of fear, dependency, and a warped desire for love and approval from her master. "I defined the world and myself for so long through her eyes. My life, my sense of self, depended on her approval."[47] Stacey lived for Myrtle's approval and yet dreamed of running away and finding a way to unlock her self-esteem from the cruel judgments of Myrtle.

As a teenager, Stacey finally found a way out of Myrtle's home when she revealed to adults at her school that she was being abused at home. After thirty days in a shelter, she was transferred to a group home where she began to forge an identity for herself separate from Myrtle. At first she heard Myrtle's voice in her head reminding her that no one will love her, no one will be there for her. "I felt like I didn't belong anywhere to anybody."[48] Drawing on her pride and courage deep inside herself, she found her way into a prestigious high school and reconnected with some of her biological family. Along the way, she developed a fragile but budding sense of who she was as a woman, a black person in America, an adoptee, an abuse victim.

DRIVING WITH DEAD PEOPLE BY MONICA HOLLOWAY

In the third physical abuse memoir, *Driving with Dead People*,[49] about growing up with an eccentric family in small-town Ohio, Monica Holloway reveals the impact on herself and her family of her violent and unpredictable father.

"As much as I hated him, I wanted him to love me,"[50] thought eight-year-old Monica about her violent and erratic father. He was fascinated with death and trauma, which explained why he always kept a movie camera on hand to capture disasters, natural and otherwise. He would pile the kids in the car and head straight into a storm or tornado, driving wildly while filming the event for later viewing as home movies. "'You're gonna love this,' Dad said, flipping on his movie camera as he drove. He glanced at our pale faces in the rearview mirror and smiled. He knew we were petrified, which made him positively giddy."[51] In addition to frightening the children, he also routinely humiliated and beat them. A typical day for young Monica was when her father became angry at her for no apparent reason. "He was mad at me for something; and I had no idea what it was. I turned and walked in another direction, feeling his eyes on me the whole way. The world wasn't safe today."[52] She tried to stay out of his way, but "Dad started yelling for me to get my ass in the house. They were saying the prayer and filling plates. I jumped and ran for it. If Dad had to call you twice, you got spanked. Inside, I grabbed a plastic orange-and-white-flecked plate, a fork, knife, and spoon, and a white paper napkin, and bowed my hand for the prayer. . . . My nose itched and when I went to scratch it, Dad slapped the back of my head, causing my plate and silverware to clatter to the floor. 'Clumsy ass,' he hissed. Everyone looked over for a second and then bowed their heads again."[53]

It wasn't just Monica who was on the receiving end of his cruelty and anger. Coming home from work one day in a foul mood, her father watched her brother playing basketball with friends. He was fuming. "Dad was standing in the kitchen staring out the window at Jamie and his friends, who had resumed their game. They were laughing. . . . Dad was grinding his teeth, his jaw moving slightly back and forth. He was thinking something mean."[54] Eventually he grabbed a sledgehammer and smashed the basketball hoop. "He beat that basketball hoop to the ground. He pounded it until the metal rim was twisted beyond recognition and the backboard lay in splinters."[55] Her sisters as well were not spared his fury. "My oldest sister Joanne had her head split open on the corner of the coffee table when we were little. Dad deliberately stuck his foot out and tripped her."[56] Particularly distressing for Monica was observing her father warmly greeting neighbors at a church gathering, acting the part of the "great guy," realizing that he was in fact capable of civility and warmth. "He was kind to everyone but us, happy to help his neighbors. . . . At home he didn't bother to step around me if I was playing Barbies on the floor, choosing instead to kick them across the room. I watched his friends enjoying his company and wondered why Dad hated us."[57]

No wonder young Monica developed a morbid fascination with death and dying, imagining her own funeral and wondering if her death at least would evoke an expression of love from her father. "It wasn't as if I wanted to be dead; it was just that I was miserable and felt in the way most of the time. There was something wrong with me."[58] She befriended the daughter of the town undertaker and was provided an opportunity to roam around the mortuary, lay quietly inside display coffins, and see the embalming room up close. Daydreaming about death, however, did not make her life any easier.

Brutal, cruel, and unpredictable, her father terrorized Monica and her three siblings, and her mother did little to protect them. Monica's mother was unavailable, preoccupied, and emotionally distant. Moments of kindness and affection were few and far between. When Monica broke her hip, her mother reluctantly took her to the doctor, who told her that she would need to stay in the hospital to heal. "We were in shock and at the same time, I felt close to my mom. She loved me, I knew she loved me, but she hardly ever showed it physically. It wasn't much, her hand on top of mine, but it was a big show of affection from her."[59] More often, however, she was inattentive or cruel. For example, while taking a drive together, Monica innocently asked about her birth, prompting her mother to casually inform her that she was unwanted. "We'd only planned on having three children but, suddenly, there you were. . . . When I realized I was pregnant again, I cried for six weeks straight. I waited as long as possible to put on maternity clothes. . . ." She looked over and saw my eyebrows pressed together. "We didn't know it was you. . . . We didn't call you Monica until you were two years old. We just kept saying, 'Get Baby' or 'Baby needs a bottle.'"[60] Her mother had little to give to her children or her new baby.

Monica and her siblings routinely witnessed their father being cruel as well as violent toward their mother, for example, by choking her until she passed out. Less violent but equally painful moments included the time when Monica's father relented to take the family on vacation to see the mother's beloved Smoky Mountains. Speeding through the scenery, he appeared to take pleasure in spoiling the experience. Monica's mother asked him to slow down so she could enjoy the mountains. "I can see fine," he responded while driving seventy miles per hour in a forty miles-per-hour zone. "I couldn't ever remember seeing Mom cry or Dad so happy."[61] Meanwhile, Monica and her sister Becky were in the backseat, "trying not to piss anyone off. If we had to pee or eat, we still wouldn't say anything. We wished we were invisible. Only we weren't. We were trapped in the car between the hatred my parents felt for each other, and probably for us."[62] Moments later her father drove into oncoming traffic and a car plowed into Monica's door. "Dad jumped out and ran to the lady in the Honda, not bothering to look back to see if Becky and I were okay. I was right when I decided in fourth grade that Dad wouldn't love me at my death scene. It was actually worse: He wouldn't even notice."[63] Monica felt some relief when the accident occurred, as now there was a physical manifestation of the pain and misery the family was in. The family vacation was over.

One summer, Monica's mother decided to finally escape the marriage, involving her children in her secret plan. Monica was employed as the lookout while her mother pilfered small amounts of money from her father's hidden stash. Monica didn't object to helping because when her father and mother fought, he would withhold money for food. Fearing going hungry, she had a stake in her mother being able to take care of the family. Around the same time, however, Monica's mother returned to college, and she became so absorbed in her budding independence and intellectual pursuits that she abdicated virtually all parenting responsibility. Monica and her siblings assumed greater autonomy and independence, supporting and encouraging their mother, happy for her that she was coming into her own. Eventually her mother rented an apartment closer to college and stayed there several nights a week, leaving the children to take care of themselves. "I was glad Mom was happier but I was seeing less of her."[64] One day Monica's mother giddily announced that she was in love with someone else and was leaving the family. Monica, despite knowing what her father put her mother through, felt badly for him. "Amazing as it sounds, I don't think he saw it coming. I'd never seen him speechless or without the impulse to hit or destroy something, but that's what happened. He just sat there looking smaller than I'd ever seen him. I actually felt sorry for him for being sucker-punched."[65]

When Monica's mother introduced her to her new boyfriend, she expected Monica to be happy for her and made it clear that she was going to be with Jim whether Monica liked him or not, declaring, "I spent my entire life taking care of kids, and now it's my turn. You can damn well deal with it."[66] Monica and her siblings were on their own. "I am off her radar."[67] Alone and uncared for, Monica began to lose weight. "My dad moved out and hates us. Mom moved out and doesn't care about anything except her new boyfriend. I don't have enough money to live on, and there isn't enough food in the refrigerator to put a meal together."[68] She desperately craved having a caring adult to lean on, cry to, but didn't trust anyone and was too embarrassed to ask for help, as if she had brought the situation upon herself.

There were times when Monica had no money for food or school supplies. Asking her mother resulted in a casual dismissal, and asking her father resulted in absolute refusal. He would gleefully consult the divorce agreement and decline to pay for anything that wasn't explicitly identified as his responsibility. Monica was furious and hurt and began stealing money from the cash register at her father's hardware store so that she could have the money to enter a debate contest. When she grabbed the money she felt its value diminished because it was not given with love. "Meaningless. Everything was meaningless. Especially me."[69]

Shortly after that incident Monica experienced a kidney infection. "I was in the most pain of my life but happy to finally be in someone's care. I was relieved. Relieved there was something wrong. Relieved I finally felt as rotten physically as I did emotionally."[70] Unfortunately, her mother was impatient and annoyed at being inconvenienced when Monica called to tell her she was in the hospital. "That night Mom hated me for needing her."[71]

Monica eventually developed a rapprochement of sorts with her father, finding ways to connect with him as a young adult. That changed, however, when her older sister Joanne disclosed that she had been molested by their father throughout her childhood. This disclosure set off a chain reaction in Monica, causing her to wonder whether her father had also molested her. She tried to piece together her earliest memories, raising questions such as why did her mother smear them with Vasoline on their genitals at night before bed? Why did their mother insist on their not wearing underpants in bed? Why did her mother warn Monica's older sister to stay away from their father because he looked at her funny? Searching for answers, Monica visited her father, hoping to resolve her concerns, but in the end she could not bring herself to confront him. She enjoyed the relationship they worked out. "I was relieved to be out the door. The problem was the next hour, the next day, the next year, the next years. As screwy as it was, I did not know who I was without him. It was death without the body."[72] Monica pulled back from the relationship without directly confronting him. Months went by. She waited in vain for him to call. In the end, Monica came to her own understanding of what her father did to her and to her family, and what she could do for herself.

Chapter Two

Making Meaning of Physical Abuse

As noted in the introduction, while definitions of maltreatment vary across states, the common link across definitions of physical abuse is a parental act or failure to act that causes harm or risk of serious harm to a child. In most definitions, how the injury/harm was inflicted is not relevant so long as the injury/harm was sustained by the child through a parental act. Unfortunately, there are countless ways that parents can inflict bodily harm to a child. Also unfortunate is that some parents would want to do so. As the stories in chapter 2 reveal, there are some children who are subjected to physical abuse over the course of their childhoods. These children suffer not only from the physical pain of the abuse but also from the psychic pain of knowing that it is their parent who is inflicting the pain upon them. Despite their parents' harsh, demeaning, and oftentimes brutal treatment, the children clung to those parents with a desperate desire for their love and acceptance.

It is well documented in the literature that physically abused children maintain strong emotional ties to their abusive parent.[1,2] Blizzard and Bluhm describe it as "one of the greatest conundrums for therapists treating abuse survivors."[3] In response to the paradox, several explanatory mechanisms have been invoked. For example, physically abused children have been compared to hostages in that both are under the control of a hostile, dominating individual in an environment in which they feel isolated, powerless, and helpless.[4] Both experience high levels of anxiety due to chronic unpredictable and incomprehensible threats. Both have difficulty fathoming the context within which they find themselves and lack the internal and external resources to manage the situation and their experience of it. Many physically abused children, especially younger ones—like hostages—are isolated and dependent on the person creating the fear and anxiety. The person who inflicts the pain is the same person who can relieve them of it. This phenomenon has also been referred to as traumatic bonding in which individuals will develop strong emotional attachments to abusive individuals under the conditions of a power imbalance and periods of positive experiences alternating with the abusive episodes.[5] Stockholm Syndrome has also been invoked to explain why abused children maintain strong allegiances to their abusers.[6]

While helpful, these analogies are applicable only up to a point. There is at least one significant difference between a physically abused child and individuals experiencing these other scenarios (other than the fact that the abuse victim is always a child while a hostage could be any age), which is that the physically abused child has a *preexisting* caregiving relationship with the person who is abusing him while the hostage generally does not. It is this single factor that is probably the most significant for understanding how children respond to and are affected by physical abuse when it is inflicted by a caregiver. Thus, attachment theory represents the most compelling explanation for why abused children maintain relationships with their abusive parents. The utility of attachment theory is explored (see "Abuser as Attachment Figure" below).

In this chapter, we present the ways in which being physically abused by a parent is experienced by the abuse victim, focusing specifically on the relationship-specific aspects of the experience as reflected in the nine memoirs listed in table 2.1. Three of the stories were described in detail in the previous chapter, and all were reviewed for the identification of themes.

THE SEARCH FOR A REASON

The physically abused children described in these stories wanted to understand first and foremost why their parents were behaving the way they were. In the memoirs, the children were searching for a meaning and a purpose for the abuse. In this way they could make sense of it in the context of their existing relationship. If there was no meaning, then there was no way to control, understand, modify, or have an influence on their experiences. If there was no reason, then they were at the mercy of the abusive parent, with no hope of changing their behavior for the better. On the other hand, if there *was* a meaning or a purpose to the abuse, then the child had hope of doing something different that could possibly alter the course of their parent's behavior.[7]

If there was a reason then there was a road map to preventing future abuse and improving the relationship. Most often the goal was not to escape the relationship, but rather to improve and repair it. The first time that Myrtle hit Stacey in *That Mean Old Yesterday*, it came as a total surprise mostly because she couldn't readily identify an immediate explanation for her mother's behavior. "I felt like the world was coming to an end. Why did she hit

Table 2.1. Memoirs of Physical Abuse

Title of Book/Author	Abusive Parent	Abuse Victim/ Author	Secondary Abuse by Parent	Role of other Parent	Major Dysfunction in Family
Unloved	Father	Peter Roche	Emotional abuse	The mother is also abusive	Alcoholic father and familial poverty
Driving with Dead People	Father	Monica Holloway	Emotional abuse	The mother failed to protect her	None
That Mean Old Yesterday	Adoptive mother	Stacey Patton	Sexual abuse and emotional abuse	Her father failed to protect her	None
Change Me into Zeus's Daughter	Father	Barbara Robinette Moss	Emotional abuse	Her mother failed to protect her	Alcoholic father and familial poverty
Storkbites	Mother	Marie Etienne	Emotional abuse and emotional neglect	Her father failed to protect her	Mentally ill mother
A Hole in the World	Stepmother	Richard Rhodes	Emotional abuse	His father failed to protect him	Familial poverty
Mommie Dearest	Mother	Christine Crawford	Emotional abuse and emotional neglect	There was no other parent	Narcissistic mother
A Child Called "It"	Mother	David Pelzer	Emotional abuse and physical neglect	His failed to protect him	None
Cruel Harvest	Father	Fran Elizabeth Grubb	Emotional abuse and sexual abuse	Her mother was unable to protect her because the father kidnapped her	Alcoholic father and familial poverty

me?"[8] Stacey assumed, based on her experience with her foster mother and the initial kindness shown by Myrtle, that Myrtle would have a reason for doing what she did. It did not occur to Stacey that her new mother would hit her for no apparent reason. There must be a reason, otherwise the world did not make sense. Even later when Stacey left for boarding school, she experienced bewilderment about why her parents were willing to thrust her out into the world. Even though she did not want them to have control over her any more, she still wanted to know why they behaved as they had and why they were unwilling to change their behavior to accommodate her. Monica in *Driving with Dead People* wanted to know why her father was able to be friendly and kind toward neighbors but unforgiving with his own children. This discrepancy demonstrated to her that he could control his temper and could bestow acceptance on others and that he was therefore making a choice to beat and humiliate her. "I watched his friends enjoying his company and wondered why Dad hated us so much."[9] David Pelzer, author of the best-selling memoir *A Child Called "It"* about his brutal upbringing, also wondered why his mother—capable of providing loving nurturance toward his siblings—was sadistic and cruel toward him. "I stood before her dumbstruck. I didn't know what to do or say. All I could think was '*why?*' I couldn't understand why she treated me the way she did."[10] In *Change Me into Zeus's Daughter*, Barbara Robinette Moss tells of her impoverished life in the South being raised by an alcoholic and abusive father. She described how on the day of her father's funeral, she and her siblings stood around the coffin wondering if their father meant to hurt them or whether it was just the alcohol. "He didn't remember hardly anything he did when he was drunk."[11]

For some, the search for an explanation did not end when the abusive parent died. In fact, it is likely that the impetus to write a memoir represented an attempt to make sense of the abuse by creating a narrative that explained and created meaning—even when the meaning was not apparent to them as children. This is probably why most of the stories (with the exception of *A Child Called "It"*) included a brief biographical sketch of the abusive parent's childhood in an attempt to understand the psychology of the abuser. Typically, it was revealed that the abusive parent had been subjected to the same extreme hardships and cruelties that they later inflicted on their children. This humanized the tormentors and helped explain why they acted as they did; so the victims constructed meaning and no longer had to blame themselves. The storytelling also, of course, allowed the adult victims to create their own interpretations of events and to humanize their child selves, something that was denied them by their parents. In *A Hole in the World*, Richard Rhodes, the Pulitzer prize–winning author who was raised in the South by his father and abusive stepmother, writes that he "woke up one morning convinced that it was time at last to write this book—to tell my orphan's story, as all orphans do; to introduce you to my child. There was a child went forth. He'd hidden in the basement all those years. The war's over and my child has come up from the basement to blink in the sunlight."[12] By bringing to light (revealing) and shining a light on (focusing) their stories of physical abuse, the authors created coherent narratives out of what was most likely experienced at the time as unfathomable pain and suffering.

What is clear in these stories is that the pain from the physical abuse was magnified by the knowledge that they were being hurt by a parent. They were unable to understand the reason for their parent's behavior toward them, reasons that were generally sadistic and irrational. Raised as a migrant farmworker by an alcoholic father, Fran Grubb wrote in *Cruel Harvest* that she tasted the blood in her mouth when her father slapped her and screamed inside, "Why . . . What did I do?"[13] The assumption was that she must have done *something* to cause her father to behave this way. Like the terrorized children described by renowned clinical psychologist Alice Miller in *The Truth Will Set You Free*, Fran tried to "interpret the mysterious actions of the parents as good and loving."[14] Miller argues that children—because they are dependent on their parents—cannot tolerate thinking of them as irrational or hurtful and therefore must search for explanations for even the cruelest and most outlandish behavior. Children, Miller argues, are forbidden "to see their parent's cruelty for what it is,"[15] and therefore they must come up with an acceptable explanation that protects their idea of their parents as good. The explanation they often come up with is that they, the children, deserved the abuse. This belief is reinforced when the parent was observed behaving kindly and respectfully toward others (be it siblings or other adults), demonstrating that they were able to control their actions. That is, they were not uniformly and consistently cruel. They were cruel only in relation to them. From there it was only a short leap to conclude that they must be the problem. They were, of course, encouraged to come to this conclusion by the abusive parents who were only too eager to deflect blame for their abuse onto their child victim.[16]

SELF-BLAME AND SHAME

The most accessible answer to the question "why does my parent hurt me?" appears to be "because I deserve it." This conclusion represents an example of the cognitive distortions that physically abused children engage in.[17] Thus, not surprisingly, self-blame was a prevalent theme throughout the stories. Peter wrote, "I believed it was no more than I deserved and that it was my fault I brought this kind of punishment on myself. I often thought that if only I wasn't so bad, I would get affection and sympathy. I was beginning to ask myself why I was always in trouble."[18] He described covering his bruises and scars with bits of rags so others wouldn't see "the evidence of the shame and punishment I'd brought on myself."[19] Not only was he protecting his parents, who had impressed upon him the dire consequences for bringing authorities into the home, but also he was protecting himself from others knowing about what he perceived to be his unworthiness. Stacey experienced the shame of her beatings, "that was my reality,"[20] and Fran believed that "up to this point I felt everything my daddy did was my fault."[21] Monica, as well, felt too ashamed to ask for help after her parents moved out of the home, leaving her and her siblings to fend for themselves. She felt that the behavior of her parents was a reflection of her lack of worth rather than of their irresponsibility and selfishness. After his mother stabbed him, David told his teachers that "mother punishes me because I am bad. I wish they would leave me alone. I feel so slimy inside."[22] Later, David looked to his father for protection and reassurance, and "knew right then that I was a 'bad boy.'"[23] He felt ashamed. "I came to believe that everything that happened to me or around me was my fault because I had let it go on for so long."[24]

The self-blame absolved the parent and created some sense of meaning and order, albeit confusing/inconsistent and illogical. It was better to blame themselves than their parents. Otherwise, they would experience intolerable anxiety that their parents could not take care of them and were bad, thus thrusting themselves into an insecure world without parents to protect and love them. Moreover, many of the abuse victims were explicitly told that they were being beaten because they were bad. In *Mommie Dearest*, Christina Crawford's mother, famed movie star Joan Crawford, told her, "You love it don't you. . . . you just love to make me hit you,"[25] as if she invoked and desired the abuse. By assuming blame they were merely adopting the parent's version of reality. As noted above, the self-blame allowed them to maintain the hope of improving the relationship as well as helped them avoid antagonizing the abuser who would not be pleased with the child considering them abusive. Self-blame also allowed them to create a relatively safe world for themselves by not rejecting their parent or having to realize that their parent was unable or unwilling to protect and take care of them. Of course, by writing their stories they were taking responsibility for their own narrative in which it was clear that they did not deserve the abuse. They were correcting their misperceptions and freeing themselves from the responsibility of their abusive past. In that way, the memoirs functioned to help the victims assume power over their abuse experiences by relieving them of the power and influence the abuser held over them. By portraying their parent as a sick, sadistic, imperfect, and a seriously flawed human being, the author became empowered by correcting maladaptive thinking and ridding themselves of the blame and shame that they experienced as children. Now as adults, their past abuse cannot hurt them as much. They have attributed the responsibility of the abuse to their parent/abuser, not to themselves.

That the children internalized the blame for the abuse is consistent with several prominent theories of human development. For example, in object relations theory, Fairbairn argues that children would rather "assume the burden of badness" upon themselves because "it is better to be a sinner in a world ruled by god than a saint in a world ruled by the devil."[26] If the child is to blame then the world makes sense, even if it requires the child to think poorly of himself. Similarly, in trauma theory, John Briere describes the dilemma abused children confront when striving to maintain the vision of the abuser as a good and rational parent.[27] He argues that in order for the child to preserve that idea, the child must conclude that he deserved the abuse meted out to him by that parent. Anything else is too frightening and overwhelming to even consider.

ABUSER AS ATTACHMENT FIGURE

Attachment theory speaks to the child's strong emotional attachment to the caregiver, even when the caregiver is abusive.[28] Harry Harlow first demonstrated the importance of this attachment bond in his research with monkeys removed from their mothers early in life.[29] Through a series of studies that most likely could not be conducted today because of concerns about animal cruelty, Harlow empirically demonstrated the importance of an attachment figure to a primate's physical, social, and emotional well-being. When given a choice, baby monkeys readily preferred a wire "mother" covered in comforting cloth over a wire "mother" offering food, especially when the baby was anxious or afraid. Harlow also demonstrated that baby monkeys will cling to and seek comfort from a mechanical mother, even abusive ones. Harlow devised abusive mechanical "mothers" who blew cold air in their baby's face and poked them with sharp spikes. According to Rosenblum and Harlow, "an aversive stimulus can also augment responsiveness to the surrogate even though the aversive stimulus is coincident spatially and temporally with surrogate contact."[30] In plain English, the babies clung to their abusive mothers, seeking comfort from their attachment figures despite the fact that the mother was the source of their fear and pain.

Humans, as well, are biologically inclined to form an attachment relationship with a caretaking adult, regardless of the quality of the caretaking.[31] According to attachment researcher Mary Salter Ainsworth and colleagues, the *quality* of caregiving affects the *quality* of the attachment, not the strength of the bond.[32] They found that early experiences with the caregiver gradually result in the formation of a set of thoughts, memories, beliefs, expectations, emotions, and behaviors about the self and about the self in relation to others. This "internal working model" allows the child to draw on specific experiences to form a general understanding of the self.[33] It is through the early relationship with the caregiver that the child comes to understand his own worthiness and lovability and the extent to which the world will be responsive to his needs.[34] Thus, children are meaning-making creatures, primed to make inferences about their self-worth based on how their parents interact with them. Parental rejection is interpreted within that framework. Self-blame in the context of an abusive relationship with a caregiver is an understandable, albeit unfortunate, result of this process.

LIKE AN ANIMAL

Ethological studies of primates were instrumental in the development of attachment theory.[35] The authors of the memoirs of physical abuse felt our animal roots quite viscerally. In fact, common throughout the stories were comparisons with animals. Peter described being put out of the house like a cat; Stacey referred to herself as an abused puppy that "never learned from the smacks and kicks,"[36] as well as a "grungy old sick cat that wanted to crawl up into some dark hole and sleep my life away,"[37] and as a fish "swimming around fish much bigger than me. Big fish eat little fish, and the ocean don't care."[38] There were numerous animal references in *A Child Called "It."* For example, "When I *was* given the luxury of food, I ate like a homeless dog; grunting like an animal at mother's commands."[39] "It was bad enough waiting like a dog out in the backyard on the rocks while they enjoyed dinner."[40] "I submerged my head, keeping my nostrils barely above the surface of the water. I felt like an alligator in a swamp,"[41] and "forcing myself not to cry in front of them, I crawled, completely dressed, under the table, and covered myself with the newspapers, like a rat in a cage."[42] Christina felt like "one of those little yellow chickens in the story from her childhood. I felt like she was squeezing the life out of me too."[43] Barbara compared herself to a "cowering dog,"[44] and Marie Etienne in *Storkbites* described herself as a "mutt with a tail-wagging desire to please."[45]

These metaphors contain several potential meanings. The first is the recognition that animals (especially domesticated animals such as cats and dogs) are generally at the mercy of their owners. They do not eat unless they are fed. They do not go outside unless someone opens the door for them. They do not receive love and attention unless their owner chooses to bestow it upon them. They have virtually no control over their physical environment. This is generally true of abused and neglect infants and young children as well. By contrast, with "good enough" parenting a baby learns that for the most part, a responsive, contingent, loving parent is available to respond to his needs in a predictable manner.[46] A baby cries out in hunger and the mother feeds him. The baby has a dirty diaper and the mother provides a clean one to relieve the unpleasant sensations. Through experience with a responsive parent, the baby learns that his actions induce the caregiver to relieve suffering, not perfectly, not all of the time, but most of the time. In contrast, physically abusive parents teach their child that his actions do *not* consistently invoke relief but often result in greater suffering. In this way, the physically abused child feels helpless in the face of his needs, as helpless as an animal that does not have a say in the care that he receives.

A second aspect of the animal metaphor is that the animals described are generally undesirable. The cats and dogs are described as old, dirty, and grungy. They are unappealing if not disgusting. That was how the children experienced themselves in the eyes of their abusive parents, and that was the self-image the children internalized within themselves. They were disgusting, dirty, and less than human. They did not have a right to have a say in their upbringing. Their needs and feelings did not consistently matter. They were not equal members of the family. They were of another species, separate and apart from the rest of the family. In this way the adult survivors saw themselves as subhuman and therefore not deserving of the normal love and nurturance inherent in most parent-child relationships.

A third aspect of the animal metaphor is that pets are generally innocent and undeserving of abuse and cruelty. Thus, the stories were suggesting that the abuse meted out to them was as senseless and wrong as beating an innocent animal. This was felt on one level, while on another—as noted above—the children believed that the abuse was in fact deserved.

A final element of the metaphor is that animals—especially dogs—are eager to please and quite forgiving of their masters—even abusive masters. In this way the abuse victims were portraying themselves as perpetually willing to forgive their abusive parents and desiring most of all their parent's love and acceptance, just as a dog will eagerly greet its master and seek affection and approval despite having received nothing but coldness and rejection in the past.

DESIRE FOR LOVE AND APPROVAL FROM THE ABUSER

Like the animals they felt themselves to be, many of the physically abused children craved the love and approval of their parents. All Peter ever wanted was to feel the love of his father. "And yet in spite of it all, for a good year after we moved house I liked to stand and watch at the front window after school to see if I could spot Dad coming home from work or the pub. Stupidly, I looked forward to seeing him. He was my dad and I wanted him to be pleased to see me."[47] Sadly, Peter received nothing but the back of his father's hand (or worse) when his father arrived home, unable to acknowledge or recognize that an eager young boy was hoping for a bit of kindness from his father.

Stacey, too, yearned for love and approval from her disapproving and harsh mother. "For all my early adolescence, I wanted to make myself perfect for Myrtle. I wanted to lighten my complexion to high yellow. I hated my brown skin because I believed she hated it. If I looked more like her, then she wouldn't beat me so much. I had the same wish as Nicodemus in the Bible: to be born again."[48] Stacey saw herself through her mother's eyes and found herself—as Myrtle did—lacking. She believed that if she looked more like Myrtle and were born from her then Myrtle would have opened her heart to her. Rather than see Myrtle's cruelty as a function of her inability to love, a flaw in her mother's makeup, she believed that *she* was the one lacking. She was too dark, or not a biological child, or too sassy, or too different. Stacey's desire for Myrtle's love and approval was a constant yearning throughout her childhood, a psychic yearning she experienced at a visceral level throughout her body. "My mind and the middle part of my body where all my feelings came from experienced relentless cravings. My yearnings for love, affection, attention, trust, and safety wouldn't let me breathe right or sleep peacefully."[49] Even after she escaped home by winning a scholarship to a private high school and Myrtle and Mr. G cut her off in response, she still craved their approval. She would call them on the phone just to hear their voice.

Similarly, David never lost the hope of winning his mother's love and would imagine finding a lost object of his mother's and "marching upstairs with my prize and Mom greeting me with hugs and kisses. My fantasy included the family living happily ever after,"[50] and later when he was left at an aunt's house while the family went on vacation he imagined running away to join them. "For some strange reason I wanted to be with my mother."[51] Christina repeatedly strived to please her mother, trying in vain to win her approval. "I yearned for the fondness and love only my mother could give me."[52] She would have given anything to please her. "I tried every way I knew to show her how much I loved her and how I hoped she'd be proud of me."[53] When Christina eventually reconciled with her mother, she experienced it as a "miracle in my life. . . . It was complete acceptance."[54] Even as a young adult, her mother's approval meant everything to her. Thus, when her mother came to see Christina perform in a play, she was crushed and heartbroken when her mother brushed her off and failed to commend her. When her mother was attentive, Christina felt "thrilled and delighted."[55] During good times she felt that a burden had been lifted. "I knew she loved and cared about me."[56] Nonetheless, she took no chances. "I called, I visited their apartment, I wrote them when they were away. I remembered all the holidays and birthdays and anniversaries. I tried to be what Mother wanted me to be."[57] So eager to please was she that she allowed herself to be humiliated by her mother on more than one occasion. She experienced her mother as the legendary Lorelei, pulling her back with her enchanting song, something she was unable to resist despite the danger she posed. "I felt the pull and lure of her song even when it was silent. It was the memory of her wishes, the need for her love, the sound of the lullaby buried deep in our past. I tried very hard to guide the ship of my life by myself, but I could feel it shudder and wander off course. Then some echo, some fragment of that song of the Lorelei would reach me and I felt the ship tugging me in that direction."[58] The feeling of obligation and longing tied Christina to her abusive mother long into adulthood.

Richard, too, was consumed with a desire for a different kind of parenting. "Against all evidence, as if wishing might ever make it so, part of me still longed for a strong father and a loving mother, a happy home."[59] It wasn't until many years later that he realized how "hazardous it is to long for an ideal father when your real father fails you."[60] Barbara, too, was so desperate for a loving parent that she convinced herself that a tortuous contraption her father constructed to force her to write with her right hand was actually fun. "I was so delighted to be smiled upon by him that I worked even harder, perfecting each letter, each number. With each writing lesson, I hoped for my father to smile at me, to shake me gently as he untied the cord on my left hand as if he were tickling me, to swat my bottom just as I moved out of his reach."[61] She fantasized about a benign and physically playful exchange in contrast to the punitive treatment she experienced in reality. Once when her father returned from a trip, she clamored for his attention. "Dad! Dad! I shout, jumping up and down. Dad, look at my cheeks. Look at my ringworm scars! Remember, I got them before you left."[62] She was starving for her father's love. She recounted a time when her father handed her the tab from the top of a beer can, saying, "'Don't say I never gave you nothing.' I laughed and muttered a sarcastic 'Thanks.' But I had a cigar box full of his beer tabs, some he had given me, saying exactly what he had just said, and some I had taken from the station-wagon ashtray. They were precious somehow, because he had held them between his fingers; so I saved them."[63] Marie as well recalled times when she yearned for her mother's love. "That day by the pool, Momma hugged me tighter than I can ever remember. I wanted her to hold me forever."[64] Physical affection was usually reserved for the family pets that Marie observed enviously when her mother doted on them. Like many children, Marie made her mother handmade gifts, crafted with love, which she presented to her mother with hope and pride. Unfortunately, her mother casually glanced at them and set them aside. Marie felt humiliated, as if she—and not just the gift—were being discarded. She was learning that she did not matter, that it was not possible to win her mother's love and approval.

While the stories revealed primarily negative parent-child relationships, this was not uniformly so. Some of the authors reported moments of connection and love with their abusive parent. For example, Christina experienced periods of closeness with and acceptance by her mother. In that way she was like many physically abused children who receive inconsistent—as opposed to consistently lacking—love and approval from an abusive parent. In fact, it may be that it is the inconsistency that fuels the efforts of physically abused children to seek the love and approval of their parents. Thus, while some of the descriptions presented in the memoirs create the impression that the children received nothing but abuse, this is not uniformly so for victims of physical abuse. Even in abusive homes, there can be a continuum of parental love and affection with some physically abusive parents able to also demonstrate warmth and affection.[65]

PARENT AS OMNISCIENT

When Marie's mother discarded her daughter's handmade gifts, she was defining the gift as garbage, as unworthy, and by extension Marie felt herself to be unworthy as well. Young children see themselves through their parents' eyes. If a parent looks lovingly at a child the child experiences himself as worthy of love and lovable. For young children, parents explain and define the world around them and their place in that world. Through the parent-child relationship children co-construct their sense of self and the world. For children who are physically abused by a parent, the reality that is created for them is that they are unlovable and deserving of pain, suffering, and rejection.[66]

For young children, their parents are God or at least godlike, all knowing, all powerful, ever present. Like God, parents create their children, name them, and provide them with an environment within which to live. The adult survivors remember the power that their parents had over them—their bodies, their minds, and their souls. Peter wrote, "I knew this feeling well. It came every time I had a beating like this, when it had got so bad that I had given up begging him to stop, and I knew myself to be completely helpless, utterly powerless."[67] Stacey referred to her mother as "my master, and I obeyed her without questioning."[68] Monica experienced her father as being able to read her mind and "always watching me,"[69] while Richard described his stepmother as his "commandant" able to control the pain in his body over time and space. Christina was totally devoted to her mother, and before the abusive rages began her mother was like a god to her. "The sun rose and set on my beloved Mommie dearest. Her laughter was the music of my life, and the sound of her heart beating as she held me close to her made me feel safe and quiet."[70] Barbara described herself as a mere object, a plaything, for her father. "My father believed he was the master of his fate. He did exactly what he wanted to do, and by manipulation or force, made those around him do what he wanted them to do. He inflicted pain recreationally, both physical and emotional. It was his hobby, his pastime. We marched before him like tin ducks in a shooting gallery, to be shot through the heads and hearts, only to pop up again and go around once more."[71] These children did not experience themselves as having agency in their lives, the ability to control their environment and to protect themselves from both the physical abuse and the unrelenting tension they experienced on a daily basis.

OBEDIENCE

As expected from their all-powerful, unpredictable, hurtful parents, the abused children were as obedient as possible.[72] After beating her, Stacey's mother extracted proclamations of love. As she dabbed Stacey's wounds that she had inflicted with soothing salves (she gave pain and she took pain away), Stacey professed her love for Myrtle. Monica jumped and "ran for it" when her father called her into the house. "If Dad had to call you twice, you got spanked,"[73] and she kept quiet despite having to go to the bathroom and being hungry. She was powerless in the face of her father's anger. Fran "never dreamed that a father could kidnap his own children. It had never occurred to me to run away or call the police. He was our dad, and we were his property."[74] Christina dutifully referred to a total stranger as "Daddy" to please her mother and be the polite and obedient girl she was expected to be. Likewise, even though she didn't enjoy sleeping in her mother's bed she would do so at her mother's request, unable to imagine doing anything but what was expected of her. She would prefer to stay awake all night trying not to wiggle, which would incur her mother's anger, than decline her mother's request. She felt she had no choice but to obey. Even when her mother made mystifying requests such as fetching a chain saw in the middle of the night, Christina did what she was told. Marie also was obedient regardless of the cost to herself. At one point she developed a painful urinary tract infection. "I knew I was dying. For weeks my urethra had burned. I felt a constant pressure on my bladder. Yet when I went to the bathroom, nothing came out. Momma would pace the white-tiled floor. 'Are you finished yet?' She'd glance at me, blowing smoke from her cigarette. Even if I failed to produce a drop and my stomach still burned, I nodded like a coward."[75] She learned obedience at an early age when her mother taught her how to pull down her own panties in preparation for a beating. "Without waiting to be told, I pulled down my underwear and lifted my gown. My panties fell to the floor as Momma swung me around."[76] She was taught to stand in place and take the abuse, no matter how painful, no matter how undeserving. "I thought about the dreams I had where I was paralyzed with fear. I couldn't remember a time when I ever tried to pull away from Momma. I always stood perfectly still. Obedient. Frightened. Hoping it would end soon."[77] We think it is important to mention that—in contrast to the authors of the memoirs—some abused and neglected children, including physically abused children, develop opposition defiant disorders. Their anger drives them to disobey and act out against others. As a matter of fact, some children are physically abused due to their "acting out" or even in response to normal independent/autonomy behaviors as a way for abusive parents to assert their power or because they are helpless to control their children in any other way but physical punishment.

EMPATHY FOR THE ABUSIVE PARENT

The abused children—despite being treated cruelly by their parents—still were capable of feeling empathy and concern for them. The parents in these memoirs—like most parents—were not all bad. Even if they inflicted pain on their children, they also provided them with some love and nurturance. In return the children cared about that parent and wanted that parent to be happy. That desire might stem in part from self-preservation. If the parent were happier perhaps he or she would be less likely to be abusive. But it appears from the stories that their concern for their abuser went beyond self-interest and was based instead on genuine love for the parent. Peter wrote, "There had never been a moment when being good got any reward, but I still tried hard to do what they wanted. Especially for my father. I wanted to be loved, but most of all, even from a young age, I wanted to make my dad happy."[78] When Stacey observed Myrtle crying from her own loss and sadness, Stacey felt her heart "balled up in the middle of my chest. Seeing her tears broke something inside me. As they came rolling down her face, fast and furious, I not only saw but I felt her pain. Forget about me. How could I be so selfish? I wanted to know where her pain was coming from. Who hurt her?"[79] Fran expressed empathy for her mother—despite her mother's inability or unwillingness to protect her from her abusive father. "I hid my feelings and forced a smile on my face. I didn't want Mama to be sad or know how upset I was."[80] Monica felt badly for her father when he learned that his marriage was over, despite years of his humiliating and painful abuse of her. "He just sat there looking smaller than I'd ever seen him. I actually felt sorry for him for being sucker-punched."[81] David's mother beat him bloody and stabbed him during an altercation. Yet David was certain that the stabbing was accidental, and in his weakened state he tried to reassure his mother that he forgave her and knew that she hadn't intended to harm him. Christina's empathy and forgiveness for her mother was evident throughout *Mommie Dearest*, reflected, for example, in an incident when her mother confided in her about her doubts and sadness. "She told me how poor she'd been and how lonely as a child. How hard it had been for her. She talked for a long time, and I tried with all my might to understand what she was saying to me. But some things I couldn't understand. I was only about seven and I just didn't know what she was talking about. So I held her hand with all my strength and concentrated on her face. I never took my eyes off her for an instant. I was trying so hard to understand, to help her. She started to cry."[82] As an adult Christina was empathic toward her mother and wanted to ease what she perceived to be her suffering. She went out of her way to send thoughtful and elaborate gifts to her despite having been banished and ignored by her for years. When she was finally accepted back into her mother's life she described the pleasure of giving her gifts. "I couldn't have been happier than I was watching her open all her presents just like a kid on Christmas morning."[83] Christina's story began with the death of her mother. She stood over her mother's dead body, thinking, "I just want to tell you that I love you . . . that I forgive you."[84] Barbara enjoyed driving her abusive father around to bars and was happy to do so because she understood that he needed her company. She was able to see things from *his* perspective—that he was lonely and fearful—despite his having been unable to generally do that for her. Likewise, when Marie's mother was in the mental hospital, Marie "lay in bed wondering if Momma was lonely and scared. Images of her . . . haunted my dreams."[85]

BEING INVISIBLE

Invisibility was a feeling described by most of the authors. In some cases the invisibility represented a wish and in others it was a fear. For Peter being invisible was a wish as it held the promise of escaping the pain that resulted from being noticed. To be seen by a parent in that family was to become a victim. Thus, invisibility was a cloak of protection. "We had all developed our own ways of surviving in this family, and mine was to be as invisible as I possibly could."[86] For Monica, invisibility was a wish so that she would have no needs. "If we had to pee or eat, we still wouldn't say anything. We wished we were invisible. Only we weren't . . . We couldn't do anything but ride it out."[87] David wished to become invisible, a nothing, so as to escape his mother's control of him; he wanted "to dissolve and be gone forever."[88] Christina learned how to endure her mother's rages "as quietly and unobtrusively as humanly possible."[89] For these children being invisible meant flying under the radar of the abusive parent as a way to avoid additional pain and suffering.

Invisibility was also written about—not as a wish for a protective barrier—but as an annihilation of the self, a denial of the needs and humanity of the child. Stacey, for example, felt that her true self was invisible to her parents. "I had become a shell. I denied what I felt. I hated without showing it. I knew how to weep without tears."[90] Stacey longed to be truly seen and accepted by her mother. In the absence of that basic acceptance, she felt invisible. She wrote about wanting to become the Thanksgiving turkey at the center of the table because only then could she imagine herself being the object of desire by her parents. Being an only child involved another kind of invisibility for Stacey, the lack of a witness to her pain. Without someone to acknowledge her beatings, she felt that the pain did not really exist. Richard wrote of another kind of relationship to invisibility, the experience of shrinking in response to his stepmother's overpowering abuse. "For two years our stepmother funneled us into smaller and smaller spaces of physical and mental confinement—less food, less room, less nurture, less hope—in order to swell her own. In time, under her vicious regimen, we might have come to occupy no space at all."[91] Invisibility was being imposed on him as a suffocating denial of his very being. Barbara felt invisible when her mother was preoccupied comforting her favorite child and soothing her abusive husband rather than tending to Barbara's needs. When Barbara became seriously ill, her mother "went blindly through the days, pretending I wasn't sick. She became irritated if I vomited or collapsed dizzily into a chair. Both of them looked through me as if I weren't there at all."[92] For Barbara, invisibility was not a shield so much as it was a barrier between her and her mother's love. Marie, too, struggled with the fear of not being seen by her mother. "I don't think she noticed how I ran through the door every day at three o'clock and headed straight for the bathroom. . . . She never said anything. Just gave me a quick hello and a blank-faced kiss."[93] Marie was unhappy. She was suffering and she wanted her mother to notice her, but she didn't. To her mother Marie was invisible.

HYPERVIGILANCE

While the children felt or wished to be invisible, the abusive parent loomed large in their psyches. The children were keenly attuned to the moods, desires, and habits of their parents in an attempt to be able to predict and perhaps avoid future abuse. Hypervigilance was probably a result of the continual activation of their fight-or-flight system in their bodies due to the chronic and unpredictable abuse. They were in a constant state of "stress response" activated by the possibility of danger. When they perceived an event as potentially dangerous—such as proximity to a parent who had a history of inflicting pain—their brains signaled the hypothalamus to release cortisol, which in turn triggered the release of adrenaline into their bloodstream. As a result, they went on high alert, with heightened and focused attention to the environmental cues that signal danger. As psychologist and journalist Daniel Goleman explains, "anxiety narrows attention,"[94] an evolutionarily adaptive response to avoiding infrequent but life-threatening dangers (such as an approaching lion). Hypervigilance is less helpful when the source of the fear is regularly present—such as with physical child abuse—as it overloads the body with stress and preoccupies the child's attention with monitoring the location and mood of the abusive parent.

Heightened attention was certainly evident in the stories, with the authors being keenly tuned into the abuser. For Peter it was listening to the sight and sound of his father's footsteps. "I learned to watch the way he walked through the door. He was always ready to give us a hiding, but if he was pissed it was certain he wouldn't need to find an excuse. He had a heavy, flat-footed way of walking that made him move around quite slowly, but if he stepped up the pace and started walking fast, I knew he was looking for a victim. He could march at the double even with a night's beer inside him, and the sound of those thumping footsteps coming swiftly, one after the other, was the sound of hate and cruelty on legs. It was the most terrifying noise I knew."[95] Peter described himself as a soldier, "on constant sentry duty, only there was never a leave, not so much as a moment when I could let my guard down."[96] Stacey wrote about walking on eggshells around Myrtle. "Listening to the night air to see if her waking breath turned into sleepy snores so I could finally shut my eyes in peace."[97] As long as Myrtle was awake, Stacey remained on high alert, her ears straining to discern the variations in her mother's breathing so she could determine whether she was at immediate risk. By age ten Stacey was exhausted from not being able to let her guard down. "That day would begin a pattern of searching for her lurking around every door and shadowy corner in every room."[98] No part of the house, no time of day felt safe for her. Monica was attuned to the muscles in her father's face, as they signaled the kind of mood he was in. "Dad was grinding his teeth, his jaw moving slightly back and forth. He was thinking something mean."[99] Barbara was attuned to her father's body. "From the backseat I could see his body stiffen, feel the scorn creep into his posture."[100] For David it was the clothing his mother wore that revealed her state of mind. "After a while I could determine what kind of day I was going to have by the way she dressed. I would breathe a sigh of relief whenever I saw Mom come out of her room in a nice dress with her face made up. On these days she always came out with a smile."[101] Christina and Marie both wrote of a pervasive sense of anxiety and dread. When Marie's mother was in a mental hospital and unable to beat her in the middle of the night, Marie was relieved. "No one came into my room at night. I could sleep. I no longer had to be so vigilant."[102] Christina wrote, "The household was in a permanent state of agitation and I was continually worried about whether I'd make a mistake or say something wrong. It was exhausting to be there."[103] It must have been exhausting because when adrenaline soars through the body it can provide the much-needed energy for a short and intense sprint to avoid immediate danger. Afterward, however, it can result in a feeling of being emotionally and physically depleted. To be on high alert all of the time is more than the body is prepared to handle without some negative consequences to well-being and functioning.

Adding to the stress was the unpredictable nature of the abuse. Despite their vigilance, it was never possible to completely predict what would set off the parent. According to Peter, "These attacks were systematic, automatic, and they were relentless. The trouble was there was never any logic to these punishments. I was told I asked for it, and yet most of the time I didn't know what I had done wrong."[104] His father would sometimes beat him for answering a question while other times he would beat him for not answering. There was simply no predicting. Likewise, both Christina and Marie were awakened in the middle of the night by raging mothers furious over what appeared to be unknown and/or minor infractions. Nothing made sense to them; the rules were constantly changing. The kind of hypervigilance described in these stories is also likely to generalize to other relationships later in life, which can create additional stress and complications for victims of physical abuse.[105]

FEAR OF ABANDONMENT

Many of the authors wrote of being afraid, not just of the physical pain but also of being abandoned. This fear was instilled in them through small doses of being cast out (a form of emotional abuse). Peter's mother kicked him out of the house every day, starting at the age of three, to wander around the neighborhood on his own for hours at a time. Stacey recalled a time when her mother unlocked the door, opened it, and pushed Stacey out. Terrified, Stacey begged to be let back in, both to the house and to the heart of her mother. "'Please, Mommy, don't make me go,' I cried . . . I was more terrified of being alone in the big, cold world, with nothing and no one."[106] Barbara's father tried the same tact. "'Let's see how long you two boneheads can make it on your own.' Dad shoved David and me into the cool night and slammed the front door behind us."[107] Monica's mother (the nonabusive parent) would regularly neglect to pick her up at school, often arriving more than an hour after everyone else had gone home, leaving her feeling alone, parentless. David was sent outside in cold, wet clothes to sit on a rock for hours until his mother deemed him worthy enough to reenter the home. One summer David was left at an aunt's house while the rest of the family went on vacation. Despite being free from physical abuse, he yearned to be with his family and fantasized about running away to be with them. "I felt like an outcast as the station wagon drove away, leaving me behind. I felt so sad and hollow."[108] Christina's mother routinely banished her from the family and the home, culminating in her being sent to boarding school year-round for over two years. Even when living at home Christina lived under the threat of "total banishment from her presence forever."[109] She saw firsthand what happened to people who displeased her mother, for there had been a baby removed from her home. "Phillip's image was ripped out of every picture in each of our books! Sometimes only his head was ripped off. Other pictures were torn down the middle to remove him completely. One or two of the photos were left with just a severed male hand sticking out beyond the torn part. Except for those mutilated photographs it was as if he had never existed at all."[110]

As Harlow's research has demonstrated, a baby monkey with nothing more than a wire mother to soothe him will cling to that mother even if the mother is cruel and abusive. With fear racing through its body and mind, the baby (monkey or human) has only one goal—to seek comfort and solace from its caregiver. That it is the caregiver who inflicts the pain—at the moment—is utterly beside the point. The parent gives pain and gives comfort, and that is all that the baby knows.

SUMMARY

The stories written by adults who were physically abused as children are moving and terrifying. In each, the authors described severe physical abuse by a parent for the majority if not duration of their childhood. In response, the children (as described in the memoirs written when they were adults) wanted to understand why they were being hurt and, in the absence of any other explanation, blamed themselves. They compared themselves to animals at the mercy of their abusers, yet they were desiring of their abuser's love and they were willing to forgive them. They experienced their parents as omniscient and were obedient in response. They had empathy for their parents and wanted to understand what drove them to act as they did. They were hypervigilant of their parent's moods and states of mind. They were afraid of losing that parent and yet wanted to be invisible to avoid further pain and suffering. They both loved and feared that parent. They craved that parent's approval yet feared that parent's attention. They lived in a state of chronic arousal. Perhaps most damaging was that the physical abuse became internalized in the child as a series of negative perceptions of the self as unworthy, dirty, and bad. The power the parents had over their children extended beyond the ability to inflict momentary physical discomfort. These parents had the power to define their children as worthy of abuse, a belief they carried within them for many years. In the end, each author reclaimed his or her voice and dignity through the memoirs they wrote.

Chapter Three

Stories of Sexual Abuse

Three memoirs written by adults who describe their experiences of being sexually abused by a parent when they were children are summarized in this chapter. The first, *How to Cook Your Daughter*,[1] was written by Jessica Hendra, the daughter of *National Lampoon* editor, Tony Hendra.

HOW TO COOK YOUR DAUGHTER BY JESSICA HENDRA

Jessica Hendra was the younger of two daughters of bohemian parents who moved to the United States from England in the 1960s. At age seven Jessie was a shy, cross-eyed girl with a crooked smile; she was insecure and eager to please. Her father, Tony, comedian, author, playwright, and onetime editor of *National Lampoon* in its 1970's heyday, was a dynamic and charismatic man whose presence loomed large in the family. Jessica's parents raised their daughters in a nontraditional lifestyle, which included communal weekends of drug-addled nudist parties. The children were tolerated, but they were neither coddled nor nurtured. Jessica described never really feeling like a child in her own home, unprotected from adult discussions and behavior. "I had just turned 7, but there wasn't an adult around me who cared that I was a kid."[2] Jessica walked in on her parents having sex more than once and had easy access to a range of sexually explicit material such as her father's collection of R. Crumb comic books. By Tony's own admission he was a reluctant and inattentive parent. She quoted him saying that he ignored and resented his children, that he was selfish and treated his family like props and possessions. One of many examples of this that she shared involved dressing his preteen daughters and their friends as pimps and prostitutes to pose for the cover of *National Lampoon*, explicitly sexualizing these young children, including his own daughters.

Tony wrote a satirical piece for *Lampoon* titled "How to Cook Your Daughter," a tongue-in-cheek account of how to prepare the body of a naked six-year-old girl for dinner. *A slight nip of the teeth will quickly reveal the precise degree of succulence. An ancient and surprisingly accurate test of readiness is to hold the buttocks one in each hand and squeeze gently. If the daughter says, "Grrrugchlllllchllll," she is not yet quite ready. If she slaps your face, you have missed your opportunity. But if she giggles, she is just right.*[3] Copies of the magazine were strewn around the home, with its message that young girls are not only delicious but before a certain age are likely to be complicit in their own consumption and objectification.

According to Jessica, her father was a charismatic, domineering man who spared no insult when his children disappointed or annoyed him. He had cruel nicknames for them, especially regarding their weight and bodies, referring to her older sister, for example, as "Thunder Thighs." He considered his views on culture and politics the final word and let Jessie and her sister know when he disapproved of their taste or choices. While endorsing an antiauthoritarian point of view in his humor and lifestyle, he didn't seem comfortable with his children holding different views or having different taste than him. "When my dad used to tell me that some song I liked was stupid or that the book I was reading was trash, I accepted his views as the unquestionable truth. . . . I had always assumed that my father's words were gospel, that his opinions should be my opinions, he delivered them so forcefully."[4] As a young girl, for example, Jessica wanted to join the Brownies. However, Tony referred to the Brownies as a fascist organization and belittled her for wanting to join. "His reaction left me feeling better and worse. Better because he made me believe that the Girl Scouts were stupid anyway; worse because now I felt stupid for wanting to be one in the first place."[5]

When in a good mood Tony could be extremely funny and fun to be with, but when he was in a dark and sour mood, everyone would suffer. "When my father was livid it seemed like he took up the entire loft. And not just with his screaming . . . There seemed to be a rage that emanated from his body, like a glow of radiation that, if you got too close, might kill you. He was like a grenade ready to explode."[6] He felt his feelings very strongly and expected others to do so as well.

When the family lived in New Jersey, Tony commuted to New York City to the offices of *National Lampoon*. He worked irregular hours and would sometimes be absent for days at a time. He expected his family to accept that he would be accountable to no one. "Before cell phones and answering machines, it was harder to track people down. You could just disappear—and my father often did."[7] His unpredictable schedule and dangerous lifestyle (drugs, physical altercations, unexplained absences) resulted in Jessica fearing that her father would simply disappear one day. "I just remember how very afraid I was for Daddy, that something terrible might happen to him. I felt better and safer when I was with him."[8] Jessica grew up with a terrible fear that someday her father might never come home. Acutely aware of his moods, she strived to please her father by comforting him when he was upset in the hopes that he would spend more time at home. "He often felt guilty about the drinking, the drugs, the affairs, the betrayals. One night I went into the kitchen and found him lurching around the loft. He flung himself down on the sofa and started to sob. I offered to sing him a song—the only thing I could think of to make him feel better. And so we sat on the sofa and I sang him all the lullabies I could remember while he sniffed and wiped his eyes and eventually fell asleep."[9]

Her desire to keep her father safe and at home was of paramount importance to her, paving the way for her acquiescence. Three times over the course of her childhood Jessica was sexually molested by her father. "One night, as I was falling asleep in my bunk bed, my older sister fast asleep below me, my father entered my bedroom and told me in a whisper that he was going out for a bit. I asked him not to do that. He said he would come into my bunk and lie with me until I fell asleep. He squeezed into my bunk, and I snuggled into his arms. As I drifted off to sleep, he asked me to take off my underwear."[10] The next time occurred while she was keeping him company during his bath, something she routinely did. He became aroused and asked Jessica to perform oral sex on him. He tried to penetrate her vaginally but declared her "too small." After one of these episodes he explained that this is how people who love each other behave. "And I did. I loved him so much."[11]

Not until she was twelve did she tell anyone what happened, and even then it was a friend who was not in a position to act on that knowledge. It was many years before she shared the information with anyone else. "Of course I told no one. How could I? What would I tell them? That Daddy made me do things I didn't understand. 'That's what people do when they love each other,' he had said and I desperately wanted to believe him."[12] She even entertained the possibility that she had asked for what happened with Daddy, "as if my interest in sex had encouraged him."[13] At the same time, she was afraid that if she brought it up with her father it would happen again. After one episode he confessed to her that he was "a drunken asshole," which led her to fear that it would happen again when he was under the influence of alcohol or drugs, a common occurrence. She also noted that "despite everything I still adored my daddy,"[14] and she obviously didn't want to upset or anger him. "For years I never told anyone. Maybe I believed that was what people do when they love each other. Maybe I was afraid my father would stop loving me."[15]

At age eighteen, Jessica, unhappy and suffering from bulimia, was trying to make sense of what happened, and she confronted her father. His response was to chastise her for feeling sorry for herself. "My advice to you is to stop picking at your wounds, Jessica. It's a bad habit to make other people respon-sible for your failures in life. . . . You are sitting around picking at old scars, bringing up history so you can make excuses for yourself. If you have prob-lems they are yours not mine. Stop being so self-involved. Much worse things have happened to children."[16] For the next fifteen years or so she maintained a relationship with him, despite the fact that "just the sound of his voice on my answering machine started an emotional chain reaction that made me feel crazy."[17] Jessica was unable to find closure or resolution for herself. "Every time I heard his voice, each time I saw him, I would simply try to preoccupy myself by focusing on the trees to avoid the forest, to try to escape the question that nagged at me: Should I have this man in my life at all after what he did? Wouldn't I be better, wouldn't it be less aggravating to never talk to him again?"[18]

Jessica struggled internally with her relationship with her father until external events propelled her toward a resolution. In 2004 Tony wrote a best-selling redemption memoir in which he revealed his sins and described his path of spiritual absolution. The omission of the sexual abuse, what Jessica considered his "greatest transgression," renewed her desire to hold her father accountable and find some peace within herself. "What should I do? What could I do? Was it better to forget it or do something? Could I forget it? And what could I do anyway? He had written a history of his life, of his sins. How could he have taken on such a project knowing that he would never tell the truth about his most egregious transgression? But, as always, I found myself back in that complicated place, and as always, I wanted to give him another chance."[19] The chance she wanted to give him was the chance to make up to her for what he had done. "I just kept hoping he might apologize. I kept hoping that it could be made right somehow. I just kept hoping that he would finally say that it was his fault."[20] In addition, she wanted a shared under-standing of what had happened between them. "What I really wanted from my father was for him to understand me. To say he regretted what he had done and that he should have come clean about it years ago. To acknowledge that he needed to do this, not only for me but to be able to live with him-self."[21] Despite all that he had done to her, Jessica would have forgiven him if he had just acknowledged how he had hurt her. "It's not that I wouldn't have forgiven him. I would have if he just asked me to."[22] In the end, Jessica wrote her own redemption memoir about her childhood in order to have her reality known. Rather than her book calling forth from her father a desire to acknowledge and atone for his parental sins, he responded by cutting off all contact, which ultimately may have been just what Jessica needed. "For 32 years I had tried to have a relationship with my father and pretending I could almost killed me."[23]

NO MOMMA'S BOY BY DOMINIC CARTER

In *No Momma's Boy*,[24] New York City journalist Dominic Carter tells of being raised by a doting extended family because his father was uninvolved and his mentally ill mother was unable to care for him. During a visit with his mother she sexually molested him while in a delusional break from reality.

Dominic Carter was born to unmarried parents, Dudley Hall and Laverne Carter, in the early 1960s. His father—although known at the time—was not listed on Dominic's birth certificate, a mark of rejection he carried with him throughout his life. Dominic lived with Laverne in various troubled and desperate neighborhoods in New York City, what Dominic referred to as a "landscape of despair . . . a poisonous environment."[25] Even more troubling for Dominic was that his mother suffered from paranoid schizophrenia and had been repeatedly hospitalized, medicated, and given ECT (electroconvulsive therapy) throughout her teen and young adult years. At her best, Laverne was an inattentive parent (although Dominic recalls fondly being treated to ice cream and trips to the zoo with her). At her worst she was harsh and cruel. During his mother's darker periods Dominic was tended to by his beloved grandmother and two aunts, who adored him. "Everyone in the family except my mother saw something positive in me."[26] The fact that his mothering was provided by others was not lost on him. "I felt like a motherless child. . . . I loved my mother just like any other fresh faced youngster does, but I sensed that she was turning on me . . . and she became more hostile with both her words and her actions. I could sense that she viewed me with scorn."[27] In addition to Laverne's intermittent physical abuse, she perpetrated a single yet harrowing incident of sexual abuse against young Dominic, who was seven years old at the time. Laverne commanded him to undress and join her in bed. Although uncomfortable and confused, he complied. "How could I not obey my mother?"[28] He struggled to make sense of his mother's unusual behavior by wondering if perhaps this was her way of letting him know she loved him. "Mommy's breath was hot when she kissed me. My mother had never kissed me on my cheek and now she was kissing me on my mouth. Was she finally making up for lost time? . . . My mommy had never shown me this much attention. . . . I was starved for her affection and I was too young to discern when it crossed the line."[29] Later that night he struggled to make sense of what had happened between them. He wondered if his mother was dirty, whether he was dirty, and whether he was to blame. Before long he began to view himself as "dirty and bad."[30]

Eventually Dominic lived with his grandmother full-time, and with the love and guidance of his extended family he graduated from high school, attended college, and began a successful career as a journalist. Despite his outward successes, he remained in emotional turmoil due to his troubled relationship with his mother. One of the last times he confronted her about her abusive and negligent parenting he was in his midthirties. "'Laverne,' I said my voice strong, 'Why did you do that to me?'[31] Her response was an emphatic, 'Boy leave me alone with that.'"[32] Furious that she was unable or unwilling to explain herself, he fumed, "The nerve of her! I'd given her a chance to confess to me and explain her sins, and she had refused."[33] Nonetheless, he felt that asking the question—despite her unwillingness to answer it—had served a purpose. "I had asked a simple question, but in that one question I had sent a lot of information to my mother. For one, I showed her that she wasn't off the hook. After years of pretending, I wanted her to look her son, her firstborn, dead in the eyes and acknowledge her crimes against me. When we looked at one another I wanted her to see how many times I had cried myself to sleep because of her abuse."[34] "I wanted her to answer my questions, and there were many, 'Why did you play games with my fragile life, Laverne? Why did you dump me in foster care when there were relatives who were more than willing to take care of me? Why did you try to fight Grandma Anna Pearl when you knew you didn't want me? What did I do to deserve your scorn?' All these questions and more were raging inside me, and I wanted her answers."[35] Dominic longed for his mother to offer an explanation and a wish to atone, for her to say something like, "Son, I love you and am sorry for how I hurt you." Laverne, however, remained steadfast in her inability or unwillingness to show remorse or guilt for her behavior. He had given her yet one more chance to redeem herself and she had refused. "If she had said anything like that, I could have embraced her, and maybe I could have finally had some closure, some semblance of peace with myself. Once again Laverne had left me heartbroken, and I was again that little boy waiting on the stoop after school, waiting in vain for my mother to come for me."[36] As long as he wanted atonement and remorse from her, she retained the power to hurt and disappoint him. "Her actions had left a gaping hole in my heart that promised to haunt me until my death, and she apparently could not have cared less."[37] In this way, her single act from long ago reverberated throughout his life.

Four years later, Laverne died. "I tried to get over her passing but had difficulty doing so. I felt bound to her by anger . . . And at times that anger was all consuming."[38] He had not yet received the reparative experience he was searching for. As a result he began to investigate his mother's past, to find an explanation in her death that she did not provide to him while alive. "My need for information became almost an obsession."[39] In reviewing the records of her hospitalizations he learned of his mother's mental illness, her own suffering and tragic losses. He also learned of the abuse that she had inflicted on him when he was too young to remember. "Tears welled in my eyes and my hands trembled as I continued to read the records outlining my past abuse of which I had absolutely no memory (he was under two at the time). I wondered what I could have possibly done to provoke such rage."[40]

Rage is what Dominic felt, evidenced by his unrelenting competitiveness and aggression, which both catapulted him to career success but also created interpersonal problems. In the end he found peace of sorts in reading his mother's history and in telling his own.

IN MY FATHER'S ARMS BY WALTER A. DE MILLY III

Raised in the South during the 1950s, Walt De Milly III was in thrall to his successful, charismatic father. At age seventy his father was caught molesting a young boy, setting Walt III on a path of self-discovery and disclosure of the sexual abuse he experienced at the hands of his father. *In My Father's Arms*[41] is his story.

Walt III was nine years old during the Cuban missile crisis. His father built one of the largest private bunkers in Tallahassee in their backyard. He was a prominent business and community leader, someone whom the young boy was fascinated with, enamored with, impressed with. "To my young eyes, my father occupied a station of influence somewhere in the upper air, beyond rank or order, beyond his birthright as a gentleman of the Southern tradition. . . . everyone in town knew him, and everyone somehow owed him approval. . . . People seemed to hold a place in their hearts for him, and they let me know it."[42]

There was, however, a darker side to the gregarious and prominent community leader. Walt's father was a pedophile, and the bunker in the backyard served a different purpose than intended. It did not protect young Walt from danger. In fact, it was in that dark and gloomy fallout shelter that Walt was molested by his father. Overriding the protests of his son, the father took what he wanted, did what he wanted. In response, Walt the child emotionally disappeared. This was neither the first nor the last time that this happened. The sexual abuse began when Walt was about three years of age and lasted throughout his childhood. Each time it occurred there was both pain and pleasure for the young boy. He loved his father, loved his attention, would do anything for him, and could not imagine questioning or disobeying him. The first time it happened, Walt's father took him camping. In the quiet isolation of the woods, Walt's father touched him, demanded things from him. Walt felt no longer real, no longer present for himself. "The father hasn't the faintest idea that he's holding a son who isn't there. . . . Walt is far away, in the company of serpents, long shards of glass, planets, messengers dressed in suits, and paintings that could come alive."[43] When he returned home to his mother, Walt "stopped short, swept dizzy by déjà vu. She certainly knew who I was. When I hugged her, she felt familiar but unreal. I wondered if she had the wrong boy."[44] Something had altered inside him, his very sense of self had been violated, and from that point forward the young boy struggled with feeling separate, apart from both his family and himself. He developed what he experienced as a different version of himself, The Other Walt, the one who became awake in the presence of his father. It was this Other Walt who was molested. "Whenever Dad appeared, the Other Walt came out to take my place. Dad didn't even have to touch me. Sometimes all it would take to switch was the sound of the front door cracking open or the rattle of the newspaper as Dad put it down. When these things happened I toppled like a tower of building blocks. The first Walt fell, and the second materialized."[45] When Walt was nine, his father began molesting his friends. Walt was guilt ridden, feeling that he should have protected his friends. At the same time he was jealous. "Daddy wasn't supposed to do that with anyone else but me."[46] Confused and overwhelmed from the experience, Walt suffered from ongoing feelings of dreaminess and a lack of realness to others and himself. "By the end of sixth grade I was intractably haunted by a sense that something was very wrong with me. The sensations flickered behind my thoughts, evading direct observation. I knew there was more to the world than I could see, and I knew that it was very wrong. In occasional flashes of comprehension, I sensed the presence of evil, and I feared—I knew—it was somewhere within me."[47] When Walt turned ten, his father took him on a camping trip. "It may not make sense that I wanted to be in his company, but I did. The everyday Walt adored his father and would go anywhere with him. At that point in my life, the other Walts—the peaceful sleeping infant, the terrified observer, the furious child-beast—kept all the knowledge of the Bad Father to themselves. There was no incest between the Good Father and me."[48] Unprotected even from himself, late at night the father did what he wanted. Back home, suffering but unable to speak the truth, Walt became ill. "Maybe the doctors would find out what's wrong with me."[49] But, of course, they didn't.

At age eleven Walt became a Boy Scout, studiously focusing on advancing through the ranks. "I swam quietly, politely through a private sea of pain. . . . I worked doggedly on my Boy Scout Badges. I read. I stared blankly into space. I looked at Dad as some kind of god. He was handsome, and he loved me. . . . He was a very good man—that was for sure."[50] There was no room in Walt's mind or heart to acknowledge the truth of what his father had done to him. He simply couldn't integrate the two realities. Although the camping trip marked the end of the incest, Walt remained emotionally trapped. "The pain lingered, pulsed, blistered. My soul, hollow and torn, lay abandoned somewhere in the forest."[51]

As his father turned his attention to prepubescent boys, Walt struggled with his emerging homosexuality. When his parents discovered his journal they were horrified. "I'd be so mortified, ashamed . . . just sickened if word got out that you were a homosexual," his father told him. "I'd rather blow my brains out than have a son who's a homosexual."[52] Walt was sent to a therapist with the intention of reversing his sexual interests, compounding his sense of being unacceptable, evil. "I continued to witness the sessions behind the curtain, and I knew the feeling that being myself meant being wrong. It is clear, as I look back on this fiasco, that therapy reinforced and compounded my mental disorder. . . . Dad had used me but the sessions with Blount made me into antimatter. I could not exist as one person."[53]

Walt continued in this state of antimatter, not mattering, throughout the rest of his adolescence and into young adulthood where he struggled with feelings of disconnection from others, from himself. He began to secretly explore his homosexuality, unable to speak the truth about what his father had done to him. In college Walt was plagued by memories of the abuse yet failed to "understand, or seem to even consider the connection between my incest and my intervals of pain and terror."[54] Walt remained depressed, lonely, alone.

The family was forced to confront the problem when Walt's father molested a neighbor boy. At this point, Walt the son was in business with his father, and he had assumed the role of the community leader/businessman. The victim's father called Walt, threatening to press charges unless the father sought treatment to ensure an end to the pedophilia. In crisis, the family finally talked with each other about what had happened when Walt was a little boy. Walt and his father took long drives, discussing the past. "I wanted him to beg for forgiveness, to cry in rage against his own malefactor, but his composure never disintegrated, I felt both frustrated and empty."[55] Walt did not find relief from his feelings of hollowness until therapy, where he could finally explore the person behind the "victim mask." Only then was he able to embrace all of the Walts that lived inside him. "I awoke. I felt like I'd suddenly appeared."[56] Newly awake, Walt began to repair his relationship with his mother from whom his secrets had kept him a stranger. "I held so many secrets inside me that she had not even existed, not as my mother."[57] In the end, Walt became real to himself and allowed himself to be real to others.

Chapter Four

Making Meaning of Sexual Abuse

Sexual abuse is both a criminal act and a child protection concern. From a child protection perspective, the federal child abuse statute defines sexual abuse as occurring in situations in which the perpetrator is a parent and the victim is a child.[1] Specifically, sexual abuse is defined as A) the employment, use, persuasion, inducement, enticement, or coercion of any child to engage in or assist any other person to engage in, any sexually explicit conduct or simulation of such conduct for the purpose of producing a visual depiction of such conduct, or B) the rape, molestation, prostitution, or other form of sexual exploitation, or incest with children. It is this last part of the definition that is reflected in the memoirs reviewed for this book: sexual acts between a parent and a child. Six memoirs were reviewed for this chapter. It is interesting to note how few memoirs of incest there were compared to other types of child maltreatment within the family. It may be that the shame associated with sexual abuse (see below) accounts for the relatively fewer books. Although there are numerous celebrities who have revealed that they were victims of sexual abuse, most such as Oprah Winfrey, Queen Latifah, and Ashley Judd did not report being sexually abused by a parent. The six memoirs written about sexual abuse by a parent that were reviewed for this chapter are presented in table 4.1. Three of the memoirs are summarized in detail in the preceding chapter, and all six were reviewed for the identification of the themes discussed.

Several themes emerged over the course of these memoirs. Each is discussed below. Some of the themes are presented as a duality, a conflict within the author in which two opposing experiences or perceptions are felt simultaneously.

Table 4.1. Memoirs of Sexual Abuse

Title of Book/Author	Abusive Parent	Abuse Victim/ Author	Secondary Abuse by Parent	Role of other Parent	Major Dysfunction in Family
How to Cook Your Daughter	Father	Jessica Hendra	Emotional abuse	Her mother failed to protect her	Narcissistic father
No Momma's Boy	Mother	Dominic Carter	Physical abuse and abandonment	His father was absent	Mentally ill mother
In My Father's Arms	Father	Walter A. De Milly III	None	His mother failed to protect him	None
Murdering My Youth	Father	Cady McClain	None	Her mother failed to protect her	Narcissistic mother
I Remember, Daddy	Father	Katie Matthews	Physical abuse	Her mother failed to protect her	None
Don't Tell Mummy	Father	Toni Maguire	None	Her mother failed to protect her	None

ENTHRALLED/DISGUSTED

In each of the stories, the abusive parent was an important person in the life of the child, a parent who had an existing relationship with the child at the point at which the sexual abuse occurred. For most of the authors the abusive parent was a dynamic, charismatic, charming parent whom the child loved and adored, such as Jessica Hendra, who wrote in *How to Cook Your Daughter*, "As a little girl I worshipped Tony Hendra, my father."[2] Tony was the editor of *National Lampoon* magazine during its heyday. He was an interesting person surrounded by interesting people. He had an outsized personality, socialized with celebrities, experimented with drugs, disappeared for days on end, was reckless with himself and his family, and hosted outrageous weekend-long orgies. For Jessica, "He wasn't trying to be cool, as I was. My dad *was* cool."[3] He loomed large in her eyes. "Dad was brilliant, charming, witty, and gregarious."[4] TV actress Cady McClain, who wrote *Murdering My Youth*, also adored her father, and loved him unconditionally. "No matter what he did. I loved him."[5] She daydreamed about him whisking her away, "him and me hanging out together on a beach somewhere, listening to the waves—a couple of pirates escaping the real world."[6] Walt as well was in thrall to his father. "He fascinated me in the way that any nine-year-old might be enamored and impressed by his father."[7] Despite the abuse, Walt "wanted to be in his company. . . . The everyday Walt adored Dad and would go anywhere with him."[8] When his father turned his pedophilic attention to younger boys, Walt felt guilt as well as jealousy. "I was just as in love with Dad as he was with me. I wanted him alone."[9] Walt looked up to his father as "some kind of God."[10] Katie Matthews, author of *I Remember, Daddy*, became obsessed with her father "so that I could think of nothing else."[11] The love these children felt for their parent was neither extinguished nor discouraged by the sexual abuse. That is not to say that the abuse had no impact on them, only that it did not stop them from feeling love for the parent who abused them.[12]

At the same time many of the authors reported feeling disgusted by that parent. Jessica, for example, observed her narcissistic father carry on about his work-related dramas and his concerns about being overweight, and she was privy to his pathetic and disgusting self-obsessed ruminations and rages. "The mornings after a binge were the worst. My father was in a horrible mood and, if he'd been doing a lot of coke the night before, the sniffing, snorting, coughing, and spitting were deafening and non-stop. And there was always the morning weigh in, a ritual more usual than the yawn-and-stretch. Daddy would stand naked in the middle of the kitchen."[13] Perhaps most relevant is that all of the children had experienced their parents in the throes of sexual desire, a state that was both frightening and disgusting. Dominic Carter in *No Momma's Boy* recalled his mother's sexual excitement as repulsive and terrifying. These children both adored and were disgusted by their sexually abusive parent.

POWERLESS

In relation to the abusive parent, the authors experienced themselves primarily as powerless. Jessica wrote that her father wasn't the type of man to ask for something, he just took what he wanted. "It was just an assumed command, as though through charm or force of personality, he could simply will the response he expected, the response he felt he deserved."[14] She felt that it was not possible to win an argument or even to make a point with him. He was never wrong, "not even remotely."[15] She found that he could outsmart her in any conversation or argument; "he was relentless, a pit bull that would lock its teeth on your throat until you simply stopped struggling."[16] Even later, as a teenager, she needed to consciously remind herself that her father was in fact fallible, that he was not God, so that she would stop accepting his views as the "unquestionable truth."[17] Toni Maguire, author of *Don't Tell Mummy*, also recalled being powerless. "My parents were my masters; my father controlled me."[18] Dominic felt that he "had no rights in Laverne's world. I was not respected in any way. When I misbehaved, she handed down her judgments like a rogue judge, swiftly and harshly. She showed no sympathy whatsoever for me, and all I could do is take it."[19] Dominic, like the others, experienced himself as having no voice, no say in what happened to his body, and in response he felt powerless in relation to his sexually abusive parent. The disregard for the child's needs and feelings that was exhibited during the sexually abusive interactions was woven throughout the fabric of the parent-child relationship. The sexual acts might have been isolated (i.e., hidden from view, kept secret), but the lack of regard for the child as a separate person was not an isolated aspect of their relationship. The child was powerless to stop the sexual abuse and was powerless in other ways as well.

The sense of being overpowered pervaded the relationship with the sexually abusive parent. From a parenting-style perspective,[20] these parents were generally authoritarian, as opposed to permissive or authoritative, and were, therefore, not likely to engage their child in discussions about their thoughts and feelings. Even Tony Hendra, who was described as extremely permissive with respect to countercultural pursuits, seeing nothing wrong with exposing his children to sex and drugs and generally being lax with respect to supervision, was nonetheless authoritarian in his relationship to Jessica, unable to accept that she was a separate person who had her own needs, thoughts, beliefs, and experiences. Therefore, she did not feel accepted by him for who she was and did not feel that her perceptions were of interest or mattered to him. The same held true for the other authors as well. And in response to having their needs and feelings generally ignored if not belittled, the children experienced themselves as lacking power and agency in that relationship.

AFRAID/SEEKING COMFORT

Some of the sexually abused authors recalled feeling frightened of the abusive parent, both during the sexual act and in their day-to-day interactions. Jessica's father, for example, terrified her by encouraging her to engage in sacrilegious behavior and then taunting her with the threat of eternal damnation, sadistically informing her that it was not possible to atone for her sins. He routinely humiliated and mocked her and was vicious in service of making a joke or teaching her a lesson. Jessica lived in a constant state of uncertainty of her father's love and care for her, off balance, vulnerable. Likewise, when Walt's father approached him sexually, Walt felt his father's anger toward him, as if his father "can't find what he's looking for. What have I done wrong?"[21] the boy wonders. He was afraid that he had let his father down, disappointed, or angered him. Katie had every reason to be afraid of her father, a sadistic man who killed her pet hamster and placed the dead body in the kitchen for her to find. Toni's father as well toyed with her love of animals by killing and serving her pet turkey for dinner. The death of the animal was perceived as an implied threat that the parent could and would do whatever he pleased to the child, who was as unprotected as a pet. Katie recalled, "I'd always been frightened of my father. Just thinking about him made the hairs on the back of my neck stand up and my stomach start to churn painfully."[22]

At the same time that the abusive parent was the source of considerable physical and emotional pain, that parent was also a protector and source of comfort. Walt loved and looked up to his father. He admired his father for being a pillar of the community, a respected neighbor, a man others turned to for help, someone he could turn to for comfort. His father built a bunker in the backyard to protect the family, he took his son camping, he paid attention to him, and made him feel important and special. Walt felt safe and protected by his father. Jessica recalled walking in the woods, holding her father's hand and feeling "as long as he was with me, nothing horrible can happen."[23] Toni snuggled up close to her father, eager for his approval; "sensations of being protected and safe swept over me as I cuddled closer, feeling so happy that his affection towards me had at last reappeared."[24] Cady, too, clung to her father, relishing the feelings of safety and acceptance she obtained from being in his presence. By creating the illusion of the protector, the sexually abusive parent was able to exploit the child's sense of safety in order to take advantage of the child sexually without him or her understanding that the behavior was abusive.

GOOD PARENT/BAD PARENT

The abusive parent was both safe and dangerous, inflictor of pain and easer of suffering. This contradiction was difficult for the children to integrate. Several of them wrote of having two fathers, a good and loving father who accepted and cared for them, and a bad father who hurt and frightened them. Toni wrote, "There were times when he came home quite early, bringing my mother and me sweets and chocolate. Those were the evenings when the jovial father would appear with hugs for my mother and friendly greetings for me. In my mind I had two fathers, the nasty one and the nice one."[25] She never knew which father would appear. Walt wrote that he had a "bad father" and a "good father." Cady spoke of her "dream father" as someone who would be all the things that she wanted him to be. For Jessica the distinction was between her intoxicated father who was unpredictable, unkind, unstoppable, and her sober father who was not. For these children, it was as if there was a monster lurking inside the parent that—when stirred—came alive and took over the good parent's heart and mind. It was that parent who sexually abused the child. When the sexual act was over, the monster subsided and the good parent returned. The thought that the good father was the same person who hurt them was too painful a reality to accept, so they created the alter ego of the bad father as a way of protecting their image of the good father. The splitting of the abusive parent into two distinct components functioned to relegate the frightening and intolerable aspects of the abuser to a separate identity in order to preserve the good aspects of the parent-child relationship. To be clear, this "splitting" of the good parent and bad parent was metaphorical and represented the child's attempt to process the confusing duality of the abusive parent's personality, as opposed to actually believing that there were two separate parents.

SECRET LIFE/REGULAR LIFE

Another duality for the sexual abuse victims was found in having two truths: the reality that they showed to the world in which they were fine and nothing was wrong and the inner truth they kept to themselves that something was in fact very wrong. The authors as children had a secret life of sexual abuse and sexual experiences that they could not talk about, could barely even acknowledge to themselves. In this way, they were not only cut off from a part of themselves, they were cut off from other people as well. None of the authors made disclosures at the time of the abuse (some did disclose during their childhood, while others waited until adulthood). This was so for many reasons; the same reasons described by the authors are well known in the field of child sexual abuse.[26] Most of the children did not have the words or concepts to describe what had happened to them. For example, Jessica wrote, "Of course, I told no one. How could I? What would I tell them? That Daddy had made me do things I didn't understand."[27] Dominic wrote, "My mother acted as though nothing happened, and so did I. I honestly didn't know at the time how to interpret what had happened. For all I knew, as a child, all mothers did this to their sons."[28] With no basis of comparison, young children have no way of knowing that the behavior is aberrant or abusive. Another reason for failing to disclose was the shame they felt about what happened and what they thought it meant about who they were. Keeping the abuse a secret allowed them to maintain the illusion that it did not happen. To say it out loud to someone else would have made it real and made them vulnerable; thus they preferred to pretend that it never happened. Walt "would have been too humiliated to expose Dad. A boy is not going to spill his sexual embarrassment before his mother and sister. Even if I'd been brave enough to do it, I knew no one would have believed me."[29] Most did not have a trusted person to tell, and many were afraid of retribution should they disclose. In some instances the abuser warned them that they would not be believed. Thus, they carried within them the knowledge that they had engaged in something scary, wrong, bad, and they were worried that someone would find out. They were afraid of being found out both for what it meant about themselves and for what it would potentially trigger in the abuser. Thus, they grew up knowing and not knowing, cut off from themselves as well as others by the secret they held within them.

The most important person from whom they were cut off from was the nonoffending parent, who in most of these families appeared to collude in one way or another with the abuser to allow the abuse to continue.[30] With the exception of Dominic who only had one parent, the nonperpetrating parents in these stories were either unwilling or unable to protect their children. This was felt as painfully by the children as the abuse itself, furthering the sadness, fear, and isolation. Early psychoanalyst Ferenczi said that the aspect of child abuse that is truly unbearable for the child and causes lasting damage is being emotionally abandoned at a moment of great need.[31] More recently, psychoanalyst Jay Frankel argued that children can cope with almost anything as long as there is someone with whom to share one's fear and pain. But if the nonabusive parent turns her back on the child, denying the child's experience, then the child is left "unbearably alone with her traumatic experience."[32] Again, it is important to remember that in the field of child maltreatment, the nonoffending parent is not assumed to have colluded. It happens to have been the experience and perception of the authors of these memoirs. However, research does show that when the nonoffending parent believes and supports the child after disclosure there is a much greater potential for that child to heal and to have more positive outcomes than children whose nonoffending parent does not believe or support them.[33]

DISSOCIATED

Keeping the sexual abuse a secret created a feeling of being separated from themselves and their own experiences. There were thoughts and feelings that they were not free to own, to speak of, or to share. There was a wall between the secret and the child. Thus, it comes as no surprise that one of the most common themes across the stories of sexual abuse was the theme of dissociation. The term *dissociation* is used to describe an array of experiences from mild detachment from one's immediate surroundings to severe detachment from—although not total loss of reality of—physical and emotional experiences.[34] Dissociation is considered a typical response to trauma.[35] A given event is not traumatic in itself but may be so in its effect on a particular individual. As was referred to in the introduction, it is the meaning the child attributes to the event or how the child perceives the event that makes it traumatizing or not traumatizing. Thus, not every individual who experiences a particular event will actually be traumatized, although some types of events are so extreme that they are likely to be traumatizing to most people. In these memoirs, the sexual abuse and the aftermath of keeping it a secret was portrayed as traumatic, and it appears that many of the authors as children dissociated in response to the pain, shock, and confusion of the sexual act and the feeling of being physically and psychologically overpowered and overwhelmed by the abusive parent. Walt wrote repeatedly of being numb, living behind a curtain, feeling dreamy, and disconnected, "falling into a cloud of anesthesia,"[36] floating "somewhere behind my own vision,"[37] hollow, not present. Walt was so disconnected that "I could have carried on a conversation while someone was sawing off my leg."[38] Walt took on the persona of the class clown as a role to play to keep himself distracted from his pain and confusion. "Sometimes I felt like I had forgotten how to know who I was. Thoughts came into my mind that felt like someone else's. I ignored them."[39] Walt was so far away from his everyday life that he failed to connect his father's relentless sexual advances with his own "intervals of pain and terror."[40]

The dissociation also functioned to protect Walt and the others from the terror of the sexual act itself. They used dissociation to distract themselves, to be less present and hence less frightened by the experience as it was happening. They could wall themselves off from the experience. While they were being abused they floated above themselves, they drifted away, they went blank. Walt spoke of feeling like there was more than one Walt, as if someone else were having the experiences rather than him. "Walt is far away, in the company of serpents."[41]

Another aspect of dissociation occurred when the abused child complied with the abuser, consenting, relenting to the abuse without protesting or fighting against it. The authors described themselves as feeling like a rag doll, a puppet, a robot, acquiescing to whatever the parent wanted to do to them, having no sense of self to protest against the abuse. Toni referred to her experience as having a puppet take over when her father made sexual demands of her, as if she were hollow inside with no agency or voice. She was just an object for him to handle. The children disappeared inside their minds and left their bodies behind for the parent to abuse.

According to the literature on sexually abused children, dissociation can be an effective coping mechanism as it protects the child from the immediate terror of the experience, much the way someone will distract himself when a splinter is being removed or a shot is being given.[42] By looking away and thinking about something else, the pain is attenuated, less acute. However, when dissociation is a persistent response to a chronic and ongoing traumatic experience, the coping strategy can have negative consequences. Dissociation can lead to feelings of alienation and isolation, not just from the self but from others as well. Toni, for example, wrote of feeling "alien to everyone in the world."[43] Later when she came to terms with her abuse she realized that she had hidden behind a mask for much of her childhood, unable to show or express her inner experiences to a caring adult. Likewise, Katie recalled feeling like an imposter. "For almost as long as I could remember, I'd felt as though I was acting the part of someone leading a normal life,"[44] as if she were hiding behind a mask. Dissociation may also help to ameliorate the guilt that emanates from the child's experience of themselves as complying with the sexual abuse. If they don't experience the event then they cannot in any way be responsible for its occurrence. In that way, dissociation may help to diminish the feelings of shame and responsibility.

DAMAGED AND DIRTY

The experience of feeling damaged from the sexual abuse was pervasive across the memoirs. The authors wrote about their experience as if the abuse said something about who they were as people, that the fact of having been abused marked them as unworthy and irredeemable. Katie recalled, "I always felt as though I was contaminated and somehow dirty."[45] Toni looked in the mirror and saw someone who was damaged. "Again and again, I washed myself, but still his smell lingered on me until I believed it had become a permanent stain on my body."[46] Cady, as well, experienced herself as corrupted and stained by the smell of the man who abused her. "I felt like my burnished innocence let off a smell akin to burnt rubber."[47] Dominic felt scarred and stained for life. "I began to view myself as dirty and bad."[48] For Walt the feeling of having been ruined from the inside out was amplified by his fear that he would become a pedophile like his father, that the damage done to him would be carried forward in his ruin of others. "When I looked at Dad, I feared that my own condition would deteriorate into pedophilia. I feared that my own blood would attack me, dissolving the little arteries in my feet. I feared that the same corrupted seed waited in my brain, dormant save for a signal from some patient gene."[49] In this way, the abuse—an external event imposed on them—was carried forward within them over the years, long after the sexual abuse itself had ceased. The abuse victims had forged an identity as dirty and shameful, and that identity became a part of their sense of self. It was not as if they wore a dirty garment that could be flung off to reveal the clean, pure, worthy person underneath. The cloak of the abuse was attached to them—or so they believed—and affected all aspects of their lives.

GUILTY

Part of the feeling of damaged and dirty came from the fact that the authors felt responsible for their own abuse, as if they had colluded in their victimization and/or asked for it. They did not realize that they had been taken advantage of and exploited by the abuser who was more than happy to let them believe that they had participated in their own abuse by not fighting against it and keeping it a secret. They were too embarrassed, confused, and frightened to reveal and discuss what had happened to them. Walt felt a permanent state of guilt, as if "wherever I went or whatever I did, I felt guilty, my senses converging into one lasting intractable state: terrified paralysis."[50] The paralysis was from the knowledge that he was helpless to end the abuse, that he had to bear the knowledge alone. "I knew no one would have believe me. Dad would have laughed if I had complained."[51] Dominic wrote that his mother acted as if nothing had happened, and he took his cue from her. "I honestly didn't know at the time how to interpret what had happened."[52] Katie felt consumed with shame, and she couldn't "bear the thought of having to live with the guilt and with the knowledge of what I thought *I* had done."[53] Toni's father took advantage of her confusion by telling her, "So, you're just as guilty as me. Your family won't love you anymore. If you bring disgrace to this house your mother won't want you."[54] He confidently assured her that if she disclosed the abuse it would be her who would suffer the consequences, not him.

FORGIVE THE PARENT/FORGIVE THE SELF

Keeping the abuse a secret not only allowed it to continue unabated at the whim of the abuser but also denied the child the opportunity to make sense of the experience and for the abuser to atone for his or her guilt. The secret kept the guilt in the heart and mind of the victim rather than in the heart and mind of the abuser. In that way the guilt fed upon itself, keeping the child locked in the role of the guilty and ashamed. Perhaps that is why a common thread among the stories is the desire for the abusive parent to atone for their "sins" and seek forgiveness for what they had done. Jessica felt the psychological pull toward her father and believed that if only he would admit what he had done and ask for her to forgive him, she would be free of the shame and guilt. She wanted him to ask for her forgiveness so that she could forgive him. "It's not that I would have never forgiven him. I would have if he had just asked me to, if he had just admitted what he had done, that it was wrong. That it wasn't my fault."[55] After reading his book in which he promised to admit his transgressions and finding no mention of the sexual abuse, she was crushed, thinking, "Daddy, why couldn't you just say that? Why?"[56] Walt, too, ached for his father to take in the reality of his behavior. "Like a naughty little boy who simply couldn't absorb the significance of the bad things he had done, Dad maintained his perplexed and concerned mein."[57] Cady wondered why her father had abandoned her. "Where was his guilt—his sense of failed responsibility? All I had wanted to hear him say was, 'I am so sorry.'"[58] Dominic's mother quietly murmured, "Boy leave me alone with that"[59] when he implored her to explain herself to him.

Each author wrote of wanting the abusive parent to ask them for forgiveness. None had that experience that they so pined for. They were never given the opportunity to look their abuser in the eye and say, "Thank you for admitting to me what you have done. I forgive you." In the absence of this desired healing experience, each had to come to terms with the fact that they would have to live their lives with this piece of unfinished business. Their task became not how to forgive an abuser who did terrible things to them but how to forgive themselves for being the victims of these terrible things. Their task was to find a way to put the abuse experience into some kind of perspective so that it didn't completely define who they were. Thus, rather than being a sexual abuse victim they could become a person who had been sexually abused as a child. They had hoped that their abuser would help them with that redefinition task, but that was not to be. In coming to the place where they could forgive themselves, they—for the first time—were no longer controlled and defined by their abuser. It was merely an illusion that they needed the abuser to participate in the healing process. When they gave up that illusion, the true healing could finally begin. It is clear in reading these memoirs that the writing of their stories was a very important part of the healing process. While it is up to the reader to decide whether or not to forgive the abuser, only the victim can truly forgive himself.

SUMMARY

Sexual abuse of a child—in addition to often being frightening and painful—violates the child's basic sense of trust and safety. The parent who should be protecting the child takes advantage of the child's trust in them. In involving the child in sexual acts, the parent is warping the child's identity as damaged and dirty, guilty and shameful. While the sexual abuse event may be of limited duration, the stain of the abuse can last for years if not decades. The desire for the atonement of the abusive parent is in many respects an illusion that maintains that parent's power and control over the abuse victim. Healing begins when the abuse victim (as a child or as an adult) forgives and accepts himself or herself and no longer needs the abusive parent to serve that function.

Chapter Five

Stories of Emotional Abuse

Three memoirs about emotional abuse by a parent are summarized in this chapter. The first, *Diary of a Stage Mother's Daughter*,[1] was written by Melissa Francis, child TV actress most well known for her role as Cassandra on *Little House on the Prairie*.

DIARY OF A STAGE MOTHER'S DAUGHTER
BY MELISSA FRANCIS

Melissa (Missy) Francis was the younger of two daughters born and raised in southern California. Her mother, enthralled with show business, involved both her children in modeling and acting from a young age. At four Missy had professional head shots and had already been cast in a series of national commercials. At eight she landed the role of Cassandra on *Little House on the Prairie*. Her mother managed every aspect of Missy's life and helped her achieve her early success, putting her in cute outfits, helping her learn her lines, doing her hair and makeup, driving her to auditions, encouraging her every step of the way. "I felt better when Mom was there, making sure I was doing my job properly."[2] Missy recalled that "when Mom and I worked together, we were an unbeatable team."[3] The day Missy joined the cast of *Little House* "may have been the highlight of Mom's life. Our two years on *Little House on the Prairie* were without question her happiest."[4] Her mother basked in the reflected glow of her daughter's success.

However, darker forces were at work. Despite her helpfulness as a stage mother overseeing her daughter's successful acting and modeling career, Missy's mother was also ruthless and cruel. "When we were at home, my sister and I lived in a state of constant wariness, always reading Mom's mood and bracing for impact when the mood turned ominous. She was mercurial, domineering, but also devoted."[5] The sisters were keenly attuned to the sound of their mother's approaching footsteps, fearing that she would burst into their room in a storm of anger. The two sisters could not always prevent their mother's anger, and Tiffany in particular engaged in her many mother-daughter battles. Once she was thrown out of a moving car because she had angered her mother. Petrified, Melissa sat in the back seat. "Tears rolled down my cheeks as I turned back toward the front and accidentally caught Mom's eyes in the rearview mirror. 'You want to go with her?' she asked. I didn't say a word. I tried to suck in the air around me and cry as silently as I could."[6] When Missy was eight she had a similar experience with her mother. "She pulled the car to the side of the road and told me to get out, 'Find your own way home. And another place to live while you're at it.'"[7]

On good days, when she had pleased her mother—especially if it involved outshining another child—all was right with the world. "On the way home in the car I felt exhausted but happy. 'You did a nice job today. Much better than poor Lisa. She was horrible, poor girl,' Mom said. I beamed. I loved it when my mom was proud of me. I knew I'd been the better child that day."[8] Her mother often gave her feedback about her appearances or performance, with the stated intention of helping Missy succeed. Missy was dependent on her mother to help her navigate the adult world of professional acting, but she also found her mother to be harsh and unkind. "A pitiless woman with strong hands had filed my nails and cut my cuticles with a terrifyingly sharp clipper. I cried, and then got scolded by Mom for making my eyes red. I felt like a dog after a particularly grueling trip to the groomers."[9] It was clear that Missy's success was more important to her mother than Missy's feelings.

Likewise, Missy's school success was of tremendous interest to her mother, who never missed an opportunity to brag about the skills and successes of her children to other mothers. Often her mother would exaggerate the truth in order to make Missy appear even more successful or accomplished than she was. "I had made the mistake of speaking up during one of Mom's stories before and learned that no one but Mom was allowed to talk. Afterward, when we'd gotten in the car, she'd pinched my arm ferociously and said, 'You are never to contradict me in front of another adult ever again. Do you understand me?' The pain shooting through my arm confirmed how serious she was."[10]

One day her mother returned from parent's night carrying a project that Missy had done. Her mother was not happy with the poor quality of her work and berated her. "This isn't good. Did you actually turn this in? . . . You can't turn in crap like this. This is truly horrible. Why didn't you tell me you had a project to do? What else are you too lazy to do properly?"[11] Her mother took command of Missy's next project, which was to build a replica of a mission, by making one herself and delivering it to Melissa to pass off as her own work. "Mom stood behind the model. 'What do you think?' There was a hesitation in her voice. I loved it and was ashamed of it. 'You can't tell anyone I helped you with this.' . . . Though I felt a little dirty I was grateful that Mom figured out the game and won."[12]

Missy's mother was intolerant of her children's subpar performance in all areas including appearance, grades, acting, and hobbies. She was constantly criticizing their eating habits and weight, and was relentless and harsh with either child who didn't appear to apply herself. In response to watching Melissa's sister ice-skate, her mother commented, "You were round-shouldered and pigeon-toed the whole lesson. Why am I wasting my money if you aren't going to try? Every time I looked at you, you were tripping over your own skates. Maybe you're too lazy to skate, or maybe you just don't appreciate the time and money I am pouring into you."[13] Her standards were impossibly high and provoked rage when not met. Missy recalled her mother saying, "I am so sick of both of you. I do everything I can to help you. I've devoted my entire life to you. My mom never cared about me like this. All she cared about was my brother, her precious son! My sisters were the only ones who took care of me. . . . It kills me that neither of you appreciate everything I am always doing for both of you!"[14] In this way she induced guilt in her children for enjoying the things that she had done for them and the things she had given to them.

When Missy's stint on *Little House on the Prairie* came to an end, Missy went on with her life, but her mother "reacted like someone close to her had died."[15] For a while she rallied and continued to oversee Missy's acting career, academic pursuits, and indulged Melissa's and Tiffany's desires for fancy clothes, horses, and private school. Eventually her mother lost interest in Melissa and sank into a depressive stupor, not even remembering to go food shopping or pick her up from school on time. "I waited at the curb in front of the school for Mom to drive up in her little white Porsche. The benches were empty, except for a couple of lingering strays like myself. I gamed how long I should wait before I went into the front office and asked them to call Mom and confirm that she'd forgotten me. The more time that went by, the heavier my chest felt. I wondered if she had decided not to come get me, or if I was just no longer a priority."[16]

When Tiffany graduated from high school, the family imploded. Tiffany tried to break away but could not find her foothold, especially when her mother refused to pay for her college. Tiffany had several bouts of drug abuse and rehab and eventually died of an overdose. That marked the end of Melissa's relationship with her mother. "She never called, never returned the money, never opened her heart to the daughter who needed her. There was nothing to forgive. And nothing to salvage. Our bond was just wiped away. Gone."[17]

SICKENED BY JULIE GREGORY

In this second memoir, *Sickened,*[18] Julie Gregory describes her experience as a victim of her mother's Munchausen by proxy, a psychiatric condition in which a parent creates, fabricates, or exaggerates medical illnesses in their child in order to gain attention and sympathy from both medical professionals as well as friends and family.

When Julie was a little girl, her grandmother babysat one evening, encouraging the little girl to root through the bottom of her purse to find a candy treat. Once the candy was finished, Grandma frantically called Julie's mother, reporting that a stranger had given Julie poisoned food. The alarmed family raced to the doctor, fretting that Julie might not "make it." This was neither the first nor the last visit to the doctor for Julie. The state of Julie's health was a primary preoccupation for her mother, scheduling a never-ending series of medical appointments, hoping to get to the bottom of what was wrong with her once and for all. Her mother micromanaged Julie's health care "with the logistical vigor of a drill sergeant."[19] Her mother seemed to come alive in the presence of doctors, soaking up their attention and interest. However, when a doctor failed to confirm a hoped-for diagnosis, Julie's mother stalked away furious, cursing and threatening to sue. At these times Julie tried to comfort her mother, offering her the only thing she seemed to care about. "Don't worry, Mom. It's okay. We'll go find another one."[20] In front of the doctors, Julie's mother displayed concern, worry, and exasperation at the mysterious illness that required so much of her time and attention. When the doctors weren't looking, her concern turned to anger and threats, digging her nails into Julie's thighs and hissing at her to show the doctors just how sick she was.

In reality there was nothing really wrong with Julie's health, although the pills that her mother gave her for migraines probably induced them rather than cured them. She also gave Julie special "suckers" that Julie devoured. "Mom pulls out a new book of matches and carefully bends back the cover to expose two fresh red rows of the minipops she's been giving me for as long as I can remember. My mouth waters when I see their shimmery crimson tips. The first one is always the best. . . . One by one I devour the pack, trying to finish it off for Mom. . . . she smiles softly at me with a sucker in my mouth as Dad clenches the wheel, lost in thought."[21]

Her father lived on the La-Z-Boy chair in the living room, tuned in to his TV reruns, oblivious to Julie except as someone to fetch for him. "If the batteries run down on the remote, he'll make you perch under the console and click through the channels as his living remote. Once cemented in his chair, Dad'll hawk into his hand, and fling it against the wall or the carpet. But if he knows you're anywhere near, you'll have to fetch him toilet paper and haul it off, clamping the dry edge of the damp wonton pouch daintily between two fingers. If you can, it's best to slip into your room when no one's looking."[22] For the most part he was a benign presence in Julie's life except when manipulated by Julie's mother to roar into brief but brutal bursts of parental involvement. "Before I know it he is behind me. My head flies back and lands in his massive palm, as he stuffs the greasy rind into my mouth. 'I said eat it girl.'"[23] Her mother smirks with satisfaction, "I told you, you better listen to your father. . . . You think he's a wimp and you can just walk all over him, huh? . . . you think he is . . . nothing but a sorry-ass faggot-assed bastard."[24]

Julie was a quiet child, sweet, and eager to please both of her parents, whom she adored despite their obvious limitations. "Mom had the most beautiful singing voice. . . . When we're alone, Mom shimmies her back to sit upright, settles her hands on the wheel, lifts her head and opens up her mouth to sing so loud it fills the whole car . . . there we are, belting out our song, her looking down at me and smiling, and me—fueled by her love—raising my voice to the heavens."[25] These are the moments Julie lived for.

Julie had so many doctor appointments that she routinely missed school, especially since her mother tacked shopping sprees onto "doctor days," eventually accumulating over two hundred pairs of shoes and a room full of clothes and goods that no one needed or used. School simply wasn't a priority for Julie's mother, who routinely instructed Julie to skip homework or to do it on the bus in the morning. At the end of one typical shopping trip, her mother told her that there wasn't time for homework since she still had chores to do. "By the time I unload the bags of grain, dog food, and groceries, feed the horses and do all the dishes after dinner, it's going to be way past my bedtime."[26] Between the intense housework and farm chores and the lack of food, Julie becomes thin and frail. "I pride myself on how little space I take up. I am going to shrink and shrink until I am a dry fall leaf, complete with a translucent spine and brittle veins, blowing away in a stiff wind, up, up, up into a crisp blue sky."[27]

Amid the chaos and harshness, Julie and her younger brother were hungry for their parent's love and approval. When her father came home, Julie and her brother came running "like hound puppies. I fling into his strong arms, while Danny tries to wrap his little ones around Dad's gargantuan rock-hard middle or just settles onto a single leg."[28]

Julie's mother was industrious and had big plans for the family, prodding her husband to build several extensions onto their trailer. Some of these rooms were for veterans, sick and elderly men whom the government paid to board there. When the old men first came, Julie's mother included them in family dinners but eventually figured out that she could get away with serving them cold leftovers and locking them in their rooms. One vet "paid" for the family's trip to Disney World, "sitting in silence for hours, sweltering, parked in the truck with the windows rolled up and the doors locked, while we wandered the theme park."[29] Later Julie's mother brought in a series of foster children whom she would berate, humiliate, frighten, and starve. She expected Julie to discipline them on her behalf. "Mom puts the flyswatter in my hand and shows me how to do it. Grab their wrists and whack the hard plastic handle over their pink baby palms."[30] Julie's mother had cruel nicknames for the children, and Julie, desperate to be aligned with her mother, joined in.

There were also periodic flashes of violence between her parents, especially when Julie's mother became frustrated with her husband's singular focus on the TV. She would block his view and provoke him out of his stupor until he raged at her, bashing her head against the wall, frightening the children. "Mom's screams swallow my head."[31] Julie and her brother flailed at their father while their mother played the role of the victim. "Let him kill me, Julie, just let him put me out of my misery and kill me!"[32] The whole family screamed and thrashed about until the situation subsided. "It is the boil-over that brings us back to a simmer."[33] Julie retreated to her room where she paged through a catalog, earmarking the items she planned to purchase, dreaming of placating and pleasing her mother. "She'll always have something to look forward to. I cannot wait to make my mother happy."[34] Her mother, however, was not happy. In fact, after one such evening she entered the room with a shotgun in hand. "She looks at me with her tear-streaked, puffy face. She holds me with her eyes, terrified like an animal in a chute, and raises her hand to cock the trigger. . . . You kids want me to kill myself, don't you? . . . I'm crying for her, telling her no we don't hate you, no, Mommy, we love you and we don't want you to kill yourself. . . . She drops the gun to her lap, her chin collapses to her chest. I cling around her like a baby monkey."[35] Appeased, Julie's mother confided in her about the horrors of her childhood gang rape and then asked, "Isn't your father a no-good son of a bitch for turning you kids against me?"[36]

Throughout are the concerns about Julie's "heart condition," which don't prevent the mother from working Julie like a seasoned farmhand. "I'm winded. I'm hungry. It's two o'clock and I have eaten yet today. I was going to school without breakfast, not getting any lunch money, and when I got off the bus at home, I had to do all the farm work: feed the horses, haul three bales of hay from the barn to the manger, chop the ice in the trough with a mallet. . . . once the animals were done, I had to load up the rug inside with enough firewood to last the night and the next day and dump out the tray of ash from the bottom of the wood burning stove. . . . Then I had to chop wood with an ax to replace what I'd put in the house. . . . I had to set the table for dinner and clean up afterward."[37]

Eventually Julie's mother found a doctor willing to perform exploratory tests on Julie's heart. Checked into the hospital, Julie beamed, "It's like a vacation or going away to camp, which I've always wanted to do."[38] Julie had a clean bed, three meals a day, and was treated like a child. "I love the hospital."[39] Her mother, too, was in her element, chatting with the nurses, befriending other mothers, and visiting children in the hospital and reporting to Julie their various illnesses and suggesting that Julie visit them. "I'll go anywhere in the hospital Mom tells me to as long as it's not home."[40] However, the fun ended when Julie realized that she was to be cut open. Shocked and frightened, Julie blurted out the truth that she didn't know that she knew, that her mother was fabricating the illness, that there was nothing wrong with her. "I can't believe I just said that! I jump to the back corner of the bed, clutching the covers up to my neck."[41] The news—so life shattering for her—did not alter the course of events set in motion by the mother, and Julie underwent painful, frightening, and unnecessary surgery. When the doctor informed her mother that there was nothing wrong with Julie's heart, she took it in stride, asking when the open-heart surgery would be scheduled. Her mother became frustrated and enraged when the doctor informed her that this was neither appropriate nor necessary.

Giving up on heart surgery, Julie's mother focused her attention on other pressing medical conditions Julie was afflicted with, such as breathing through her mouth. Facial surgery was arranged, followed by a series of tests and consults for digestive and intestinal functioning, culminating in a painful and intrusive catheterization. Eventually Julie's mother lost interest in her health and decided that at age sixteen Julie should meet an older man and leave home. She posed Julie suggestively in a series of snapshots that she carried around in her purse in case some nice older man came along. Julie's mother arranged for her to get a job at the hospital, and through her connections there Julie decided to try to become emancipated by telling a caseworker what was going on in her home. She was moved to a group home while waiting to testify for the state against her parents. She believed that the hearing would result in the removal of the foster children from the home, but Julie was misled by her parents to believe that the case was against Julie. At the last moment she decided not to testify. Julie returned home, and life reverted to routine for a little while until her parents conspired to burn down the house. Her parents shared the insurance money but went their separate ways, leaving Julie and her brother as latchkey kids, raising themselves in a camper. Only later did her mother confess to causing the fire, which inadvertently killed Julie's dog. Julie eventually moved after graduating from high school. Neither parent attended. She maintained periodic contact with her parents until she discovered that her mother was once again taking in foster children and seemed to be identifying mysterious medical conditions that required extensive medications and ongoing testing of them. Horrified that another child was being put through this ordeal, Julie felt compelled to try to put a stop to it. "I have come back to prosecute my mother, to tell her secrets, to rip from her a veil burnt, sewn, crusted onto her skin. I pick up the phone and call Children's Services."[42]

HOUSE RULES BY RACHEL SONTAG

In the third memoir of emotional abuse, *House Rules*,[43] Rachel Sontag describes being raised by enlightened, liberal, educated parents in Evanston, Illinois. According to Rachel, her father emotionally abused her while her mother—too afraid to speak the truth—allowed it to continue.

Rachel was the eldest of two daughters of Ellen and Steve Sontag. Her childhood was marked by the many privileges of wealth (e.g., European vacations, nice homes, good education). It was also marred by her father's extreme protectiveness, control, and domineering personality. His approval meant everything to Rachel because he insisted that he was the only one who knew what was smart or right or good. She strived to be accepted and admired by him. "I was my father's daughter."[44] To fail to please him, to give the wrong answer, was to mortally wound him, to disappoint him, and to incur his anger or hurt, to risk being ousted from his acceptance and good graces. While he was allowed to tell jokes at everyone else's expense and the children were expected to laugh with good humor, if Rachel told a joke that her father failed to see the humor in or found insulting, he punished her by refusing to speak to her for the rest of the day. Rachel recalled a time when she impressed her father with her near-death experience and went to sleep that night on the couch, "where I remained worthy of my father's attention."[45] Because his love and approval were so unattainable, Rachel and her sister desperately wanted to please him to "feel our way to his heart."[46]

But it wasn't possible for Rachel to please her father because he changed the rules (what was acceptable one day was not acceptable the next) and because his expectations were often not appropriate. He was relentless in his desire to teach his children a lesson even if the punishment inconvenienced or humiliated his children or wife. When his children packed Barbie dolls to take on vacation against his express wishes, he insisted that Rachel's mother find a locker in the airport to store the dolls, resulting in the family missing their flight. His rules were to be followed at all costs.

Rachel's father exercised a degree of control over her that was excessive and inappropriate, for example, locking the phone in a metal box when he left the house and insisting on an "outline of how I would use my 'unmonitored' time at the library."[47] When she got older her father measured the length of her fingernails, did not allow Rachel to make any phone calls, and had strict curfews. When she was thirteen her mother got into a car accident near the house. Rachel was in the car, unharmed. Her mother instructed her to walk home to notify her father about the accident. Furious that she had "left the scene of an accident," her father locked the doors and sent her back to her mother. It was more important for him to teach her a civics lesson than to address her emotional or medical needs. She had to concede that technically he was correct, she *had* left the scene of an accident, which was why once again she was left feeling bitter and confused. She wondered "what he saw in me that caused him to break up inside."[48]

Likewise, when she lost her house keys he refused to let her in the home and left her in the cold for several hours to teach her responsibility. She pressed her nose against the glass doors and watched her family sitting in the living room, watching a TV show together. She rang the doorbell but no one answered. They could see her outside in the cold but no one dared let her in until the father felt that she had sufficiently paid the price for her mistake. "I stared at the side of Mom's head, pressed my lips into the window. Had there been no glass pane dividing us, I could have touched her shoulders with my lips. I knocked once more but she didn't look away from the TV."[49]

During a family vacation in Europe, Rachel's father put her in charge of holding everyone's passports and then he derided and humiliated her for holding them in her hands rather than placing them in her fanny pack as he would have preferred. Rather than offer a constructive suggestion, he sarcastically commented to her mother that Rachel was so confident in her abilities that she held the passports in her hands, mocking her hubris for risking the family's life and vacation. Rachel's sister Jenny was in charge of the maps of Europe that the family were to consult during their trip. However, Jenny inadvertently left the maps on the airplane. "When she finally realized what she'd done, she started heaving the kind of terrible bodily sobs that made me embarrassed for her. We were different in this way. Jenny let it all hang out. I checked out. My mind faded to a calming state of numbness. I simply evaporated, removed myself completely from the situation until the situation had passed. Jenny had no ability to turn herself off, to mentally escape a situation that she was physically trapped in."[50] In response to their mistakes her father condemned both daughters. "I don't even want to be here with you two,"[51] he declared, failing to see that perhaps he had asked too much of them or given too little support and supervision to allow them to successfully carry off their assigned tasks. Off the hot seat, Rachel was so relieved that her father was mad at someone else that she "basked in the aftermath of Dad's affection."[52] Later in the trip Rachel tried to impress her father by exchanging money on the black market, something she had seen him do numerous times. Unfortunately, the money she received was not real and her father had nothing but scorn for her. "You've got to be kidding me, Rachel. Counterfeit. You fell for the oldest trick in the book."[53] Once again she failed to please him, and what she cared about most was "how I'd lost not money but Dad's respect."[54]

He was particularly harsh when he felt that Rachel was not sufficiently chaste in her clothes and demeanor. When her hair was too long he berated her. "I used to know girls like you . . . girls who hated themselves."[55] Rachel felt her father's disapproval of her hair, her clothes, her changing body. "She's fourteen and she's got hair hanging in her eyes like a . . . like a cheap girl. It's cheap!"[56] Once when she wore lipstick he lectured her that what she was doing was "dangerous, walking around with that stuff on your face. It's provocative, stupid. It's going to attract the wrong person and then it's going to be all over. . . . And it's going to be your fault. You walk around looking like that, you pay the price. You got it, Rachel?"[57] It was almost as if he were wishing something bad to happen to her so that he could have the satisfaction of having been right.

Rachel's mother was also called out repeatedly for her failures and imperfections, as if she were another child in the family. "She did everything wrong, from buying that expensive ice cream to trying too hard to speak French in public and sounding like an idiot."[58] During these times, Rachel was in her father's favor. "On nights like that, it almost felt like Dad admired me, like I reminded him of himself when he was a boy."[59] At the expense of her relationship with her mother, Rachel was intermittently allowed to receive her father's love and approval.

Appearances were vitally important to Rachel's father, and one of his most strongly held beliefs was the importance of not discussing family problems with others. When his own mother was in the hospital and took a turn for the worse, he accused Rachel of bringing on the illness by confiding in her grandmother about tensions in the family. "Rachel, you are going to kill her with the things you say."[60] Rachel tried to reassure her father that she didn't say bad things about him to his mother, but he insisted that she had done so and for that he condemned her as "negligent and selfish."[61] Likewise, if she spent time with his family he wanted to know in detail what they spoke about and whether she had made negative comments about him.

When Rachel behaved in a way that upset her father, which was quite often during her teen years, he would summon her to the living room for lengthy and emotionally draining "discussions" during which he grilled her about her infractions and mocked her speech and ideas when she tried to respond to his questions and commands. As a teenager she developed an interest in theater and worked on acting scenes for the speech team. She often found herself reverting to one of her characters in her mind in order to protect herself from her father's onslaughts and humiliations, to help her be physically present in the room with him without being fully emotionally present. It was as if her character were being humiliated and berated rather than her. "That was how I separated and protected who I was from what was happening with Dad. I excavated emotions of characters to distract me from my own. Dad could see it I was sure. He could feel me becoming someone else."[62] Many of the sessions ended with a final judgment against her, with him declaring, "I'm ashamed to say you're my daughter, disgusted and ashamed."[63]

During her teen years Rachel and her father continued to clash. She seemed unable to please him, and the more she displeased him the more she rebelled against his rules. She was engaged in a battle for his approval, to know that he loved her no matter what. "I wanted to know that Dad was there for me. That if something happened, something threw off Dad's worldview, he might still be there."[64] She also secretly thought that he admired her for standing up to him. This allowed her to view their struggles in a more positive light. Through it all she maintained a keen appreciation for his values and the life lessons he tried to instill in her. "It killed me to see parents ruining their kids with TVs and phone and video games. . . . This was something I thought Dad did right . . . infusing us with values that would inform our entire lives. . . . I knew it even then, even in the midst of everything, that I'd forever be grateful for this."[65] And Rachel felt protective of her father as well, often seeing her mother as he did, as weak and pathetic, an annoyance. "I understood Dad's frustration. There she was, discouraging us from pushing our limits, doubting Dad's ability to lead us through the Canyon after dark."[66] Rachel sided with her father in this dispute. "I ran after Dad, my arms flailing everywhere, chasing after the respect I'd earn in not being a quitter."[67]

At one point Rachel was removed from home because her relationship with her father had become volatile. When she returned, things remained untenable between them. "Whatever it was Dad saw in me, it was something he struggled with, and I hated him for seeing me like that, and I hated myself for being whatever it was he saw."[68] She harbored fantasies of being adopted by a new family who would love and appreciate her and help her feel that she belonged. "I would be their child. That's what I wanted, to be somebody's child."[69] Back home, during one of their frequent conflicts, her father compared her to Saddam Hussein, seeing her as conniving, manipulative, and cruel.

One of the more insidious forms of punishment Rachel's father instituted was to create situations in which Rachel had to betray herself. He would hand her a piece of paper and insist that she take dictation as he tossed out insults at her. He would throw out words such as *selfish*, *rotten*, and *worthless* and insist that she write them down in full sentences about herself and submit her paper for his inspection. During one of these sessions, he wanted her to write that she was the scum of the earth, like a snake, and then he threatened to kick her out of the house. Rachel's mother was often involved in these sessions as well, being commanded by her father to join him, to own his opinions as her own. "Say it Ellen. You are ashamed that she's your daughter. She can't just hear it from me."[70] At his most cruel, he informed Rachel that he wished she had never been born.

Rachel and her father continued to struggle against each other until she left for college and began to live on her own. There were periods of closeness and periods of distance that culminated in the end of her contact with both parents in order to free herself of the burden of trying to please a man who could not be pleased.

Interestingly, her father and mother appear to have created a website devoted to refuting Rachel's claims about them. However, rather than provide an opposing point of the view, the tone of the website as well as the many documents posted on it are consistent with Rachel's description of her father as petty and cruel. The tone of the website is sarcastic, inappropriate, and generally out of touch with the emotional needs of children. For example, the website contains a typed letter purportedly written by Rachel's father to her in which he outlined the kind of apology letter that he insisted on receiving from her. He described that her apology letter must be perfectly neat and contain detailed explanations of how she was wrong. Consistent with Rachel's description of her family throughout her book, the letter contains no warmth or emotional connection. Consistent with her description, Rachel's father appears to care more about being right than in having a loving and mutually respectful relationship with his daughter. Rachel tried for many years to win her father's approval but in the end found that it simply was not possible for him to give her that which she so desperately craved.

Chapter Six

Making Meaning of Emotional Abuse

According to the American Professional Society on the Abuse of Children (APSAC), there are six types of psychological maltreatment (that is the term used to encompass maltreatment that is not physical or sexual in nature).[1] The six types are spurning, terrorizing, isolating, exploiting/corrupting, denying emotional responsiveness, and neglecting the child's medical or mental health needs. The last two are addressed in other chapters in this book (denying emotional responsiveness is addressed in the emotional neglect chapter and neglecting the child's medical/mental health needs is addressed in the physical neglect chapter). The first four are rightly subsumed under the header of emotional abuse and are taken up in this chapter. Unlike physical or sexual abuse, there is no bright line between poor parenting and emotional abuse. What differentiates poor parenting from emotional abuse is the frequency and severity of the behaviors and the overall quality of the relationship.

Twelve memoirs about the emotional abuse of a child by a parent were read. Three of the memoirs were summarized in the previous chapter, and all were reviewed for the themes described in this chapter. Table 6.1 presents an overview of these stories.

Below, common themes are discussed. Because of the variety of ways that a parent can emotionally abuse a child, the first half of this chapter is devoted to descriptions of those types while the second half of the chapter focuses on the meaning of those experiences from the adult child's point of view. What is notable is that in all of these stories the emotionally abusive parent was the mother and the victim/author was a daughter. We suspect this is not a coincidence as women in general may be more able to express themselves emotionally and are more open to working through their trauma experiences, in this case by writing their memoirs. As women are the primary

Table 6.1. Memoirs of Emotional Abuse

Title of book/ Author	Abusive Parent	Abuse Victim/ Author	Secondary Abuse by Parent	Role of other Parent	Major Dysfunction in Family
Who Do You Think You Are?	Mother	Alyse Myers	Physical abuse	Her father was deceased	None
The Sky Isn't Visible from Here	Mother	Felicia C. Sullivan (Lisa)	Physical neglect	Her father was absent	Drug-abusing mother
Her Last Death	Mother	Susanna Sonnenberg	None	Her father was ill and absent	Drug-abusing and sex-addicted mother
You Ain't Got No Easter Clothes	Mother	Laura Love	Physical neglect and abuse	Her father was absent	Mentally ill mother
Lies My Mother Never Told Me	Mother	Kaylie Jones	None	Her father was deceased	None
Diary of a Stage Mother's Daughter	Mother	Melissa Francis	None	Her father failed to protect her	None
House Rules	Father	Rachel Sontag	None	Her mother failed to protect her	None
Why Be Happy When You Could Be Normal?	Mother	Jeanette Winterson	Physical neglect	Her father failed to protect her	Depressed mother
Sickened	Mother	Julie Gregory	Muchausen by proxy	Her father failed to protect her	None
With or Without You	Mother	Domenica Ruta	Physical neglect	Her father was absent	Drug-abusing mother
Falling Leaves	Stepmother	Adeline Yen Mah	Physical neglect	Her father failed to protect her	None

Title of book/ Author	Abusive Parent	Abuse Victim/ Author	Secondary Abuse by Parent	Role of other Parent	Major Dysfunction in Family
The Three of Us	Mother	Julia Blackburn	None	Her father was absent	Sex-addicted mother

caregivers their relationship with their children may be more important for their children and may become the primary focus of the child victim's experiences.

TYPES OF PSYCHOLOGICAL MALTREATMENT

Spurning

Spurning is defined by APSAC as "hostile, rejecting/degrading, verbal and nonverbal caregiver acts."[2] There are four types of spurning. Each is described in table 6.2 along with examples from the memoirs. (There are different numbers of examples for each type of emotional abuse because some were more present in the memoirs than others.)

Terrorizing

Terrorizing is defined by APSAC as behaviors that threaten to or are likely to physically hurt, kill, abandon the child, or place the child or child's loved ones or objects in recognizably dangerous situations.[3] There are five types of terrorizing, which are described in table 6.3 along with examples from the memoirs.

Isolating

In the APSAC definition of psychological maltreatment, isolating consists of "consistently denying the child opportunities to meet his/her needs for interacting and communicating with peers or adults inside or outside the home."[4] There are two types of isolating. They are described in table 6.4 along with examples from the memoirs.

Exploiting/Corrupting

According to APSAC, exploiting/corrupting is defined as encouraging the child to develop inappropriate behaviors (self-destructive, antisocial, criminal, deviant, or other maladaptive behaviors).[5] There are four types of exploiting/corrupting. They are described in table 6.5 along with examples from the memoirs.

Table 6.2. Spurning

Book	Example
Spurning Type 1: Belittling, degrading, and other nonphysical forms of overtly hostile or rejecting treatment	
You Ain't Got No Easter Clothes	Laura was subjected to her mother's routine putdowns and rages, such as "One wintry Sunday morning, Mom walked into the living room and kicked me awake from a sound sleep on the floor of our apartment, I sprang to my feet clad only in underwear, to the sound of her piercing voice, 'Neither one of you lazy-ass niggers thought to get up before noon and bring me the goddamn Sunday paper. I suppose I'm not worth half a shit to you now since I told you I might just walk outta that goddamn job and not look back. The only thing I'm worth to you little parasites is the paycheck I bring home.'"
Lies My Mother Never Told Me	Kaylie's mother made cruel comments throughout her childhood, "You're a mean, spoiled, and ugly girl . . . You bore me to death, I can't wait for you to grow up . . . You have ugly legs, not like me . . . I was much prettier than you when I was your age . . . You're a klutz." When Kaylie is accepted into college her mother urges her to "'get around and meet some future doctors and lawyers' . . . She was still convinced, and told me so at every possible occasion, that I'd never be able to take care of myself and was heading for a miserable life of drudgery and want."
House Rules	Rachel's father told her that he wished she had never been born. Once, when she became separated from the family during a vacation in a foreign city, he was furious with her and berated her. "How unbelievably selfish, to run off with my camera." In ninth grade her father's response to her wearing makeup was "there's a girl who hates herself."

Book	Example
Who Do You Think You Are?	Alyse struggled with her mother's ongoing negativity and rejection toward her. "My mother always told me how beautiful my daughter was. 'She doesn't look like you did when you were a baby' she would tell me. 'You were pretty ugly. I was always so embarrassed when people would look at you and tell me you were cute when I knew you weren't.'"[8] "'You're just like your father' she said, 'You only do what's good for you. You take after him and his goddamn family.'"
The Sky Isn't Visible from Here	Felicia's mother was a drug user who was unpredictable in her ability to be loving and kind to her daughter. "I always reached for her. She was never as close as I wanted her to be; her body was always at a remove. She alone would determine how close I could get."
Diary of a Stage Mother's Daughter	Missy's mother stage-managed her acting career and her life, cruelly cutting down her daughter. "A week later, Mom brought the tambourine home from Parent's Night. 'This isn't good. Did you actually turn this in?' I didn't say anything since the answer seemed obvious. 'You can't turn in crap like this. This is truly horrible. Why didn't you tell me you had a project to do? What else are you too lazy to do properly?'"
Why Be Happy When You Could Be Normal?	When Jeanette's mother was "angry with me, which was often, she said, 'The Devil led us to the wrong crib.'" She wrote, "Once it was decided that I was the Wrong Crib, everything I did supported my mother in that belief."

Spurning Type 2: Shaming for showing normal emotions

Book	Example
Lies My Mother Never Told Me	When Kaylie's family moved to a new city, her medicine was left behind. Sick and in pain, she approached her mother. "'Mommy,' I said, nervous, upset, my voice shaky. 'I can't breathe through my nose. I'm really not feeling well.' Sitting at the edge of the large, creaky, still unfamiliar bed, she said sorrowfully, 'You're so neurotic.'" Likewise, her mother routinely forgot to pick her up at school. "Back home, not remotely calmed, I went downstairs to my parents' room to confront my mother. She might be lying back on her round bed with its faux fur cover, her eyes closed; or taking a bath, getting ready for her evening out. 'You forgot to pick me up at school again!' I shouted. 'Absolutely not!' she retorted, offended. 'And don't talk to me that way. God you're so neurotic!'"
House Rules	When Rachel was upset about the conflict in her relationship with her father, he accused her of being insincere and manipulative. "Are you going to cry for us, Rachel? Are you putting on a little show?"
Her Last Death	Susanna's mother accused her of being melodramatic when she complained or had a negative reaction to her outrageously inappropriate behavior, such as sleeping with her boyfriend, stealing, lying about having cancer, or overdosing. "Bitch. Look at me when you speak to me, you little. Melodramatic. Bitch. Are we going to talk again about poor Susy's childhood because her mother did drugs? Jesus, *get over it.*"

Spurning Type 3: Singling out child for less rewards and/or greater punishment

Book	Example
Falling Leaves	Adeline described the many ways in which her father and stepmother favored their children over the father's children from his first marriage. "Besides a large double bed and an ornately carved dressing-table and mirror, it contained an alcove which overlooked the garden and served as a sitting area. James was to nickname their bedroom 'The Holy of Holies.' It was separated by a bathroom from the 'antechamber,' Franklin's and Susan's bedroom, which opened on to a balcony from which Franklin often threw food or toys down to Jackie prowling below. When we first arrived from Tianjin, we, the 'have-nots,' were relegated to the second floor. Ye Ye had his own room with a balcony, Aunt Baba and I shared a room, my three brothers another. It was tacitly understood that we, the second class citizens, were forbidden to set foot in the antechamber or the Holy of Holies. However, 'they' the first-floor residents, roamed our quarters at will."

Spurning Type 4: Public humiliation

Who Do You Think You Are?	Alyse recalled that her mother often put her down in front of friends and neighbors. "My mother would always tell everyone how lucky she was that this one was so easy, pointing to my middle sister, and that the baby was too, thank God. Not like the big one, she would tell everyone, looking at me." When Alyse got her clothes dirty, her mother coldly berated her in front of the neighbors. "'You stupid idiot,' she hissed at me, grabbing my wrist with her hand."

Book	Example
The Three of Us	Julia recalled her mother's reckless embarrassment of her in front of others. "She was in a very odd mood. I remember we went for a swim and I had forgotten to bring my knickers and had to walk back to the house with a bare bottom under my skirt. We were going up the steps and there were lots of people around. 'Julia's got no kickers on! Julia's got no knickers on!' sang my mother at the top of her voice, laughing at my angry embarrassment."
Falling Leaves	Adeline felt shame in the weekly ritual of the boarding school announcing which children had parents who delivered eggs for them. "Those eggs became symbols of rare privilege. They were cheap and readily available in the markets, but having your number called by Mother Mary meant that someone from home loved you enough to bring the eggs so that you could eat a nourishing breakfast. Just because your family was rich did not mean that you would automatically receive an egg. You could not charge eggs to your account like milk or piano lessons. The breakfast egg, more than anything, divided us into two distinct and transparent groups: the loved ones and the unloved ones. Needless to say, I remained eggless throughout my tenure at Sacred Heart."
With or Without You	Domenica recalled the time she had head lice. "My mother made me walk up and down the street and confess this to any neighbor whose house I'd ever entered. Like a registered sex offender, I had to knock on their doors and identify myself as the carrier of a plague."

As can be seen in the tables, there are many specific ways for a parent to be emotionally abusive to a child. The common thread appears to be the parent's inability or unwillingness to factor in the needs and experiences of the child. Fundamentally, their parents do not register the child's needs and desires. That does not mean that the parents are always inattentive or unloving, because that was not the case. What it does mean is that they were unable to consistently take into account that their children are separate indi-

Table 6.3.   Terrorizing

Book	Example
Terrorizing Type 1: Placing a child in an unpredictable or chaotic circumstances (frightening the child)	
Who Do You Think You Are?	Alyse recalled that as a teenager her mother kicked her out of their apartment in a rage. "I was asleep for only an hour when my mother came into my room and ordered me to leave the apartment. She said I couldn't use the phone to call anyone and told me that if I wasn't out of the house in fifteen minutes she would call the police and have them take me away. She said she was going to go back into her room, and that if I was still there in fifteen minutes—and she showed me her watch, pointing at the time when the fifteen minutes would be up—she would call them."
The Sky Isn't Visible from Here	Felicia wrote, "Ever since I was ten, I've sat alone in hospitals while doctors dispensed tranquilizers to my mother, tried to calm her down because she loved cocaine and she kept doing too much of it." Her mother also left her in the care of her sister who was a drug addict.
The Three of Us	Julia recalled her mother's rages at her. "I was having a shower when she suddenly burst into the little bathroom. She pulled back the curtain and, fully clothed, stepped in under the drenching hot water. She put her face close to mine and she began screaming accusations at me, about how I had destroyed her life for ever. I remember thinking that maybe she had a knife and she was going to kill me."

Book	Example
With or Without You	Domenica described her mother, Kathi, as "a screamer. Sometimes she opened her mouth and the screech that came out sustained for minutes without breaking or getting hoarse. She used to bend down to scream directly in my face, and I would get lost at the black fillings in her molars, the heat of her breath touching my skin like a finger." Her mother was a periodic drug user and was unpredictable in her nurturance of her daughter. "Asking my mother for help could be risky. It required perfect timing. Her waking hours were mapped by a wave of chemical highs and lows. If I asked her to hem my skirt, I could get a cold shrug of the shoulders. I could get a temper tantrum and an ashtray flung very close to but not exactly at my head. I could get a wild shopping spree for a new wardrobe but not a new uniform. I could get roller skates, a puppy or the following: 'Get the fuck away from me. I can't stand the sound of your breathing right now.' I could get kicked out of my own house, banished to my grandmother's, or simply ignored for the next three days."
Her Last Death	Susanna's mother told her that she (the mother) had leukemia and was going to die shortly. When Susanna asked who would take care of her and her sister, her mother explained that she hadn't decided yet, with no awareness of how frightening that would be for her children. More than once she had seizures in front of Susanna from overdosing on her pain medications or from mixing alcohol and drugs. Susanna's mother taught her how to inject her intraveneously and tend to her infected wound sites.

Book	Example
Why Be Happy When You Could Be Normal?	Jeanette's mother had a view of the world as bleak and dangerous and explained many routine objects and incidents in frightening ways. "Mrs. Winterson had terrible stories about fridges—they gave off gases and made you dizzy . . . children got trapped inside and couldn't escape . . . and froze to death." She appeared to hate her life and let her daughter know how miserable she was. "Every day Mrs. Winterson prayed, 'Lord, let me die.'"

Terrorizing Type 2: Placing a child in recognizably dangerous situations

The Sky Isn't Visible from Here	Felicia reminisced with one of her mother's boyfriends. "We talk about her rages; the time she threatened to burn down the house while we lay sleeping; the time she hurled Christmas dishes over our heads because we grumbled about the film of grease on the cutlets."
Sickened	Julia, whose mother induced illnesses and conditions onto Julie for the benefit of the attention from having a sick daughter (formerly known as Munchausen Syndrome by proxy and currently referred to by the American Psychiatric Association as Factitious Disorder Imposed on Another), recalled a time when her mother manipulated her father to beat her. "Mom has told him [her father] that I drop them (Kleenex) so that he will have to pick them up; a premeditated attempt to sicken my father with clever trickery. He takes the Kleenex, and as his voice gains momentum, my mother's trails off. Like a relay race in which she just puffed through the first leg, he is stepping in and now she can let go. My eyes are frozen wide, this cannot be happening."

Book	Example
You Ain't Got No Easter Clothes	Laura's mother attempted to kill herself in front of her children. "She did eventually find the yellow rope and she tied it onto an exposed pipe. She pushed a kitchen chair up under that rope, climbed onto the chair, slipped her head through the knot, and walked forward as if simply stepping off a curb. . . . She was my mother and she was swinging from a yellow braided laundry rope right in front of our faces, with her tongue turning blacker by the second." Laura also wrote, "Lisa and I were threatened with bodily harm and abandonment if we ever discussed our mother's past with anyone."

Terrorizing Type 3: Setting a rigid or unrealistic expectation with the threat of loss, harm, or danger if they are not met

Diary of a Stage Mother's Daughter	Missy's mother was deeply invested in her daughter's acting career and appeared to care more about Missy's acting successes and appearances than she did about Missy's happiness. She would sometimes complete Missy's homework for her in order to ensure that she received top grades. Nothing less than perfection was acceptable, and Missy feared her mother's wrath and rejection should she fail to meet her expectations.

Terrorizing Type 4: Threatening to perpetrate violence against the child

Who Do You Think You Are?	Alyse wrote about her mother, "Whenever she got angry at me—if I didn't clean my room, if I was on the phone too long, if I didn't put the milk back in the refrigerator—she threatened to go after me with one of my father's belts."

Book	Example
Falling Leaves	Adeline lived in fear of being cast out, knowing that she had no standing in her father's new family. "'What's going to happen to me?' I asked fearfully. 'We're not sure,' was father's cruel reply. 'Since you're not happy here, you must go somewhere else.' . . . I saw myself wandering aimlessly along the streets of Shanghai. I had seen abandoned babies wrapped in newspapers lying on the roadside and children in rags searching for food scraps in garbage cans. . . . I was terrified."
You Ain't Got No Easter Clothes	Laura's mother threatened to abandon her children if they let others know about how they lived. "She told us she could not forgive us if we ever revealed our family secrets, and that we would have to fend for ourselves if we did, because she would be called home to be with God in the event of our betrayal."
Terrorizing Type 5: Threatening or perpetrating violence against a child's loved ones or objects	
The Sky Isn't Visible from Here	Domenica's mother "destroyed all of my writing, years of handwritten stories and poems torn up with her hands."
Why Be Happy When You Could Be Normal?	Jeanette's mother found books hidden under her bed and burned them.
You Ain't Got No Easter Clothes	Laura's mother instructed Laura to hang her cat before killing her mother killed herself.

viduals with legitimate, independent experiences of their own, and then modify their behavior accordingly. Instead, these parents steamrolled over their children's needs, failing to see them altogether or discounting them as invalid. There was usually something more important to the emotionally abusive parent than accommodating the unique needs and experiences of the child. That is, the abuse occurred when the child's needs and wishes were not consistent with those of the parent's. During the times when the child's needs *were* aligned with the parent's desire, then the parent was not abusive and could in fact be loving, attentive, and appropriate. Thus, the parent was unwilling (or unable) to meet the child on the child's terms. Underlying that unwillingness or inability could be any number of factors such as mental illness, cultural beliefs, religious beliefs, unrealistic expectations of children's capabilities, stress, lack of parenting knowledge, and addictions. Sub-

Table 6.4. Isolating

Book	Example
Isolating Type 1: Confining the child or placing unreasonable limitations on the child's freedom of movement within his or her [physical] environment (such as confining the child to a closet or other small space)	
	(no examples were found in the memoirs)
Isolating Type 2: Placing unreasonable limitations or restrictions on social interactions with peers or adults in the community	
Falling Leaves	Adeline was placed in a boarding school year round with orders for no contact with outsiders.
Sickened	Julie was not allowed to engage in any extracurricular activities.
You Ain't Got No Easter Clothes	Laura and her sister were isolated from her mother's family. "We had hardly ever been allowed to meet and develop any relationships with our relatives."

stance abuse was a factor in some of the stories, and the argument could be made that the choice to use drugs generally puts the parent's needs above the child's needs (although not all substance abusers emotionally abuse their children).

Rachel Sontag's father in *House Rules* needed to be in control and right all of the time. Thus, he appeared to be a caring and involved father so long as he maintained control and no one challenged his opinions or choices or failed to follow his rules. But when Rachel didn't live up to his expectations he was harsh and cruel and would accept nothing less than a soul-crushing apology from her in which she demeaned and denounced herself. She had to completely submit to his authority in order to be accepted by him. Questioning his decisions or beliefs was not allowed. Julie's mother's desire for sympathy and attention from medical professionals was more important than her daughter's need for physical health, the truth, or integrity in her body. Speaking the truth, therefore, was not allowed. In both *Her Last Death* by Susanna Sonnenberg and *The Three of Us* by Julia Blackburn, the mothers needed constant affirmation of their sexual allure and viewed everything else as secondary to that goal. Their lust and insecurity blinded them to their children's need for a responsible and nurturing adult. If the choice presented itself to take care of their child or have a new sexual adventure, both mothers readily choose the liaison over their children. Adeline Mah's stepmother, as described in *Falling Leaves*, needed to be the dominant parent. That need outweighed Adeline's need for acceptance and love. For the stepmother, accepting Adeline in the family would have threatened her place as the

Table 6.5. Exploiting/Corrupting

Book	Example
Exploiting/Corrupting Type 1: Modeling, permitting, or encouraging antisocial behavior (e.g., prostitution, performance in pornographic media, initiation of criminal activities, substance abuse, violence to or corruption of others)	
The Three of Us	Julia remembered how her mother arranged for her daughter to have sexual experiences. "A little while ago my mother wanted to go to Geoffrey's cottage and when she saw me looking sad, she invited a boy I hardly knew to stay with me. . . . 'I bet you'd like to look after her this weekend.' . . . When my mother was leaving she winked at him and said, 'Have fun, won't you?'"
Lies My Mother Never Told Me	Kaylie wrote, "After our father dies, my brother and I were spoiled rotten in many ways. We didn't have to pay for anything or answer to anyone; on any summer weekend we would throw all night parties, free-for-alls with the inevitable skinny dip in the pool, dancing in the big kitchen with the music blasting, which didn't bother Gloria in the least because she'd be out at her own parties, or dancing right along with us, or passed out upstairs."
Sickened	Julie's mother instructed her to physically abuse the young foster children in their home. "Mom puts the flyswatter in my hand and shows me how to do it. Grab their wrists and whack the hard plastic over their pink baby palms." Her mother also encouraged her to eat matches. "Mom pulls out a new book of matches and carefully bends back the cover to expose two fresh rows of mini-pops she's been giving me for as long as I can remember. My mouth waters when I see their shimmery crimson tips. The first one is always the best. . . . One by one I devour the pack, trying to finish it off for mom."

Book	Example
With or Without You	Domenica's mother was crude and impulsive. She took her daughter with her when she smashed the windows of a car because she was mad at its owner. She was foul-mouthed in front of her daughter. "If cursing has a matriarchal order, and for the Rutas it did, then *cunt* is the Queen Mother. This was how I knew when Mum was really, really, *really* mad. She called me so many things, but this Grand Dame of words she saved for special occasions." Her mother also chose to accept welfare rather than work and then recklessly spent the month's money in a few days. "Then there were periods when my mother was just as happy to sleep all day and collect welfare. On the first of the month she would hop around our apartment, waving her check at me and singing 'Free Money Day. Free Money Day!' . . . My mother would spend every dime of her welfare check immediately on cocaine, new clothes, new coloring books and dolls. . . . By the end of the month we'd be fisting the couch for loose change." Her mother also supplied drugs to her daughter. "Mum remembered fondly the pleasure potheads found in salty and sweet snack foods, so once I started getting high she made sure the cabinets were stocked with good 'munchables.'"
The Sky Isn't Visible from Here	Felicia's mother told her that when she was a teenager, she practiced black magic. "My mother proudly recounted stories about the people she'd maimed and others who had suffered at her hand." Her mother also was a drug user. "I see my mother's shoulders quake, remember her nose, the bleeding, everything always stained red. Nights I see her hand slithering into my drawers, snatching my paper-route money. Her rent money squandered on glassine bags."

Book	Example
Her Last Death	Susanna's mother was addicted to both painkillers and sex, speaking about both to her young daughters constantly. "'He's getting the *Turning Point* for me,' she said. 'I *have* to see it. Don't you think it'll be better than sex?'" She purchased pornography for her daughter and then referred to her as "my little pervert," and she arranged for her to have sexual relationships and slept with her boyfriends. She also was a liar and a thief when the occasion called for it. "'I just walked into Bloomingdales and stole everything we needed—the coats, the sleeping bags, this'—She pulled a necklace from under her collar." When Susanna was ten her mother taught her how to administer painkillers intravenously. At age twelve her mother took her to Venice and got her drunk, referring to her as "my little lush."

Exploiting/Corrupting Type 2: Modeling, permitting, or encouraging developmentally inappropriate behavior (e.g., parentification, infantalization, living the parent's dreams)

Book	Example
The Three of Us	Julia's mother discussed adult matters with her daughter and relied on her for comfort and companionship. "One day in 1956 my mother told me that my father was having 'an affair' with a woman called Patricia. I didn't know what the word meant. 'It means he loves her and he doesn't love me,' she said, 'and he sleeps in her bed and has sex with her, but I suppose you don't know what that means either.'"
Diary of a Stage Mother's Daughter	Missy's mother micromanaged her acting career, learning her lines for her, watching everything she ate, commenting on every aspect of her appearance. Her mother made cruel comments about the other children competing for roles at auditions, such as "You did a nice job today. Much better than poor Lisa. She was horrible poor girl." When the TV show that Missy had a role in went off the air, "Mom reacted like someone close to her had died."

Book	Example
Lies My Mother Never Told Me	On the day her father died, Kaylie's mother "collapsed on the living room couch and lay prostate for days with a bottle of scotch on the floor beside her, while worried friends stood vigil. In a kind of twilight state, she ranted that she was going to walk into the ocean and drown herself. 'Where's my daddy?' she kept saying . . . But this wasn't her daddy, this was my daddy who had just died."
Her Last Death	Susanna's mother "called from hospitals after back surgery. She phoned from airports, dinner parties, and the lobbies of movie theaters in which she stood weeping over a love story. She needed me, she said, to calm her down."

Exploiting/Corrupting Type 3: Encouraging or coercing the abandonment of developmentally appropriate autonomy through extreme overinvolvement, intrusiveness, and/or dominance

Book	Example
The Three of Us	Julia felt that her budding physical development set off a reaction in her mother. "But for my mother the tiny rounding of my eleven-year-old nipples created a different awakening. It was as if she had been waiting impatiently for this moment and now she was eager to share with me everything she knew about sex." One day her mother decided to introduce her to "something very special," she said, proudly displaying a dildo. "I masturbate every night if I haven't got a man with me. So why don't you? Has no one told you how? Would you like Mummy to teach you?"
Sickened	Julie experienced her mother as "cannibalistic. That she wanted to ingest my living flesh, to tear chunks from my body. That the closest she could come to cannibalizing me was to lift me onto the serving platter for the men of the medical community to carve."
The Sky Isn't Visible from Here	Felicia's mother asked her, "'Why do you need friends?' she kept asking. 'You have me. You don't need anyone else.'"

Book	Example
House Rules	Rachel's father was overinvolved in her daily life, dictating how long her hair and nails could be grown, what channel to listen to on the radio, and creating elaborate rules for the most mundane aspects of daily life. Rachel could hardly imagine a life away from his control and intrusion. "I was thrilled to be away from home, and a little terrified that without the challenge of my father I'd amount to nothing. It was not him but the weight he held in our world that left me feeling slightly devoid of purpose. . . .There was nothing real like Dad had been real, there was nothing anchoring me down." For her, "Our lives became a series of rewards and punishment. Years later we'd reminisce about occasions with a certain nostalgia, not because of the occasion itself but because all of us still remember the intricate details of whom Dad was mad at and why."
Diary of a Stage Mother's Daughter	Missy wrote about her mother, "Her vigilance was also a leash, one she could pull tight enough to strangle." That leash was evident when Missy contradicted her mother in front of other people. "I had made the mistake of speaking up during one of Mom's stories before and learned that no one but Mom was allowed to talk. Afterward, when we'd gotten in the car, she'd pinched my arm ferociously and said, 'You are never to contradict me in front of another adult ever again. Do you understand me?'" Her mother was also vigilant about what she ate. "'You don't have to eat so fast,' Mom said, slapping my hand as I grabbed for another fry. Then before I could eat anymore, she said, 'That's enough' and dumped our trays."

Book	Example
Falling Leaves	Adeline's stepmother dominated the house and manifested her dominance by insisting that she and her siblings only receive bus money if they begged for it. "It's your father's wish that you should walk to school! Your father and I want you to know that you will no longer bother Ye Ye or Aunt Baba for money. If you think you need money, come directly to me. . . . we want each of you to come to us individually. Apologize for your past behavior. Admit that you have been spoilt. Turn over a new leaf. Come to us and beg for your tram fare, and we might give it to you." Her stepmother's control extended to every aspect of Adeline's life.
With or Without You	Domenica's mother encouraged an unhealthy enmeshment. "The other girls in your dorm can't stand you because you're so gorgeous. You should see the way they look at you. They want to kill you. But you're lucky. You have me. Mummy will always be your friend. I'm your best friend." She recalled, "Did I tell you about the time when you were brand-new, lying on Nonna's bed, reaching for me, and you were so cute I wanted to hit you. I mean really hit you! I leaned over and bit your foot and you started to cry. Oh, the face you made!"
Why Be Happy When You Could Be Normal?	"Mrs. Winterson never respected my privacy. She ransacked my possessions, read my diaries, my notebooks, my stories, my letters."

Exploiting/Corrupting Type 4: Restricting or interfering with cognitive development

With or Without You	"During Kathi's sedentary spells, which could last anywhere between a couple of days and several weeks, she lay regally in her bed consuming four or five movies in a row. . . . 'Honey you have to watch this movie with me.' 'I'm doing homework.' 'This is more important. I promise. You'll thank me later.'"
Her Last Death	Susanna's mother gave her narcotic painkillers for anxiety the day before her school entrance exam, reducing her chances of going to boarding school.

Book	Example
Why Be Happy When You Could Be Normal?	Jeanette's mother forbade her to have books in the home and kept her back from school for a year.
Sickened	Julie was routinely pulled from school for shopping trips and "doctor days."
You Ain't Got No Easter Clothes	Laura's mother "said that since no one seemed to care, we didn't have to go to school anymore if we didn't want to. We didn't, so Lisa and I began staying home and listening to our radios all day."

supreme and only mother. Missy Francis's mother was so enamored with her daughter's acting career, as described in *Diary of a Stage Mother's Daughter*, and the family's brush with fame it afforded her that nothing else was as important or as real to her. While she may have appeared to be devoted and involved, it was primarily in service of appeasing her craving for celebrity status. Kaylie Jones, daughter of noted author James Jones, wrote in *Lies My Mother Never Told Me* that her mother was so devastated by the death of her beloved husband that she failed to recognize that her child just lost a parent and was in need of comforting as well. Lisa's mother as described in *The Sky Isn't Visible from Here* was a thrill-seeker whose desire to be interesting and to be stimulated overrode her ability to provide a predictable, nurturing environment for her child. Alyse Myers described her mother in *Who Do You Think You Are?* as experiencing her (Alyse) as difficult and "alien," and in doing so, failed to see what was special and unique about her. Her mother was resigned to her limited life and was not open to the possibility that her daughter wanted and deserved more. Jeanette Winterson, acclaimed author of *Oranges Are Not the Only Fruit*, among other works, experienced her mother's need for order and structure as denying her free spirit, creativity, and curiosity. In each story the parent was blind and deaf to the unique needs and voice of their children.

How that blindness and deafness manifested itself varied across the stories. The four specific types of emotional abuse (spurning, terrorizing, isolating, and exploiting/corrupting) occurred as different forms of negative parental responses to the child's needs. Spurning occurred when the parent ridiculed the child for thinking, feeling, or wanting something that the parent did not want the child to feel, think, or want. The message was something like, "How dare you be something other than what I want you to be? How dare you expect something from me that I don't want to give? How dare you have needs at all or how dare you impose yourself on my life? Or, how dare you be imperfect like I am, so I will punish you like I was punished or would punish myself." Terrorizing occurred when the parent failed to take into account the child's need to be protected. The message was something like, "I am going to do what I please regardless of how frightening it is for you and if you dare question me or express your needs in a way that is inconvenient for me I will be unavailable and/or cruel." Terrorizing was also a way for parents to vent their anger and express their sadistic needs to punish and hurt the object (child) for frustrating or embarrassing them. Exploiting/corrupting occurred when the parent failed to recognize the impact on the child of satisfying their own desires. The message conveyed by the parents to their children was something like, "I am going to pursue my pleasures (for sex, drugs, admiration) regardless of how it makes you feel. Moreover, I will assume that you are as depraved as I am because it is exciting for me when you violate society norms." In this way the parent wanted the child to be corrupted like them and enjoyed the pleasure of seeing their child violate social norms. This reflected a narcissistic need and/or sadistic pleasure to see the child suffer or be "bad" as a way of having the child join them and be "bad" like them. (Isolating was relatively rare in these stories, and thus it was not possible to glean what kind of parental "message" that behavior would send to the child.)

IMPACT OF EMOTIONAL ABUSE

Research on brain functioning demonstrates that the pain caused from psychological wounds (being socially rejected, for example) activates the same regions of the brain as pain caused from physical wounds.[6] As far as the brain is concerned there is no difference between physical abuse and emotional abuse. Thus, it should come as no surprise just how painful the emotional abuse was for the authors of the memoirs. Below we explore the specific ways in which children made meaning of their painful, emotionally abusive relationships with their parents.

Message: I Am Not Accepted for Who I Am

Children who more often than not received the message "how dare you be something other than what I want you to be" responded by feeling that there was something fundamentally unacceptable about who they are. They understood that their thoughts, feelings, needs, and wants were not appropriate or acceptable to the parent. The predominant response to this emotional abuse message by a parent was a profound feeling of being unwanted, unloved, and rejected. In *Falling Leaves* Adeline "was considered inferior and insignificant,"[7] and she "knew that I was the least-loved child because I was a girl and my mother had died giving birth to me. Nothing I did ever seemed to please Father."[8] She felt "total rejection,"[9] like the ugly duckling, "despised and unwanted."[10] Rachel felt so unacceptable to her father that "it doesn't matter what I do, there is something in me he just doesn't like,"[11] feeling, "I'd never be loved by Dad the way I wanted."[12] Lisa, author of *The Sky Isn't Visible from Here* about growing up with a volatile single mother, "wondered why she had to make me feel like I was always a chore, an obligation that needed tending,"[13] and singer Laura Love, author of *You Ain't Got No Easter Clothes*, "saw myself as a monster."[14] Children who are called names, put down, ridiculed, and shamed come to the same conclusion: that there is something inherently undesirable about them. Jeanette wrote simply, "I never believed that my parents loved me."[15]

The feeling of rejection experienced by these children resulted in a heightened desire for that parent's love and approval.[16] The emotionally abused children longed for something that they never really had: the unconditional approval from a seemingly disapproving parent. That doesn't mean that they didn't have an attachment with that parent, because they did. It's just that most did not recall a time before the disapproval was felt. They did not experience a fall from grace so much as a desire to attain a state of grace. Adeline wrote, "I wished above all else to please my father. Oh, so very much! To gain his acceptance. To be loved. To have him say to me, just once in my life, 'Well done, Adeline! We're proud of you!'"[17] She experienced her need for her father as a "basic need: a longing for acceptance, a craving for my rightful place in the family, a primal cry to be included—all of which had been denied in my youth."[18] She wanted what her father and stepmother were able to give to their other children but had been denied to her. Regardless of the years of exclusion and cruelty, as a young adult she scrimped on herself in order to buy presents to gain the affection of her family, and she continued to seek the approval of both her father and her stepmother. She was delighted when her father wished to participate in a real estate venture she developed. Even after he died she was intent on finding some proof of her father's love for her so that she could comfort herself with the thought that "perhaps he loved me after all."[19] Rachel wrote about her dominating and critical father that "my need to be accepted by him was stronger than ever."[20] His constant put-downs and criticisms induced in her a desire for him to find her worthy. He held himself as the arbiter of judgment within the family; his opinion was the only one that mattered, and thus his approval was of paramount importance to her. "He loomed over everything I did."[21] After all of the disapproval that Mrs. Winterson heaped onto her daughter, even as an adult Jeanette still wanted her mother to recognize her achievements—to find her worthy. "More money in the slot [payphone] and I'm thinking, as her voice goes in and out like the sea, 'Why aren't you proud of me?'"[22] As a child she clung to the belief that "there was God in Heaven who loved me like I was the only one who mattered,"[23] because it was virtually impossible to imagine that she would be able to receive the love she craved from her mother. Although not reflected in these memoirs, at some point some victims of emotional abuse detach themselves from their emotionally abusive parents as a defense against the pain of rejection. They no longer care or feel a desire for, although on a fundamental level they still crave, their abusive parent's love and acceptance.

Message: I Am Not Safe

If the consistent parental message is "I am going to do what I please regardless of how frightening it is for you and if you dare question me or express your needs in a way that is inconvenient for me I will be cruel and/or unavailable," then the child's response was to feel unsafe and unprotected. The parents' terrorizing tactics and threats to abandon the child or hurt the child left the child feeling not safe by the person(s) who was supposed to provide them with the protection and safety they required in order to develop normally. Lisa wrote about her mother that "with her, love and fear were one and the same, with every kiss came a pinprick, with every hug came a lashing out. My mother was my first hurt."[24] She wondered why her mother was unable and/or unwilling to protect her and keep her safe. "Why wasn't she there when I was ten, crossing the intersection to buy Cheese Doodles from the store on the other side?"[25] Adeline recalled sitting at the dinner table with her stepmother inspecting her. "An oppressive fear invariably gripped my whole being and my appetite would vanish."[26] Jeanette felt that she was never safe at home because of the oppressive weight of her mother's perpetual gloom, anger, depression, and bizarre thoughts about apocalyptic end of times. Her home was not a safe haven. "I couldn't relax at home, couldn't disappear into a humming space where I could be alone in the presence of the other. What with the Departed Dead wandering round the kitchen, and mice masquerading as ectoplasm, and the sudden fits of piano playing, and the sometime-revolver, and the relentless brooding mountain range of my mother, and the scary bedtimes . . . well, home wasn't really a place you could relax."[27]

At no time did these parents seem to consider or care that their children would be overwhelmed, confused, or frightened by their behavior or choices. The children experienced their emotionally abusive parent as willing to expose them to any and all sorts of inappropriate people and experiences, including drug addicts, frightening ideas and places, sexual misconduct, pornography, pedophiles, drinking, and violence. Nonetheless, the children still viewed their parents as their primary attachments and desired their love and approval, although it was highly likely the attachment would be considered insecure (as opposed to secure) in style.

Message: I Am Not Important

In response to the consistent parental message, "I am going to pursue my pleasures (for sex, drugs, admiration) regardless of how it makes you feel," the child felt unimportant, small, insignificant, invisible. According to Lisa, "When you wronged her, when she left you, you ceased to exist."[28] When Rachel's father decided to have a several-hour-long family discussion in which he berated her and specified all of her faults, Rachel felt she had no choice but to submit to his humiliating lectures and diatribes; there was no place for her. "Dad was infuriated to the point where he couldn't see either Mom or me sitting in front of him."[29] There are several references to her being unnoticed and invisible throughout the book, indicating that she felt that her father was responding to her based more on who he thought she was rather than on who she actually was. Whatever was bothering him had little to do with the person standing in front of him. For Susanna, her mother's lies designed to evoke pity or admiration were "blunt and obvious. I felt I didn't matter."[30] Julie felt that despite all of the attention on her medical needs, she as a person was not real to her mother. Her mother was interested in her only as a vehicle to have her needs for attention met. "I pride myself on how little space I take up. I am going to shrink and shrink until I am a dry fall leaf, complete with a translucent spine and brittle veins, blowing away in a stiff wind, up, up, up into a crisp blue sky."[31]

TRAUMATIZING NARCISSISM

In these stories the emotionally abusive parents varied in their educational background, socioeconomic status, cultural affiliations, professions, and life-styles. What they shared, however, was their overwhelming inability to recognize that their children were separate people with their own experiences, perceptions, and subjectivity. In other words, they meet psychologist Daniel Shaw's definition of a "traumatizing narcissist."[32] Shaw defines a traumatizing narcissistic parent as someone who cannot foster or tolerate intersubjectivity, the experience of a mutually negotiated reality. Instead, the traumatizing narcissist, according to Shaw, will go to great lengths to preserve his or her dominance by suppressing the validity of the subjective experience of the other person, in this case the child. That is, these parents only feel wholly alive and loved when their point of view is accepted as the only valid experience and perception. In this way, the child's experiences and perceptions are threatening to the parent and must be invalidated. Shaw describes the narcissistic parent as relating to his or her child with the expectation that the child will serve primarily as a gratifying object. For this obedience the child is rewarded with the parent's approval. However, the child is simultaneously punished—that is, unrecognized—for her efforts to assert her separate reality. Thus, these parents refuse (or fail) to engage the child in what Shaw refers to as "mutual recognition,"[33] which he defines as the space between them in which a shared understanding exists. That means the child is denied the opportunity to be understood for who she really is, to be affirmed for herself. As long as the child affirms the parent, the child is accepted and loved, but the love is wholly conditional on the child's emotional enslavement for the parent's gratification. As Shaw points out, because children will go to great lengths to preserve their idea of their parents as good and loving and because they know no other reality other than that of their parents, they will adopt the distorted relational style of the narcissistic parent as right and good. In essence, they will turn themselves inside out to become what their parents want them to be in order to be accepted and loved by their parents. However, even then the love of the narcissistic parent is conditional and tenuous, based on the false premise that the child has no sense of self. "Any opposition from the child is characterized by the parent as signifying the child's moral failure, punishable by the withdrawal of the parent's love and the administration of contempt."[34] Thus, in being loved for whom the parent wants him to be, the child experiences a profound sense of not being loved for who he is. Moreover, as Shaw points out, the narcissistic parent cannot tolerate the unacceptable parts of his own personality and must project them onto others, usually their children because they are so willing to internalize these bad messages about themselves. In order to feel good about themselves they must denigrate others.

This dynamic is seen throughout the stories of emotional abuse. For example, Susanna's mother referred to her as a lush and a pervert when these qualities applied to her, not her child. Thus, in order to be loved by her narcissistic parent Susanna needed to hate herself, and hence experience herself as unlovable.

Shaw outlines four characteristics of the traumatizing narcissist (TN). The first is intergenerational trauma, referring to the narcissistic parenting that the TN herself experienced as a child. The TN, according to Shaw, has typically been exposed to her own cumulative relational trauma throughout her development in the form of shame-based parenting by parents and/or other significant caregivers who are narcissistically disturbed. The TN's parent resents the dependency needs of her child and demands that the child "recognize the exclusive validity of the parent's needs and wishes—which means of course that the child is to be ashamed of his own needs and desires, and view them as the parent does—as irrelevant, or as contemptible."[35] The future TN grows up unable to feel that her needs and experiences are valid and worthy of attention. She must cut off her own needs in order to be seen and loved by her parents. Most of the memoirs reviewed for this chapter contained examples of how the author's parent was himself or herself a victim of a narcissistic parent, confirming Shaw's view of the intergenerational transmission of traumatic narcissism.

The second aspect of the TN relational system is "delusional infallibility and entitlement."[36] The TN parent is "obsessed with maintaining a rigid sense of omnipotent superiority and perfection—of infallibility, self-sufficiency, and entitlement."[37] The TN parent will defend and justify her beliefs and rules with all of the vigor and energy she can muster. To question her authority provokes rage, outrage, and cruelty if necessary. She must maintain her stance and position of superiority at all costs and will repudiate any sign of weakness in herself. "Since, for the traumatizing narcissist, insufficiency is equated with mortifying dependency and the ensuing sense of impotence and inferiority, it is crucial for him to keep the destabilizing shame of these repudiated aspects of self from being released into consciousness."[38] The TN feels entitled to maintain her superiority by shaming, belittling, and controlling her children and projecting onto them the parts of her personality that she finds (meaning her own parents found) unacceptable in herself. In doing so, she squashes the child's sense of self and self-esteem but continues to bolster her own sense of power and rightness. This was apparent across the stories. For example, Rachel's father exhibited a need to control and humiliate everyone else in the family. Anyone who crossed him was subjected to brutal condemnation and casting out, and it appeared that he relished creating situations in which someone would be humiliated so that he could feel and exhibit contempt and disgust.

Shaw's third element is "externalization of shame."[39] In order to avoid feeling self-loathing that accompanies dependency needs, the TN assigns those unacceptable feelings to the child. The TN becomes obsessed with demonstrating the weaknesses and unacceptability of others in order to reassure herself that they are "out there" and safely away from herself. "The traumatizing narcissist virtually colonizes others, using the other as a host, as it were, onto whom to project and control his unwanted and disavowed affects and self states connected to dependency—especially the shameful sense of neediness and inferiority."[40] Keeping Julie in a sickened dependent state, for example, allowed her mother to derive gratification of being the protector and the healthy one.

The final relational dynamic between a TN parent and child highlighted by Shaw is "suppression of the subjectivity of the other."[41] The TN parent experiences only his own needs as valid and acceptable and finds any expression of neediness on the part of the child as selfish and unacceptable. The TN is unable to allow the child to have a separate and valid reality and needs that are real and require attention. Thus, while the TN needs the child to be needy in order to protect himself from his own neediness, she cannot actually bear to attend to the needs of the child, who is, therefore, placed in a double bind of having to be shamefully weak but then being told that her needs are selfish. "Unable to be anything but dependent, yet still attempting independence, the child of the traumatizing narcissist parent is condemned either way. She comes to associate dependency with shame and humiliation, and independence with rejection and abandonment."[42] An example of this can be found in Felicia's mother's bizarre desire to bite her infant daughter when she reached for her.

SUMMARY

At the heart of each story of emotional abuse is a parent whose heart is not in the right place, a parent who—because of depression, mental illness, or addiction—is too self-absorbed to be emotionally present and consistently loving to their child. Psychological abuse takes many forms, all of which involve a parental act that creates in the child a belief that he or she is unloved or unworthy. Inherent in this definition is the fact that parents have tremendous power over their children's self-esteem and sense of self. Parental acts that fall within the category of emotional abuse can penetrate the very being of the child and shape their sense of whom they are, casting a long shadow on their lives.

Chapter Seven

Stories of Emotional Neglect

Twelve memoirs about emotional neglect were read, three of which are summarized in this chapter. The first, *The Kiss*[1] by Kathryn Harrison, is the story of an only child growing up with virtually no contact with her father and only periodic and unpredictable contact with her emotionally neglectful mother.

THE KISS BY KATHRYN HARRISON

Kathryn, the only child of young parents, was raised by her mother and maternal grandparents, her father having been banished from the home and family. Even his photographs were removed by Kathryn's grandmother. "I sit on the foot of her bed and watch her edit the family albums, a task she undertakes with a kind of grim determination."[2] Kathryn's mother, bereft over being denied the man she loved, could not rise from her depressed stupor. "My mother sleeps. For as long as she lives with us, in her parent's house, she sleeps whenever she can. She sleeps very late every day, as much as six or seven hours past the time when I am up for breakfast. I stand beside her bed."[3] As a young child, Kathryn yearned for her mother to wake up. "Her eyes closed and hidden behind her satin sleep mask, her face as flat and white as the mask . . . one mask under another."[4] However, even when awake, Kathryn's mother was emotionally asleep. "If I wake her she doesn't talk to me. She stalks around her room, as if enraged, a wild and astonished look on her face. I make myself small. . . . and often she doesn't seem to know I'm there . . . her eyes, when they turn at last towards me, are like empty mirrors. I can't find myself in them."[5] In such a lonely home, Kathryn turned her hopes toward her father, who remained a ghost for much of her childhood, "an absence, a hole."[6] When Kathryn was six years old, her mother moved out of the home, leaving her with her grandparents. "She is gone, but her room remains just as it was."[7] Young Kathryn stood over her mother's unused bed trying to conjure her mother's presence, and she went to her mother's closet to surround herself with the clothes her mother left behind. "I push my face into the smooth fabric, a hundred times more lovely than any other thing in the house. If a dress like this was not worth taking, how could I have hoped to be?"[8] Her mother maintained a relationship with Kathryn, but only on her own terms. "She sees me often, but she comes and goes at her own discretion: she does not want to be summoned by fevers or nightmares or lost teeth."[9] During her visits, Kathryn's mother tried to teach her to speak French, but Kathryn was resentful of her mother's absence and was unwilling to learn. "Once she throws the flash cards down and slaps my face."[10] Striving to please her mother, Kathryn cheated in order to pass her French exam, but she was then devastated by her mother's enthusiastic approval of her high grade. "My mother's love for me depends on my capitulation. She will accept, acknowledge, see me only in as much as I will make myself the child who pleases her."[11] Throughout her childhood, Kathryn was both in thrall to and furious with her mother, who came and went as she pleased. Kathryn meant so little that her mother couldn't bother to be on time. "My mother's lateness is so extreme it transcends hostile insult . . . it implies she exists in another temporal frame . . . I never get used to it."[12] Later she began a relationship with her father, enjoying their shared bond with the woman who could never love them. "Two people spurned by the same woman . . . in thrall to her, spiting her—the person neither of us could ever know or possess—we hold on to each other. She is more compelling than we are, because she always eludes us. For half of his life and all of mine, we have defined ourselves as those who love her, the one who won't love us back."[13] Kathryn eventually transferred her enthrallment from her mother to her father. "I feel that my life depends on my father seeing me."[14] She seemed to mean "see" both as in spending time together as well as in understand, validate, appreciate. When her father kissed her sexually she was so desperate to not lose his love she denied the reality of the kiss. "I think of the kiss not as what he did but as what happened. I've separated him from the act; I've made the adjustment of regarding the kiss as I would a more helpless physical transport, a seizure, perhaps, or a spasm of coughing. If the kiss was an accident, outside of human control, then it doesn't pollute the love he has for me. It doesn't demand that I turn away from what I want."[15] When her mother responded to the inappropriate relationship forming between father and daughter, Kathryn recast it as her mother's inability to imagine that anyone could love her. Her mother—through her unavailability and rejection—had lost the credibility required to help Kathryn see her father's intentions clearly. In fact, it was her mother's reaction that solidified Kathryn's unhealthy bond to her father. "If she won't love me, then the only way not to fall into the abyss of the unloved is by clinging to him."[16] Her father's love, however, was all consuming, jealous, rageful. Eventually her father's desire to possess her physically and emotionally suffocated her, which coincided with her need to reclaim her relationship with her mother before she died of cancer. In the end, mother and daughter form a rapprochement of sorts before her mother leaves her one last time, symbolized by Kathryn cutting off her long hair and offering it to her mother. "When I was a small child my mother would sit at her vanity table and brush my hair. The vanity table had opposing mirrors at its sides, and if I turned my head to the left or to the right I'd see the two of us multiplied endlessly, and I would read in that spatial infinity a message of temporal infinity as well: No matter the future I would always see myself standing as obediently as possible, under my mother's hands as they worked, the two of us united in the bond that would always define us, our trying to make me into the child she can admire and love."[17] Before her death, Kathryn's mother was able to, in her own way, express her love for her daughter, and Kathryn was able to return that love. Although her mother's headstone bears no words, the book is dedicated to her, beloved.

BEFORE THE KNIFE BY CAROLYN SLAUGHTER

Before the Knife[18] is Carolyn Slaughter's story of growing up during England's rule of Africa. Her father was preoccupied with governmental affairs while her mother was chronically depressed and emotionally unavailable.

Carolyn was the middle daughter of upper-class English parents, who in the waning days of English rule over India moved to British-occupied Africa—a "singularly beautiful place"[19]—Carolyn was three years old. Her father was "one of those men who strode around wearing hard hats, khaki uniforms, and knee-length socks of the Empire,"[20] and her mother was a glamorous woman raised to be beautiful. Carolyn felt a special bond with her mother, who was primarily focused on herself. Carolyn was allowed into her mother's world only when she was dressing up for the evening. Carolyn was permitted to watch her mother select her outfit and prepare her hair and makeup. "I used to stand behind her watching her flirt with her own face. She set me little tasks like dunking the powder puff in the Helena Rubenstein box, and she let me dab silky powder onto her white shoulders. She was proud of herself: my waist is still twenty-two inches small, she crooned. . . . Then she glared at her teeth: they aren't as strong as they used to be, she said, you two used up all my calcium."[21] For much of her first three years, Carolyn was raised by nannies, but when the family left for Africa on the ocean liner, her mother was forced to spend more time with her children. Carolyn recalled this attention from her mother as deeply satisfying. "I remember her walking around the decks with us, and sitting with us while we had our meals in the children's dining room. She would even bathe and dress us, comb our hair. . . . Once when I was feeling seasick, she sat with me in a deck chair in the evening air, and we watched the stars come out, wrapped up in a blanket together, safe."[22] At that time Carolyn felt that she had a special bond with her mother, while her older sister was closer with her father. Once in Africa, Carolyn took to the wild beauty and connected with the land, animals, rivers, and people. Her mother was not as pleased. Originally a domineering presence in the household, overseeing the many servants to ensure they performed up to her exacting standards, Carolyn's mother lost the energy even for that. Carolyn's wildness was such a problem for the family and the two older girls were too taxing for their mother that they were sent to boarding school five days a week, a frightening and unhappy place. Despite Carolyn's loud protests, her mother made it clear that she was to attend the school. "My mother was miserable as sin, and I was contributing to her unhappiness. My rage about being thrown out of the house was upsetting everyone but my father. . . . My mother made it clear to me that my screaming and carrying on had to stop. But I couldn't stop. I was devastated by my mother's abandonment."[23] Around that time Carolyn's younger sister was born, and her mother informed her that she needed to grow up and be her mother's helper. She tried. "I trailed after her as she carried Susan in her arms; I offered to do things for her, and she swatted me aside impatiently."[24] For Carolyn there was nothing she could do to capture her mother's attention. "My mother suddenly couldn't stand the sight of me, and the more I wailed and sobbed, the more she turned away from me."[25] The removal of the two older girls to boarding school did nothing to lift their mother's spirits, so they were summoned home to prepare for the family's move to the Kalahari Desert. In a photograph taken at that time, Carolyn recalled that her mother's head "is hanging down and her body is slumped sideways. She doesn't have the energy to lift her head and there's a deep sense of sadness about her."[26] Carolyn was also in the picture with a matching expression in an effort to remain connected to her mother, absorbing her mother's mood and making it her own. Her mother took to her bed, and Carolyn was bereft. "She fell into a depression that we were both powerless to contain. I spent hours of my day hanging around her door, or creeping close to her bed to press my face up against the mosquito net rising and falling with the slight breeze of the overhead fan. I stood and watched her, staring in through the gauze as she lay on her bed with the back of her hand on her forehead and her eyes closed. Her body was locked against touch or communication, curled around as if sheltering some empty space. She was terribly sad and lonely, and all I could think was: What shall I do? What shall I do?"[27] Periodically, Carolyn's mother brightened. "She was smiling again, she was happy, everything was all right."[28] Moving the family seemed to help her rally, but then the inertia would resettle over her and she returned to bed. Dutiful, Carolyn stood by her mother, asking if she could bring her something, but her mother wanted nothing she had to offer. "If I spoke to her she often ignored me, or made a mute shrug, or turned and walked away. Her silence was laden."[29] After mustering courage, Carolyn asked her mother, "Do you love me?" Her mother "whipped around and looked at me as if I was some strange insect that had alighted on her bed. 'Don't be silly' she snapped, and turned back to the wall."[30] Carolyn retreated into the African bush, further alienating her from her mother, who found her to be dirty and incomprehensible. Then, surprisingly, upon another family move, her mother "picked up the maternal role a bit more."[31] She threw birthday parties and was able to share in her children's pleasures. Too soon the darkness descended again and her mother retreated back to her bed with a steady stream of headaches. "I watched her go down, and before long I, too, was as low as a snake in a well."[32] There were additional ups and downs, but from that point on Carolyn's mother was primarily unavailable to her daughter. When Carolyn was a teenager, her family left Africa and returned to England, leaving the older sister behind to finish her schooling. By that point Carolyn would have preferred staying, but as usual, her preferences were unheeded and her voice was unheard.

SWALLOW THE OCEAN BY LAURA FLYNN

Laura Flynn was the middle daughter of middle-class parents raised during the 1970s on the West Coast. In *Swallow the Ocean*,[33] Laura describes the impact of mental illness on her mother's ability to care for and nurture her.

As a young child Laura was enchanted with her beautiful and intelligent mother. Laura and her sister shared mornings with their mother while their older sister was in school. She recalled walking through the rose garden in Golden Gate Park, the cherry blossoms in bloom, the sun shining on them. "My mother had an uncanny ability to create a private universe."[34] At the enchanted Tea Garden, they basked in the glow of their mother's love. "We were lucky that way: born in this beautiful of cities, our future on the whispering sliver of paper pulled from the fortune cookie, bread for the ducks, a penny for the pond, the stories of good deeds for the next life. With the weightless motion of the water striders, we moved on the bright plane of our existence. And, of course, we thought my mother walked on water."[35] As a young girl the biggest challenge in Laura's life was the Mulligan children, neighborhood bullies, but generally life was good. Her mother stayed at home to care for the three girls; her father went to work with a briefcase each morning and came home for dinner each evening. By the time Laura was five, her father knew something was wrong with her mother. He thought that it was something that could be fixed with time and attention, so he packed the family off for a three-month cross-country trek. But the magic of the country did not stop the unraveling of Laura's mother. "All that year my mother would sit for hours in that high backed armchair by the window in the living room, her legs tucked up under her."[36] She was lost in her own thoughts. "It was not a question of not seeing the forest for the trees—because she saw all that, the pine needles, the branches, the trunks, and the forest. Beyond that she saw the way the light flooded the forest canopy. And then the even deeper, untold meaning, the connection of the trees to the light and the branches to the needles."[37] While engrossed in the mystical connections between all living things and the feeling of energy that emanated through the fog and the air, Laura's mother was not able to see her children. She was captivated by the currents of power she felt, the knowledge that a battle was being waged between good and evil. She heard the whispers of information in the air and needed to concentrate, to hear the messages meant just for her. The voices of her children no longer interested her. Laura's father believed that he was the source of the mother's anguish and left the family, hoping that her own parents would be able to convince her to seek help. "He doesn't think of taking us because we are still more hers than his."[38] After her father left, "the shades went down, and the acacia tree in the front yard grew up and over the windows. My mother didn't leave the house for months at a time, and for three full years no one came inside. Days slid into night, and night into day. My mother more and more manic. Retreating to her room or the enlarged universe inside her head."[39] Trapped inside the house, the children were caught in the fog of their mother's illness. They played games with the dolls, all of which begin with them as orphans, "stories of loss, abandonment, and escape."[40] Much of the time Laura's mother was lost in her reveries, unavailable to her children, a "vacant absence."[41] She also had rages triggered by internal demons. She transformed into an undefined person with grey hair wearing a trench coat. Sometimes Laura would go into her mother's closet. "If I pressed my cheek to the sleeve, ran my nose over the soft fur of the cuff, I could still catch a whiff of my parents' romance, could imagine my mother stepping down the stairs of her hotel in Paris. That was the woman I aspired to be, even if she no longer did."[42] On rare occasions her mother was able to "summon her former magic" and attend to the needs of her children, such as baking a birthday cake for Laura's ninth birthday, "the most charming I had ever seen—have ever seen."[43] By the time Laura was in fifth grade her mother was consumed by her schizophrenia, alternating between intrusive overinvolvement and total absence, absorbed with her thoughts and fears. At one point she moved her mattress into the living room so that she could feed papers into the fire, purging after years of hoarding. When Laura was ten her father gave her a notebook so she could become a writer. Every day after school she worked on a story. Some days her mother was in the kitchen with her, other days she was locked away in her bedroom, "a deep silence echoed from within, broken only by an occasional riffle of laughter, something half stifled that slipped under the threshold of the door."[44] Other days Laura could hear her mother sobbing in her bedroom. Laura worked diligently over several weeks if not months filling her notebook only to awaken one morning to find that her mother had fed it to the fire. "Why did she burn it? . . . Maybe she didn't even see it. Just picked it up and tossed it into the fireplace without knowing."[45] Eventually Laura's father won custody of the three girls as her mother fell deeper into her mental illness. After a long period of no contact, Laura and her sisters reestablished a tenuous relationship with their mother, who "lived alone, shrinking further and further into herself with each passing year, like an imploded star."[46] She refused to get treatment or to even tell her children where she lived. For Laura, knowing her mother was like "a funeral that never ends."[47] She never again had the loving attention of her mother with the magic touch.

Chapter Eight

Making Meaning of Emotional Neglect

According to the American Professional Society on the Abuse of Children (APSAC), psychological maltreatment has several components, one of which is referred to as denying emotional responsiveness (DER).[1] DER is for all intents and purposes synonymous with emotional neglect. APSAC defines it as "acts that ignore the child's attempts and needs to interact and for affection,"[2] and they include being detached, uninvolved, inattentive, and unaffectionate. Twelve memoirs were read in which emotional neglect was the primary or only form of child maltreatment perpetrated by the parent. These books are listed in table 8.1. Three of the stories are summarized in the previous chapter, and all were reviewed for the identification of themes discussed in this chapter.

THE SEARCH FOR LOVE

The stories of emotional neglect are stories of love and loss. They are stories of attachment and separation. They are stories of yearning against improbable odds for a parent to awaken from the slumber of self-absorption to once again look upon the child with love and affection. The stories are dreams of longing that never end, not even with attainment of adulthood nor the death of the parent. A visual depiction of this yearning is found in the movie *A.I. Artificial Intelligence*, in which a mechanical boy, David, becomes psychologically bonded to his human mother when she chooses to activate his emotional life. In response, he adores her unconditionally, wanting only to look in her eyes and see her love for him reflected back at him. Halfway through the movie she casts him out of her heart and her home; he no longer meets her needs. Desperate for her acceptance, he cries, "If you let me, I will be so real for you."[3] But she will not let him. After a dark and dangerous

Table 8.1. Memoirs of Emotional Neglect

Title of Book	Abusive Parent	Abuse Victim/ Author	Secondary Abuse by Parent	Role of other Parent	Major Dysfunction in Family
Swallow the Ocean	Mother	Laura M. Flynn	Physical neglect	Rescued child	Mentally ill mother
In Spite of Everything	Mother	Susan Gregory Thomas	None	Abandoned child	Alcoholic father
My Mother's Keeper	Mother	Tara Elgin Holley	None	Absent	Mentally ill mother
Dead End Gene Pool	Mother	Wendy Burden	None	Absent	Alcoholic mother
Before the Knife	Mother	Carolyn Slaughter	None	Enabler, abusive	Depressed mother
Other Side of Paradise	Mother	Stacyann Chin	None	Unknown	Narcissistic mother
Running with Scissors	Mother	Augusten Burroughs	Physical neglect	Absent	Mentally ill and narcissistic mother
Fiction Ruined My Family	Mother	Jeanne Darst	None	Enabler	Alcoholic mother
Three Little Words	Mother	Ashley Rhodes-Courter	None	Absent/ unknown	Drug-using mother
Chanel Bonfire	Mother	Wendy Lawless	None	Cut off	Alcoholic mother
Memory Palace	Mother	Mira Bartok	None	Abandoned	Mentally ill mother
The Kiss	Mother	Kathryn Harrison	None	Cut off	Depressed and narcissistic mother

journey David ends up stranded in a helicopter at the bottom of the ocean, where he remains for two thousand years, pining away for his mother's love. It is that innocent longing that is captured so poignantly in each of the memoirs of emotional neglect.

At the end of the movie, David is allowed one perfect day, which he constructs out of his wishes and desires. In that day he fulfills his dream of a perfect mother-child reunion. He spends the day alone with his mother doing everyday things such as waking up, eating breakfast, getting washed, and getting dressed. In each act the mother is delighted by her child. This perfect day for David is every child's perfect day—to be the light of the parent's heart, to have that parent shine her love upon the child, for the child to please the parent and to experience himself as pleasing to that parent—to have a day of precious moments, within each one a pure distillation of parental love and acceptance.

Each of the memoirs of emotional neglect read for this book contains within it the wish for that perfect day. In *The Kiss*, Kathryn Harrison wanted her mother "fervently" and feared that without her mother's love she would "fall into the abyss of the unloved."[4] Tara Elgin Holley, whose mother's schizophrenia is chronicled in *My Mother's Keeper*, wrote, "I had a mother I loved, and I did not forget her. I thought about her, dreamed about her. Every night without fail."[5] Tara fantasized about being with her mother, how she would "sweep me into her arms and hug me, and we would never be parted again."[6] She imagined that her mother would be like other mothers, baking cookies for her, helping her fix her hair, talking with her teachers, guiding her, telling her she was doing okay. Like David, she wanted to share the small moments of her life with her mother, to have those moments matter. "I remember that more than anything I wanted her in my life."[7] Ashley Rhodes-Courter, author of *Three Little Words* about growing up in foster care, "remembered aching for my mother . . . desperate to climb on her lap."[8] The memories and desires for her mother acted "like magnets connecting me to her no matter how much time passed or circumstances intervened."[9] Ashley had a fantasy of what the reunion would be like down to the color of the car her mother would drive and how many hugs her mother would give her when she came to pick her up from school, experiencing the longing as an "irrational throbbing for my mother that came in waves."[10] Staceyann Chin, author of *The Other Side of Paradise*, also dreamt of being with her mother. She grew up in Jamaica with only periodic contact with her mother. "In my dreams I speak fluent French. My mother takes us to restaurants."[11] She imagined her mother coming for her, a beautiful stranger who loves her most of all. Jeanne Darst, author of *Fiction Ruined My Family*, described desiring a mother who didn't drink, a mother who took care of herself, a mother who took care of her. Even after her mother's death, she longed to be loved by her.

These descriptions of the child's longing for the mother are wholly consistent with what we now know about how infants form and maintain attachment relationships with their first caregivers.[12] Infants are born with a predetermined capacity and need for attunement and connection with a caregiving other. This is a basic emotional need that is part of the human makeup.[13] Thus, the longing in the infant for the mother/caregiver is hardwired and present from birth, and it remains of paramount importance to the child throughout childhood and beyond. The longing described in the memoirs is a poignant reminder of the power of the attachment bond.

Like David in *A.I.*, the adults who wrote these memoirs recalled having a powerful desire to be loved and taken care of, to matter. That desire was fueled by the memories of an attachment bond with the parent. As Mira Bartok in *The Memory Palace* wrote, "Our bond with her is inexplicable, before the beginning of time. She is fierce love; she is sorrow. She is a howling in the wilderness we can never see, calling us home. She is what we fear—and what we long to return to—the heat of the cave and the animal closeness, before all civilization and reason."[14] The parent-child bond these children had may have been imperfect, but it existed, and through its existence it created an expectation and a desire for its continuance. Just as David waited at the bottom of the ocean for two thousand years, never wavering in his desire to be real for his mother, the authors wrote of never ceasing to want to return to that time and place when they were loved by the parent who had since lost interest in them, who no longer attended to them, who no longer saw them. Perhaps the memories of the relationship were positive because the relationship was actually positive, or perhaps the memories became distorted over time. It cannot be known by the reader, and perhaps not even by the writer. What is clear in the stories is that the authors recalled a time when they resided in the garden of their parent's heart, and they wanted nothing more than to return to that time and place.

Carolyn Slaughter, author of *Before the Knife*, described her early attachment to her mother as a shared special bond. "There are many photos where I am close to my mother's side; her arm around me, her hand placed tenderly on my chubby arm. . . . I [am] fused to her hip and she's smiling, her bobbed curls blowing in the wind."[15] She also recalled those rare and magical times when her mother was able to respond and attend to her. "On the boat she was different. I remember her walking around the decks with us, and sitting with us while we had our meals in the children's dining room. She would even bathe and dress us, comb our hair, part mine on one side and sweep it up out of my face with a pin shaped like a bow. Once when I was feeling seasick, she sat with me in a deck chair in the evening air, and we watched the stars come out, wrapped up in a blanket together, safe."[16] Actress Wendy Lawless, author of *Chanel Bonfire* about growing up with an alcoholic mother, experienced rare moments when her mother "was happy and everything was going to be fine. That day, Mother gave Catherine the night off and even fixed dinner for us, and we all ate together in the kitchen."[17] Tara, too, recalled early loving moments with her mother, "playing with me in the park, singing the songs I remember to this day."[18] She also recalled that her mother "would come into my room at night and hold me when I was frightened of the dark,"[19] revealing that she was a little girl with "a mommy who loved me."[20] That her mother was able to comfort her and reassure her that she was safe created the desire and the expectation that her mother would always be there for her. Ashley had many vivid memories of being with her mother, for example, one visit that "is encased in my mind like a scene in a snow dome. The door opened, and I saw her silhouetted in the window light. I ran into her arms, claimed her lap, and forgot about Mrs. Moss, who hovered in the corner. A raw sunburn blotched my shoulders. She examined the red dots that mottled my limbs. . . . My mother fretted over each blemish, sending accusatory glances in my foster mother's direction,"[21] and another visit in which "the moment I saw her, I felt my heart would leap out of my chest. She wrapped her arms around me and told me everything would be all right—and I believed every word."[22] Ashley described the "rush of joy as I fell into her arms."[23] For Ashley her mother was the object of pure love and desire. Likewise, Laura Flynn, author of *Swallow the Ocean*, wrote, "My mother was my life. I listened to her. Took in every word she said. . . . I lived in her world, was latched to her side."[24] In these stories, the tie to the mother was visceral, a strong, physical bond in which the child's heart and mind and body were tethered to the mother's. In the acclaimed memoir *Running with Scissors*, about growing up with a mentally unstable mother, Augusten Burroughs described feeling the psychic umbilical cord that tied him to his mother's body. These memoirs are rich with descriptions of the child's need for nurturance, care, and love that are the building blocks for the infant's developing sense of self and other.

Scent of the Mother

One manifestation of the parent-child bond was the strong connection to the mother's aroma. Most of the authors conjured up the specific smell they associated with their mother, a smell that lingered in their minds as a trace, a remembrance of the relationship. Kathryn found her mother's dresses in her closet. "I duck under the skirt of one and let it fall around me like a yellow tent, a tent the color of the sun and smelling of flowers. I push my face into the smooth fabric, a hundred times more lovely than any other thing in the house."[25] Tara remembered her mother as a "feeling that comes back, as evocative as a remembered fragrance, and I am calm and happy."[26] Stacey-ann wrote about the first time her mother returned. "My mother smells of talcum powder and coffee beans. . . . She smells like something else but I cannot think what it might be. Something like Christmas fruits soaked in rum and sugar."[27] When Ashley reunited with her mother, she "breathed in the familiar smokiness that mingled with a soapy sweetness,"[28] and when they weren't together she was "aching for my mother, desperate to climb on her lap, smell her musky perfume, have her stroke my hair and call me 'Sunshine.'"[29] Wendy Burden in *Dead End Gene Pool* touched her mother's skin, "slippery from the tanning oil. It smelled of her own bittersweet perfume:

coconut, perspiration, Diorissimo, Prell shampoo, citrus, and booze. I would close my eyes and rest my cheek on the warmth of her shoulder."[30] Augusten hugged his mother and "loved the smell, Chanel No. 5 and nicotine,"[31] and Wendy's mother in *Chanel Bonfire* "leaned toward us, opened her arms, and drew us to her. She smelled like her new perfume, which was very sweet and expensive. It even had a name that went with her new life: Joy."[32] Mira held a photo album to her nose and smelled her mother's scent, a mix of cigarettes and Tabu, her favorite perfume.

Mira described the sense of smell as "the strongest memory trigger of all, the only sense that travels directly to the limbic system in our brain."[33] This observation is supported by research on the biology of olfaction. As psychologist Rachel Herz explains in *The Scent of Desire: Discovering Our Enigmatic Sense of Smell*, "The neurological interconnection between the sense of smell (olfaction) and emotion is uniquely intimate. The areas of the brain that process smell and emotion are intertwined and codependent as any two regions of the brain."[34] That is why "more than any other sensory experience, fragrances have the ability to trigger our emotions."[35] The sense of smell was the first sense to appear in middle life-forms that emerged on earth, and the "ability to experience emotion grew directly out of our brain's ability to process smell."[36] Olfactory bonding (linking memories to smells) occurs very early, is very powerful, and lasts throughout life, something brought to awareness by Proust, as described in *Remembrance of Things Past*[37] when he tasted and smelled the madeleine cookies that transported him back to his childhood bedroom. Smell can be a powerful trigger for memories, especially memories that are laden with emotionality. The smell of the mother is one of the first smells infants experience and is strongly associated with the experience of being cared for.

Peekaboo: Intermittent Reinforcement

Not only was there an existing attachment bond between mother and child, but the mothers in these stories were able to intermittently psychologically return to their children. They did not disappear all at once, but rather in bits and pieces, over time and never completely. There was a thread of a connection that lingered, like the smell of their mother's perfume. This thread kept the children in a state of perpetual longing. The intermittent attention they received kept the bond alive and reinforced the child's needs and expectations for that parent. In learning theory, reinforcements (psychological or material rewards) that are provided sporadically in response to a stimuli (an event or experience) produce associative learning that is the most difficult to unlearn.[38] A child who receives parental love and attention on an intermittent basis, sometimes—but not consistently—has become conditioned to persist in hoping and waiting for that love to return, often beyond reason. The desire for the mother's love is not one that can easily be extinguished. In fact, it may never be extinguished. It may be modified, transferred to another object or person, repressed, or sublimated, but it is a basic human need. Thus, once having felt their mother's love, these children remained in a state of longing to feel it once again.

Wendy in *Dead End Gene Pool* wrote about how her mother would rally on her (Wendy's) birthday and "behaved like a mother,"[39] and that while her mother normally did not have the "time of day" for her children, "in her studio she took on her birthday persona. We would run amok there and she just laughed. We ripped into the clay like mice into a bar of soap, and made action figures . . . and dipped our arms and legs in buckets of wet plaster she made for us."[40] In that singular time and space Wendy's mother was able to tolerate (and perhaps even delight in) her children. It is no wonder that they found their mother's art studio such a wonderful place to be. Staceyann, too, had periodic moments of connection with her mother. When her mother made a grand reappearance in her life, Staceyann was in awe of her and felt that she was "the luckiest girl in the world."[41] Simply because her mother bestowed her presence (and presents) upon her, she felt like "somebody special." For these children it was the presence of the parent that was the present they most desired.

However, these mothers never stayed long enough. They came and went—physically and psychologically—entering and exiting their children's lives in unpredictable ways. For some, the absence and withdrawal was due to alcoholism; for others it was mental illness, narcissism, or a combination of factors. According to Tara, "My mother did not come down to breakfast that morning but her absence was not unusual. For me my mother was more like the fairies who attended Sleeping Beauty; she drifted in and out of my life."[42] Tara's relationship with her mother was like one long game of peeka-boo with her mother's face there and then not there. "She was away for longer and longer periods of time."[43] Even when her mother was present, Tara learned that "the mommy for whom I yearned might be there for me, and then again, she might not. A sad mother, preoccupied and distant, might take her place."[44] Tara never knew whether her mother would be emotionally available or not, and whether she, Tara, would be real to her mother. In *Chanel Bonfire*, Wendy's mother "became even less interested in her role as a mother and reworked herself as a jet-setter."[45] When Staceyann's mother came to visit, her presence was entirely unpredictable. She swooped in with great fanfare and commotion and just as suddenly became bored and irritable with her children, demanding that they fashion themselves to her needs rather than the other way around. "The next day she leaves after breakfast. Elmer Fudd chases Bugs Bunny across the TV screen for most of the day. Delano (her brother) is jittery and irritable. . . . We hear the latch on the gate opening before we see her. As soon as she walks through the door she tells us to pack our things."[46]

Sleeping Beauty

In *A.I.*, David's perfect day begins when he wakes his mother up. Sleeping, literal and/or metaphorical, is a theme that permeates these stories; sleeping is how many of the children experienced their mothers. In sleep, the mothers were physically present, tantalizingly close, but completely shut off from relating with their children. Kathryn's mother sleeps. "For as long as she lives with us, in her parents' house, she sleeps whenever she can. She sleeps very late every day, as much as six or seven hours past the time I get up for breakfast. I stand beside her when she sleeps. Wake up. Wake up. I think the thought so loudly inside my head that it seems as if she will have to rise, she can't remain insensible to my imploring her—my wanting her—as fervently as I do."[47] She stood beside her mother's sleeping body, intently studying her masklike face, impervious to the yearning girl standing there. One time, her mother woke to find Kathryn standing there. After that her mother's bedroom door was locked and Kathryn took up her post outside the bedroom door, waiting for her mother to wake. Carolyn's mother, as well, retreated from her family into her bed. "I spent hours of my day hanging around her door, or creeping close to her bed to press my face up against the mosquito net rising and falling with the slight breeze of the overhead fan. I stood and watched her, staring in through the gauze as she lay on her bed with the back of her hand on her forehead and her eyes closed. Often she lay with her face turned to the wall, her body was locked against touch or communion, curled around as if sheltering some empty space."[48] Jeanne's mother was a "stay-in-bed mom."[49] She also was drunk most of the time, doubly unavailable. Stacey-ann's mother also has difficulty being awake and present for her children. "The next morning Mummy is tired. All day we fetch glasses of water for her. She only comes out to use the bathroom."[50] She takes to her bed while Staceyann and her brother wait patiently for her to appear and tend to their needs, a rare event. "We spend the day quietly reading. Lunchtime passes without food. In the evening Mummy calls Delano and tells him to make bread and butter for dinner."[51] Laura's mother, as well, did not get out of bed. "The next year—fourth grade—I didn't make it to school every day. The alarm clock would go off in the bedroom and my mother would call me to get into bed with her."[52] When Mira's mother slept, Mira placed drawings by her bed in an attempt to connect and heal her.

For some children, sleep and death are confused;[53] the parent is physically present but emotionally absent. The body is there but not the heart and mind. Comingling of sleep and death is also evident in fairy tales such as Sleeping Beauty and Snow White, in which the princess lingers halfway between the two. For the children in these stories, their mother's unavailability was like a death for them because their need for their mother to be awake and alive to whom they were was not fulfilled.

The Forgotten Child

Even awake, these mothers were not particularly attentive to their children. Many of the stories contained episodes of the children literally being forgotten by the mother, constituting small doses of abandonment that echoed their ongoing concern about parental availability, heightening the anxiety and insecurity they felt about the parent's ability and willingness to take care of them. Mira's mother disappeared during a trip to a museum. Over the loudspeaker Mira heard that the gallery was closing, and she fretted, "It's getting late. I want my mother to come back. But what if she never does? I could wait here an hour or a year, set up a bed in the museum. Seasons could change. The weather could get cold, it could snow and still she might never return."[54] Kathryn was "always in tears, always sure that this time she wouldn't come at all but would leave me forever with the dentist or the Russian ballet mistress . . . and so in hallways and foyers, on dank stone benches or the vinyl-upholstered couches of waiting rooms, I silently rehearsed my grandparents' phone number and their address, to which the police should return me."[55] Laura's mother, as well, "was invariably late, which was excruciating. . . . Each day as the schoolyard emptied and I willed the station wagon to appear, I was filled with shame."[56] Carolyn's mother sent her away to school or other people's homes for long stretches, turning her back on her broken-hearted daughter. In *Chanel Bonfire*, Wendy's mother played dead. "She would ghoulishly limp to her bed and flop down on the mattress, and my sister and I would scream and jump on her, poking her and pleading with her to wake up. The game would always go on a little too long . . . and we would really start to believe that she was dead. . . . we'd start to cry and it was only then that she would open her eyes and come back to life at the sound of our tears. It was her way of gently reminding us that she was all we had."[57] These experiences functioned as rehearsals for what would ultimately become the near if not total loss of the parent.

Gone But Not Forgotten

In most of the stories, the balance between present and absent shifted and the mother was more absent than not, taking up negative space as opposed to actual space. Staceyann's mother moved out of the country without providing any means of communication and connection. Augusten's mother abdicated parental responsibility by allowing her therapist to assume guardianship of him. Ashley's mother failed to meet the requirements for regaining custody, resulting in Ashley remaining in foster care most of her childhood. For others, the parents changed homes and husbands so often that their children experienced themselves as for all intents and purposes forgotten, left behind. In *Chanel Bonfire*, Wendy missed her mother. "These days, it seemed I only spent time with my mother when she was getting ready to leave. My brother and I recently came to view her as a glamorous lodger who rented the master bedroom suite."[58] When her mother gave her a gift it awakened warmth in Wendy toward her mother. "She stunned me by putting her arms around me and awkwardly kissing the side of my head. I, in turn, nearly forgot myself and leaned in to receive it—but then I remember that she had only just arrived from Miami and was leaving for Haiti in the morning."[59] When Kathryn was six, her mother moved out of the home to live nearby in an undisclosed location. "She is gone, but her room remains just as it was. . . . She moved to a nearby apartment . . . she never tells us what street she lives on, nor does she give us her phone number. She sees me often, but she comes and goes at her own discretion; she does not want to be summoned by fevers or nightmares or lost teeth."[60] She is both mother and not mother. There and not there. For others the mothers slipped into permanent states of unavailability by way of mental illness and alcoholism—present but not present. While this may be true of all parents to some extent (parents do not pay attention all of the time to every need, wish, desire, thought, and feeling of their children), it crosses the line from poor parenting to emotional neglect when the experience of the child is one of pervasive inattention, as was the case in these stories.

Invisible

Because of their mother's unavailability and lack of interest in them, these children experienced themselves as invisible, small, unseen. Mira mused, "I close my eyes and make myself so small I could be a tiny creature inside a shoe box filled with moss and clumps of clay."[61] Kathryn wrote, "If I wake her she doesn't talk to me. She stalks around her room as if enraged, a wild animal, an astonished look on her face. I make myself small; I back into the corner by the door, and often she doesn't seem to know I'm there. Her eyes, when they turn at last toward me, are like two empty mirrors. I can't find myself in them."[62] She felt that she didn't exist unless and until her mother sees her. Like David in *A.I.*, she is not real to her mother. "As I stand watching her sleep I feel the world open behind me like a chasm."[63] Later when Kathryn became a teenager she developed an eating disorder, literally making herself smaller and smaller "until I disappear."[64] Tara experienced her mother as "more attentive to the voices in her head than to me. I would stand beside her chair, showing her my schoolwork or something I had drawn, but my mother couldn't concentrate. Rocking back and forth she would stare at the papers and nod, and then she would whisper and laugh to herself."[65] She knew that her mother "could be sweet and loving, but I also knew even when I refused to admit it to myself, that I could never quite break through to her. . . . she was focused inward, on herself."[66] Laura found that over time, "my mother grew both vaguer and sharper. Her presence in the house shifted between a kind of vacant absence, when for hours at a time she was unaware of us"[67] . . . "if we didn't call attention to ourselves, she forgot us,"[68] and Augusten observed, "Because I was sitting at an angle to the window, I couldn't see my reflection, just the rest of the kitchen, and this made me feel like a vampire. I was invisible."[69] Later in middle school he learned that because he had no friends he could cut classes and no one would notice, making "my invisibility even easier."[70] When his mother returned from a prolonged absence, he joyfully ran to greet her. "'You're back' I cried, running barefoot out of the house, over the dirt path to the street, to her window which was rolled all the way up. She continued to stare straight ahead, even as I banged on the glass."[71] Susan, author of *In Spite of Everything*, felt that she lost her bearings after her parents' divorce, lost to herself and her parents. "I didn't know where to go, what to do—not then, not in the weeks and the months that followed. . . . My mother alternately frantic about keeping her job and swooning with grief over my father's leaving us, did not really register that I essentially vanished."[72] At age thirteen, she dropped out of her extracurricular activities, started smoking and hanging out with a different crowd, and took up recreational drugs. No matter what she did to show her mother that she was hurting and confused, no matter how many red flags she waved to signal her pain, her mother failed to pay attention. In *Chanel Bonfire*, Wendy, too, experienced moments of feeling unreal and unseen, especially when her mother gave her the silent treatment. "Refusing to speak to us for extended periods was her most effective tactic. It made us feel small, almost like we'd disappeared,"[73] and when her mother came to see her in a school play, Wendy realized that "Mother hadn't come to the play just to see me—she had come to be seen."[74] As with all children, when these authors were not attended to by their mothers (their primary attachments), they experienced themselves as unreal to themselves, as if they didn't exist at all.

Distracted

Unfortunately, the mothers in these memoirs were too distracted by their own interior life to look outward to their children. They were blinded to their children by mental illness, narcissism, and alcoholism. Their desire for escape from their inner pain drove them to seek comfort in sleep and drink; they psychically numbed themselves, rendering them unavailable to their children. As can be seen in table 8.1, every mother experienced depression, schizophrenia, alcoholism, narcissism, or a combination of these factors. They lacked the capacity and/or the interest to attend to the emotional needs of their children. Their own needs—be it for alcohol, admiration, or escape— were so pressing to them that they had no mental space left for their children's needs.

In a sense it didn't matter what the cause of the inattention was because in most cases (the exception being the children with schizophrenic mothers) the children experienced the absence of maternal attention as a choice, and were consequently hurt. What was important was not so much the real cause but the child's perception or attribution of the mother's behavior. Jeanne described, "The worst feeling I had as a kid was that my mother was willing to miss my life for a drink, that she wouldn't stop for me, no matter how much it hurt me."[75]

Carolyn's mother was predominantly depressed but was able to rally when called to play the role of the glamorous wife of an important government official, a situation that activated her narcissism. "When she was adorning herself in front of the mirror, she was most perfectly herself. I used to stand behind her watching her flirt with her own face. . . . She was proud of herself: my waist is still twenty-two inches small, she crooned, even after having you two. Then she glared at her teeth: they aren't as strong as they used to be, she said, you two used up all my calcium."[76] Carolyn's mother enjoyed being the object of her daughter's fascination, rather than the other way around. Augusten's mother was involved in her personal feminist journey for self-discovery as a woman and an artist; she had little time or interest in her role as a mother. "Unless I was holding a spare typewriter ribbon or standing next to the record player when she needed the needle moved back to the beginning of a song, she had no use for me."[77] When she informed him that he would have to stay in the home of his guardian for another three years, Augusten was devastated. Her response was, "I don't have the emotional energy right now to deal with you,"[78] and that was that. In *Dead End Gene Pool*, Wendy's mother was more interested in appealing to her new husband than attending to her children, even if that meant dressing in a crocheted micromini dress with no underwear underneath and spending most of her time jet-setting around the world. Jeanne's mother was both depressive and alcoholic, a woman who had "a light cry going most of the time."[79] As the drinking progressed, so did the histrionics. "The crying was like a Tony Kushner play—it started one night and ended three nights later,"[80] and it included various complaints and threats of suicide. In *Chanel Bonfire*, Wendy's mother reinvented herself as an international jet-setter, leaving her children to fend for themselves.

Enthrallment

As is typical of some children of narcissistic, mentally ill, or alcoholic mothers,[81] the children in these stories were enraptured by their mothers. Kathryn described her relationship with her father as a shared experience of being in thrall to her mother, "the person neither of us could ever know or possess."[82] When her mother appeared coincidentally on the scene of a car accident Kathryn and her grandmother had been involved in, Kathryn experienced awe. "Her sudden materialization, the way she sprang nimbly out of the blue car, seeming angelic, magical."[83] Carolyn observed her mother's face, "stricken for a moment in the golden light,"[84] and Tara was "constantly trying to piece together the puzzle. I was obsessed with this woman who, to me, was more than just my mother; she had become a goddess,"[85] and she described her mother as having an "uncanny" way of investing songs with meaning. "She was singing, but at the same time, speaking just to you."[86] Wendy in *Dead End Gene Pool* imagined her mother being featured in *Glamour* magazine in a flattering enlargement of fashion "dos," while Wendy in *Chanel Bonfire* found that "even half dead, Mother was beautiful. She had the icy good looks of a Hitchcock heroine."[87] Ashley looked up to her mother and was enchanted by all that she did, "her smiles, her songs in the shower, the way she painted her eyes and lips with color."[88] Jeanne felt that her mother's suggestions offered her "the magic word that set me writing."[89]

Parentification

These children were empathically attuned to their mothers and were only too willing to take care of them when the need presented itself. From an early age Carolyn tried to take care of her mother, tend to her needs, and tried to rouse her from her stupor. "I was there because I had things to put down at the altar, next to the Bayer Aspirin bottle and the quinine tablets: a glass of water with a slice of lemon, or an orange cut into quarters; a painting of trees and blue sky, or a crayon drawing of a poinsettia I'd spent that morning doing."[90] If her mother was out of bed, Carolyn was at her feet, asking how she could help or offering her tea. Tara was obsessed with the notion of rescuing her mother. She became convinced that only she had the power to heal her, to save her from herself. "I would be the one to give her that chance, I would rescue my mother and lead her out of the darkness that kept her confused and off balance."[91] She had become the parent, and "watching my mother deteriorate was like watching a child being abused or a house burning down with people inside."[92] Her position as the adult was evident when she reassured her mother, "'Don't cry, Mommy' I told her over and over, tears streaming down my face. 'Things will be better now. I'm going to be here for you. I'm going to help you.'"[93] The desire to rescue was born from a sincere love for that parent as well as a desire to repair the parent who could then parent the child once again. The role reversal was also evident when Laura's mother relinquished custody. Laura was torn between a desire to be free of her mother's neglect and the thought that she should stay and take care of her mother. "I couldn't bear to see her cry."[94] Even as a little girl, Ashley was responsive to her mother's needs rather than the other way around. When her mother brought her a present that was not quite what she wanted, she reassured her, "I stroked the polished lid. 'That's ok' I slipped into my mother's lap."[95] Ashley was not free to express her disappointment because she was preoccupied with her mother's state of mind. Augusten's mother cast him in the role of her supporter and audience, a role he willingly played in order to please her (any attention was better than no attention), telling her what he thought she wanted to hear even if he didn't understand what he was saying. His role was to bolster her ego rather than to be authentic. Completing the denial of her parental role, he was instructed to refer to his mother by her first name. "She liked to think of us more as friends than as mother and son."[96] When Staceyann's mother claimed to care for her children despite her obvious lack of maternal warmth and attention, her daughter not only believed her but also felt the need to comfort and reassure her. "I understand Mummy. I think about you all the time, too."[97]

SUMMARY

The memories of emotionally neglected children are stories of unbearable longing. These children want nothing more than for their parents to awaken from their self-absorption and see them for the adoring children that they are. Unable to see through the fog of their parent's depression, mental illness, and addiction, the emotionally neglected children were stranded, as David in *A.I.* was, desiring the love and attention from a parent who was unable or unwilling to provide it. They were trapped by their desire to reclaim the love of a parent who was no longer emotionally present.

Chapter Nine

Stories of Physical Neglect

Six memoirs of physical neglect were reviewed, three of which are summarized in this chapter. In the first, *The Glass Castle*,[1] Jeannette Walls describes the physical hardship imposed on her family because of her parents' unwillingness to live a conventional life in which parents worked and provided for their children.

THE GLASS CASTLE BY JEANNETTE WALLS

At age three Jeannette accidentally set herself on fire at the stove while cooking hot dogs for herself, unsupervised. Her father was on one of his regular drinking binges, and her mother was preoccupied with artistic pursuits. The hospital where she received skin grafts seemed like a great place to young Jeannette, unaccustomed as she was to indoor heating, three meals a day, and doting attention. When Jeannette's younger brother fell and sustained a serious head injury, the family's response was that one child in the hospital was enough. They bandaged him up as best they could and expected him to do the rest of the healing on his own. The family laughed at how the floor probably was more hurt than the little boy's head, despite there being blood everywhere. Worried that child welfare services would get wind of their family situation, Jeannette's father whisked her away from the hospital, "Rex Walls style" (i.e., in the middle of the night, without paying the bills), failing to ensure that Jeannette received the full course of treatment. Shortly after returning home from the hospital, Jeannette was once again hungry and without a parent to feed her. Her mother commented upon seeing Jeannette back at the stove that it was good to not let her fear of fire get the best of her.

Unconventional, artistic, and antiauthoritarian, Jeannette's parents shunned routine employment and subjected their children to hunger, cold, and unsanitary living conditions as a result. When money did come to them, the father spent it on alcohol and the mother on art supplies and secret stashes of candy. "If we asked Mom about food—in a casual way, because we didn't want to cause any trouble—she'd simply shrug and say she couldn't make something out of nothing. We kids usually kept our hunger to ourselves but we were always thinking of food and how to get our hands on it."[2] One day Jeannette ate the last item of food in the house, a stick of margarine, and her mother was furious, saying she had been planning on using it for bread despite having no flour with which to make bread and no oven in which to bake it. "'It was the only thing to eat in the whole house' I said raising my voice. 'I was *hungry*.' Mom gave me a startled look. I'd broken one of our unspoken rules. We were always supposed to pretend our life was one long and incredibly fun adventure. She raised her hand, and I thought she was going to hit me, but then she sat down at the spool table and rested her head on her arms. Her shoulders started shaking. I went over and touched her arm. 'Mom' I said."[3]

There were frequent moves when Jeannette was a young child. When the family had to "skedaddle" out of town in order to avoid bill collectors and landlords, favorite items were usually left behind. A cat was thrown out of the car window because the parents decided not to bring it on their latest excursion, and the mother opined that it was lucky to now be free. Unwanted kittens were drowned and should consider themselves lucky for having lived at all. Tears were admonished as silly and sentimental. "Mom always said people worried too much about their children. Suffering when you are young is good for you, she said. It immunized your body and your soul, and that is why she ignored us kids when we cried."[4] On a family outing, Jeannette was inadvertently thrown from the car. Shocked and in pain, she saw her parents' car disappear down the road. When they finally retrieved her, her father announced enthusiastically, "You busted your snot locker pretty good!" and the whole family had a good laugh.[5] "Mom was not one of those fussy mothers who got upset when you came home dirty or played in the mud or fell and cut yourself."[6]

Jeannette idolized her father when she was younger. In her mind, "Dad was perfect," even though he had a "little bit of a drinking problem."[7] She described him as charming, handsome, charismatic, witty, and full of life and big ideas. He told stories about his adventures as a young man. "Dad always fought harder, flew faster, and gambled smarter than everyone else in his stories."[8] He had an infectious enthusiasm for his dreams that made everyone around him—at least for a while—think that just maybe he could pull them off. "Dad told me all about his plans and showed me his pages of graphs and calculations and geological charts, depicting the layers of sediment where the gold was buried. He told me I was his favorite, but he made me promise not to tell Lori or Brian or Maureen. It was our secret. 'I swear, Honey, there are times when I think you're the only one around who still has faith in me' he said. 'I don't know what I'd do if you ever lost it.' I told him I would never lose faith in him. And I promised myself I never would."9 Jeannette was so hopeful about the plan for the glass castle that she tried to dig the foundation herself, only to be instructed by her father to use the hole as a garbage dump.

One summer Jeannette's mother attended a college program out of town for the purposes of renewing her teacher certification, leaving Jeannette in charge of food for the whole family, as the most responsible person. As it turned out Jeannette was no match for her father's wheedling for the money for his own purposes. When she tried to resist he explained that he needed the money to make money. "'Have I ever let you down?' Dad asked. I'd heard that question at last two hundred times, and I'd always answered it the way I knew he wanted me to, because I thought it was my faith in Dad that had kept him going all those years. I was about to tell him the truth for the first time, about to let him know that he'd let us all down plenty, but then I stopped. I couldn't do it."10 Upon returning from the summer program, Jeannette's mother had renewed enthusiasm for her art career on which, she announced, she would be working full-time rather than getting a teaching job. When Jeannette expressed her concern about the family finances, her mother responded angrily, "Why do I always have to be the one who earns money?"11

Exasperated with their parents, Jeannette and her older sister devised a plan to save their babysitting money so that they could move to New York and have a life of their own. After they saved for over a year, their father broke into their piggy bank and drank away their money. "He insisted he wasn't trying to prevent Lori from leaving for New York, but if she had the sense that God gave a goose, she would stay put. 'New York is a sorry ass sink-hole' he said more than once, 'filled with faggots and rapists.' She'll get mugged, and find herself on the streets, he warned, forced into prostitution and winding up a drug addict like all those runaway teenagers. 'I'm only telling you this because I love you' he said 'and I don't want to see you get hurt.'"12 Lori moved to New York at age seventeen anyway, and Jeannette found a way to finish high school there so that she could go to college in state. Her mother broke into tears when told of the plan. "Don't be sad, Mom. I promise I'll write," Jeannette reassured her mother. "I'm not upset because I'll miss you," Mom said. "I'm upset because you get to go to New York and I'm stuck here. It's not fair."13

Shortly before she left, Jeannette's father tried to entice her to stay by resurrecting his plans to build the glass castle. It was too late, even for that. On the eve of her departure, Jeannette's mother declared that she was not an early riser and would not be seeing her daughter off. "I know what you look like," she said. Jeannette had last-minute doubts. "I studied my face in the mirror and wondered what New Yorkers would think when they looked at me. Would they see an Appalachian hick, a tall gawky girl, still all elbows and knees and jutting teeth? For years Dad had been telling me I had an inner beauty. Most people didn't see it. I had trouble seeing it myself, but Dad was always saying he could damn well see it and that was what mattered. I hoped when New Yorkers looked at me they saw whatever it was that Dad saw."[14]

Over the next few years, each of the four Walls children made their way to New York and, helping each other, made lives for themselves. Then, unexpectedly, Jeannette's parents found their way to the city as well. Shunning their children's offers of help, they squatted in untenanted buildings, ate from dumpsters, and claimed to be living the life they wanted. In the end as in the beginning, her parents were unable to adjust their lives to the standards and expectations of conventional society or their children.

BURN DOWN THE GROUND BY KAMBRI CREWS

In *Burn Down the Ground*,[15] Kambri Crews tells of growing up in rural poverty with her deaf father and partially deaf mother. Her parents, struggling financially and in their marriage, moved the family to a remote plot of land that caused even greater physical hardship for Kambri and her brother.

Born in the mid-1970s, Kambri Crews was the second child of two deaf parents. She and her older brother David were both hearing. Kambri's parents were attractive, fun-loving, sociable people who valued friendship, dancing, and good times. Parental supervision ranked low on their list. "During my seven years . . . I was a typical latchkey kid. Why would parents bother paying for a babysitter when they could tie a key around their kids' necks with a piece of yarn and let them watch cartoons for an hour or two until they got home from work?"[16] Her father in particular was lax with rules, a charming and charismatic man whom Kambri recalled, "like a deaf Elvis. Tall, muscular, and handsome with dark hair combed back into a modern pompadour, he could charm the skin off a snake."[17] She adored her father. "Ever since I could walk, I'd been at his side, helping him on projects by handing him tools, sweeping up, fetching him a fresh Coors Light. He paid me with rides in a wheelbarrow, by having me sit in his lap to steer the Chevy, or by letting me take the first sip of his beer."[18] In response to her husband's philandering, Kambri's mom relocated the family to a plot of land deep in the woods. "We're going to start a whole new life . . . It'll be like a long camping trip."[19] The family loaded their few possessions and the two young children into the bed of the truck and sped along the highway to their new homestead. Without water, electricity, or shelter, the family managed with few possessions or provisions. They were isolated and poor; nonetheless, the parents continued to find money for alcohol, cigarettes, socializing, and smoking marijuana, often in front of the children. "When our parents weren't around, my brother and I practiced making 'joints' with rolling paper and loose tobacco collected from my father's cigarette butts and argued over which of us would inherit their bong when they died."[20] A frequent family adventure involved going to the beach where—unsupervised—Kambri would go out as far as she could and would often lose track of where her family was on the shore. "It was terrifying to emerge from the surf to realize no one was watching after me."[21] Kambri was a sensitive child and wanted to understand who her parents were and would often pester them about their childhoods. Once her father told her a story of how when he was just three years old his father drove him to the other side of town and left him there. "Remembering that day . . . made me feel sad and confused."[22] Those feelings allowed Kambri to believe that her parents had had it worse than she. Kambri looked up to her parents and felt proud that her father was so cool, strutting around in his tight jeans and shades, charming the cashiers at stores with his silly antics and good looks. "My father's accomplishments . . . were extraordinary . . . and when a young man driving a large truck filled with sand caused the bridge on Boars Head to collapse, he became a superhero,"[23] a superhero whom she "desperately wanted to please." It was hard for her to enjoy things such as movies and music that he could not partake in (her mother had limited hearing and could join in these activities), feeling a "pang of guilt seeing the curiosity and hurt on Dad's face."[24] Being deaf did not interfere with her parents' partying, which they often brought into the home, introducing the children to alcohol and drugs at an early age, laughing when the children acted stoned or "half baked." For a while both parents were able to hold down low-income jobs a distance from home. "Our parents logged so many hours working and traveling to and from their jobs that most times my brother and I were left at home in the woods without any supervision. Life on Boars Head developed into a Southern *Lord of the Flies*."[25] In the absence of a father figure, Kambri's older brother took to bullying and beating her, about which her parents were unsympathetic. Routine hygiene was also not on their radar. "At home I never brushed my teeth unless my gums were puffy and bleeding."[26] Food was scarce. "I balled up slices of bread, sucked on dried sticks of spaghetti, gummed spoonfuls of butter, or ate peeled and salted potatoes, tomatoes, and cucumbers plucked from our garden."[27] Between work and partying, her parents did not have much time or attention for their children. In response, Kambri threw herself into school and extracurricular activities in order to find a place for herself, something her parents showed little interest in. "One evening at a basketball game . . . I heard a familiar voice coming from the stands and was surprised to see my father sitting alone on the top bleacher. My heart fluttered. No one had ever come to see me play."[28] She did win her father's approval when he taught her how to drive at the age of thirteen, when she went to work at the age of fourteen, and when she joined her father on the dance floor in a drunken bout of Travolta-like moves. "I was sweaty and happy."[29] She was "thrilled" when her father asked her to shoot some baskets with him after having been out all night, unaware that his young daughter missed him. When the family lost their home, again, and had to move, again, Kambri was instructed to leave all but her most treasured possessions, and she rationalized that she really didn't need that much. During her freshman year of high school her mother took a job in another state. "She had been away for weeks and I had barely laid eyes on my father. He still technically lived with us, but he was rarely home. I had no idea where he was."[30] With both parents MIA, "there was no food in the refrigerator and no air-conditioning in the shed."[31] Finally her mother found a place to live and wanted Kambri to move in with her, and her father helped her do so. By this point Kambri's parents were separated. On moving day Kambri couldn't find her dogs and sadly concluded that most likely her father had killed them as he had in the past when a dog or litter of puppies or kittens were unwanted. On her first day of her new school her father brought her to register and encouraged her to forge her mother's name on the forms. "My eyes grew wide. I was a fast thinker, and immediately calculated that this would give me full authority to cut school without my parents ever knowing. . . . Dad put his index finger to his lips. 'Shhhh.'"[32] Sad but not surprised, Kambri was forgotten by both parents on her sixteenth birthday. "No one seemed to remember. No one seemed to care."[33] Shortly after that her mother took her to an amusement park for a day of fun, with mother and teenage daughter sharing joints and munchies. "It was one of the best days of my life."[34] Throughout her high school years Kambri's parents remained legally separated, although her father would frequently stumble into their apartment and pass out drunk. Sometimes he was belligerent and aggressive, and at least once he was arrested for domestic violence. As the violence escalated, Kambri's mother stayed at her sister's house, leaving Kambri alone in the apartment to deal with him. "Even though his beef wasn't with me, I was still afraid."[35] One night he found Kambri's mother in the home and attacked her, with the apparent intention of killing her. The police were called and life settled down for a while. Despite the intermittent chaos and lack of nurturance, Kambri graduated high school, summa cum laude. Nonetheless, she didn't have a bright future, having married at age seventeen and lacking a clear direction toward a better life. While Kambri was working towards self-improvement and her mother was blossoming outside the confines of her unhappy marriage, Kambri's father continued to get into trouble with the law. The most serious offence he was arrested for was trying to murder his girlfriend. After one hour of deliberation by the jury, Kambri's father was convicted and sent to prison for twenty years. Over the next several years Kambri maintained a relationship with her father. It was painful for her to see him in jail, diminished in his looks, resources, and charm, and she worried that he would be hurt or discriminated against. She worried about how he would protect himself. After a recent visit she left the prison at peace, finally able to accept her father for who he was. She also accepted her mother to whom she was "eternally grateful"[36] for giving her an interesting life.

BREAKING NIGHT BY LIZ MURRAY

Breaking Night[37] is the memoir of growing up in the Bronx with an older sister and two drug-addicted parents. The family lived in squalor, with Liz and her sister constantly hungry, dirty, and unsupervised.

Liz was the younger daughter of two drug-addicted parents. Her father was in jail when her mother became pregnant. She already had a one-year-old and a long-term drug habit. "Ma used coke, shooting dissolved white dust into her veins; it traveled through her body much like lightning, igniting her, giving the feel, however fleeting, of something forward-moving, day in and day out."[38] She had run away from home as a teenager, escaping physical and emotional abuse, and met and fell in love with Liz's father, a literate and charming young drug abuser. When the children were born and the father was in jail, Liz's mother became sober, at least for a while. Her father was released when Liz was three years old, and both parents slid into their old ways quickly. "In the months that followed, Ma grew more laid-back about keeping up with things. Chores were neglected; dirty dishes sat untouched for days in the kitchen sink. She took us to the park less often. I sat at home for hours waiting to be swept up in Ma's activities, and couldn't understand why they no longer included me."[39] The family subsisted entirely on handouts from family and government payments due to Liz's mother's blindness. Each month when the check arrived, the parents would plan how to spend the money, with funds for coke being the highest priority, followed by the electric bill and bologna for the kids. Liz recalled adoring the time she had her mother's attention while Liz waited with her in the check-cashing line, having her undivided attention for those few precious moments. Around the same time Liz's mother began (or resumed) excessive drinking, which also took her away from the home and her children for hours every day. The night before Liz began kindergarten her mother remembered that she would need school supplies, but Liz had already scrounged up a used binder and a few pencils on her own. School became a source of both pleasure in learning and pain at the shame she felt wearing dirty clothes. Compounding matters was the fact that Liz had head lice that went untreated for months, calling attention to her differentness in the eyes of her peers. "In the first grade, when I had told and retold myself I would be a perfectly 'normal' kid, the lice had ruined everything."[40] She felt that "the world was filled with people who were repulsed by me."[41] Being an outcast was only part of Liz's problems. She also was hungry. Early each month, her parents had used the SSI check for drugs and the family was broke. Her mother would beg or prostitute herself for enough money for a hit. Liz's older sister would become furious with her parents for spending their food money on drugs. Listening, Liz would see the validity of Lisa's argument, but she would also see that her parents needed the drugs to ease their pain. "Ma said she needed drugs to help her forget bad memories that haunted her, the thoughts of her mom and dad that caused her to suffer all day long. And even though I wasn't sure what exactly in his past Daddy got high to forget, I knew it must be something very painful, because if Daddy didn't get high, then he would spend days collapsed on the couch in a withdrawal-induced depression."[42] Liz was torn between empathy for her parents who were not doing well themselves and a desire for them to be more attentive parents. "They had no intention to hurt us. It wasn't as if they were running off during the daytime to be better parents to some other kids and then returning home at night to be awful to us. They simply did not have it in them to be the parents I wanted them to be. So how could I blame them?"[43] When Liz did try to hold her mother accountable, for example, when her mother stole her five-dollar birthday gift to buy drugs, her mother would cry and beg for her daughter's forgiveness. "'I can't stop. Forgive me, Pumpkin?' Then I was crying too; we both were."[44] Liz forgave her mother that night and again when her mother sold the turkey given to them by the church for Thanksgiving, and many times after that. Liz recalled that while she forgave her mother, she was heartbroken nonetheless; she just didn't blame her mother. She blamed drugs; she blamed addiction. Sometimes at night her mother would take a break from shooting up and sit by Liz's bed and sing to her, and Liz felt loved by her. Her father, too, was able to talk to her about ideas, about books, and Liz felt loved by him. "Drugs were like a wrecking ball tearing through our family . . . I couldn't help but feel that Ma and Daddy were the ones who needed protecting."[45] Liz was a conscientious child who would stay up at night to make sure her parents came home after their drug runs, and then she would stay up into the early morning listening to her mother's childhood stories and being a comfort and companion to her parents. "Every night was like this. While Ma and Daddy injected themselves with cocaine and ran in and out, like a tag team, I stayed close by and shared the night with them."[46] When her mother's stories turned dark, Liz stayed up to soothe her. "I abandoned my needs . . . Her pain blanketed me in its urgency, so that it became difficult to realize that there was any distance—age-wise or responsibility-wise—between us."[47] Tired in the morning from the late nights, Liz skipped school. Months passed with no school attendance, which worked well for Liz because she preferred to stay home and keep watch over her mother. Despite her vigilance, Liz's mother had what the family referred to as a breakdown but was most likely a reemergence of her schizophrenia, possibly brought on by her intensive drug abuse. When her mother was in the hospital, Liz's father rose to the occasion and provided food for his children. Without the mother's drug habit to fund, the family was able to stretch their dollars further. "I learned with some degree of relief, as well as hurt, that all three of us could go an entire month eating dinner each night, and usually with something to eat during the day as well."[48] Once Liz's mother came home, however, the family reverted to its usual routine of drugs, hunger, late nights, and skipping school. The family was in crisis, and Liz's parents' marriage finally imploded. By the age of nine, things at home and at school were so unpleasant for Liz that she spent her days roaming the neighborhood, finding ways to make money for herself so that she wouldn't go hungry. She learned how to pump gas for tips, how to bag groceries for tips, and when all else failed how to steal food from the store. Liz's mother continued to cycle in and out of psychiatric hospitals. One time she returned distraught, and zombie-like she informed Liz that she had been diagnosed with AIDS. By the time Liz was twelve, she stopped attending school, fending for herself during the days and nights as neither parent was able or willing to tend to her needs. Some days she rode the subway all day just to feel the comfort of the rumbling train. A few times caseworkers came to the home to reprimand her for truancy, but none offered to help or tried to hold her parents accountable. Surprised, Liz was promoted from sixth grade to middle school, although no one came to her graduation ceremony. "In the hallway of my building, I removed my cap and gown before entering my apartment so that Ma wouldn't feel bad for missing the ceremony."[49] Shortly after that Liz's mother moved into a boyfriend's apartment. Liz's sister chose to go as well, but Liz felt that she couldn't leave her father alone so she stayed behind with him. Her father shut down, and Liz was essentially on her own. Not for long, though, because child welfare removed her from her father's care and placed her in a home for troubled girls. She was released into the custody of her mother's boyfriend, although she spent most nights sleeping on the sofa of various friend's homes. By the time Liz was seventeen she had missed most of high school and was homeless, drifting between friends who were only slightly better off than she was. After her mother died, Liz began to take stock of her life and entered an alternative high school. She realized that unless she took control of her situation, nothing would get better for her; no one was looking out for her, so she would have to look out for herself. She was very fortunate to find a small school that was able to nurture her intellect and academic achievement, despite being homeless. She finished four years of high school in two years and was accepted to Harvard. Today Liz Murray is an inspirational speaker and author, with a life purpose to empower others to lead their best lives despite their early hardships.

Chapter Ten

Making Meaning of Physical Neglect

The federal government defines neglect as a failure to act in such a way as to present an imminent risk of serious harm to a child.[1] As with other types of child maltreatment, each state has its own definition of neglect in their child maltreatment statutes. In most states, several different types of neglect are articulated, including physical neglect, medical neglect, inadequate supervision, environmental neglect, emotional neglect, educational neglect, and giving birth to an infant who is addicted to drugs. Physical neglect is the subject of this chapter. However, in the memoirs read, some of the parents engaged in other forms of neglect as well. Physical neglect has several subtypes: abandonment (leaving the child unattended), expulsion (refusing to exercise custody of the child), shuttling (repeatedly leaving the child in the care of others), nutritional neglect (failing to provide proper nourishment such that the child is undernourished and/or chronically hungry), clothing neglect (failing to provide the child with appropriate clothing), and other (inadequate hygiene, reckless disregard for the health and safety of the child).

Two controversies have existed in the field of child maltreatment with respect to the definition and identification of neglect. The first pertains to whether parental intentionality must be present. That is, is it necessary to determine that the parent intended to harm the child in order for neglect to be identified? The consensus is that parental state of mind—something that is difficult at best to ascertain—is not essential for a finding of neglect. The second dilemma is whether there must be harm to the child in order for neglect to have occurred. Again, the current thinking is that this is not required, mostly because with several types of neglect the harm is not evident until some point in the future. Thus, a parent could fail to provide proper dental care and it would not be necessary for the child's teeth to rot and fall out to determine that neglect has occurred. As with other types of maltreatment, there is not always a bright line between poor parenting and neglect. However, in the memoirs reviewed for this chapter, there is little room for doubt that these children experienced serious and chronic physical neglect, in addition to other forms of neglect as well. The six memoirs read for this chapter are presented in table 10.1. Three were summarized in the previous chapter. All were reviewed for the identification of themes discussed below.

For the authors of these memoirs, physical neglect involved being hungry, being dirty, and not having a clean and safe home. These authors as children did not have their basic needs for food and shelter met. For all there was a serious limitation on the part of the parent—such as mental illness, alcoholism, or drug abuse—that made it difficult for the parent to provide adequate care. The deprivation was felt deeply by these children. The authors wrote quite poignantly about what it felt like to not have enough to eat, to not have a clean and safe home to live in, to not have clean clothes to wear every day, to feel tired, and hungry, and dirty. For example, Frank McCourt, award-winning author of *Angela's Ashes* about growing up poor in Ireland, wrote about his home being flooded downstairs and smelling from the nearby latrine that was shared by all of the families in the row houses. It was so cold that Frank and his brothers pulled the planks off the walls and burned them in the hearth to keep warm. On most days they had nothing more than bread and water to eat. Frank's father was an alcoholic who rarely worked and drank away his paycheck when he did. Likewise, Jeannette Walls's father was a drinker. In addition, her mother, who had a teaching degree but refused to teach, chose to spend her days instead reading and painting. Because their parents refused or were unable to work, Jeannette and her three siblings often went without food. They moved frequently so as to avoid paying rent and scraped by with what little they had. The family could not afford air-condi-

Table 10.1. Memoirs of Physical Neglect

Title of Book/Author	Abuse Victim/ Author	Neglectful Parent	Major Dysfunction in Family
Breaking Night	Liz Murray	Both	Drug-addicted and mentally-ill mother and father
Angela's Ashes	Frank McCourt	Both	Alcoholic father
Burn Down the Ground	Kambri Crews	Both	Alcoholic father
The Glass Castle	Jeannette Walls	Both	Alcoholic father
Coming Clean	Kimberly Rae Miller	Both	Both parents are hoarders
Dirty Secret	Jessie Sholl	Mother	Mother is hoarder

tioning, so the parents opened all of the windows and doors, allowing both homeless people as well as wild animals to wander in and take up residence in their home. As described in *Breaking Night*, both of Liz Murray's parents were mentally ill and drug addicted. Her home was often overrun by unsavory characters who spent time with her parents while they were getting high, being high, or looking for their next high. The apartment was disorganized and filthy most of the time. Kambri Crews's parents moved the family to an uninhabitable cabin deep in the woods without plumbing or electricity. And Jessie Scholl, author of *Dirty Secret*, and Kimberly Rae Miller, author of *Coming Clean*, wrote about living in homes that were foul and disgusting due to the hoarding problems of one or both of their parents. None of these children had the experience of knowing what it felt like to live in a clean and safe environment.

The womb is our first home. It is generally a warm and comforting place (with the predictable rhythmic sounds of the heartbeat and the gentle rocking motion of the mother to lull the fetus into a perpetual state of relaxation and calm). Once born, most infants around the world are placed in a womblike setting such as a bassinet or crib for sleeping and resting and a swaddling blanket or carrier during the day. These, too, are generally small, warm, and clean spaces for the baby to feel contained and cared for. The preference of infants for small spaces has been borne out in research, which has found that swaddling can decrease crying in infants.[2] The bassinet or crib is usually placed within a larger holding space: the baby's room itself is situated within the larger home (be it a house or an apartment). Thus, babies are located in a series of nested holding environments starting with the crib and moving outward to the room and then the home. In this way, the home is an extension of the womb, as it represents safety and comfort. Unfortunately, for the authors of these memoirs their homes did not represent that safety and comfort. Rather than being contained within a holding environment, they experienced themselves as outsiders.

OUTSIDERS

The theme of outsider-ness was reflected in the memoirs in at least four ways. First, the authors spent an inordinate amount of time literally outside of their homes. Being outside was for some of them a more attractive option than being inside the dirty and smelly home. That was certainly the case for Frank, for example. His home offered little by way of comfort. Rather than being a place of safety and security, the home was a place to avoid, to stay away from as much as possible. Being outside also served as a distraction from the hunger that plagued him. With the dirt, filth, and dangerous people and animals wandering through the homes of these authors, the distinction between inside and outside was less differentiated than in other homes. Typically, the home provides a kind of protective barrier, a shield, between the outside world and children as a way to keep them safe from harm. In these families that protective barrier was porous at best and in some cases nonexistent.

The second way in which the authors wrote about feeling like an outsider was in relation to their own family. In a well-functioning, nonmaltreating family, the members of the family form a cohesive unit with an identity (i.e., the Jones family!) and a coherent set of rules and roles. In the families written about in the neglect memoirs, the children experienced a sense of "every man for himself." The parents were preoccupied with their own concerns (getting high, being drunk, staying in bed, hoarding possessions) such that they appeared to spend very little time seeing to and thinking about the day-to-day experiences and life of their children. These parents didn't just fail to provide proper food, clothing, and shelter, they failed to attend to the needs and experiences of their children (getting them to bed at a proper time, providing them with predictable meals, getting them to school, doing homework with them). In this sense, the children experienced themselves as very much on their own. Liz was roaming the streets of the Bronx at a very young age earning loose change at a local gas station or supermarket. At nine she was applying for jobs, hoping to be able to provide for herself and her family. She knew that if she were going to eat, it would be up to her to earn the money to buy the food. No one else was going to do that for her. Likewise, it was up to her to find loose-leaf paper in the trash and a binder under her sister's bed if she wanted school supplies for kindergarten. Her mother only became aware of this need at 11:30 p.m. the night before her first day of school.

Another way in which they felt like an outsider in their own family is that their parents—for their own reasons—tended to minimize the impact of the neglect on their children. Thus, the authors as children did not have a shared experience with their parents of what their life was like. The parents did not commiserate with the children about how terrible it was to be hungry or dirty, and the children knew that it was taboo to speak about their pain and suffering. Jeannette's mother, for example, responded to Jeannette's complaint that her winter coat lacked buttons by pointing out that the coat was 100 percent wool and was imported from France. When Kambri screamed for her father to slow down when he was driving recklessly, he sped up, breaking into a big smile, as if to say that what he was doing wasn't all that bad. When Kambri complained to her mother that her brother was beating her up during their long hours as latchkey children, she scolded her for being a "tattletale." Jeannette told her mother that she had been molested by her uncle, and her mother responded that she was probably imagining it and that poor Uncle Stanley was probably lonely. Jeannette was told not to make such a big deal out of everything. Bugs in the food were simply things to be picked off and eaten around. "Just slice off the maggoty parts,"[3] her mother directed her. "Harmless drunks" were allowed to wander into the home and stay overnight. The general childrearing attitude of Jeannette's mother involved ignoring or denying the discomfort of her children, especially discomfort that she would be responsible for addressing. "Mom always said people worried too much about their children. Suffering when you're young is good for you, she said. It immunized your body and your soul, and that was why she ignored us kids when we cried. Fussing over children who cry only encourages them, she told us."[4] There was no room in the family for the children to cry or complain about their hunger, cold, fear, or pain. The children colluded in this denial by keeping their hunger and fear and discomfort to themselves as a way to avoid angering or hurting their parents. But the collusion in this lie came at a great cost as it prevented the children from feeling close and emotionally connected to their parents. The one time that Jeannette recalled speaking the truth to her mother, she felt immediate shame and guilt, knowing that she had broken the unspoken rule that everyone was supposed to pretend that it was a great adventure to live the way they did.

The fourth aspect to the outsider status of these children was that they felt separate and apart from the normal, everyday life of their friends and neighbors. They felt cut off from society in general. The experience of being hungry and dirty led them to feel as if they didn't belong, as if they didn't deserve to belong in the company of other children. The experience of pressing their noses to the bakery window to get a peek inside at the sumptuous display of delicious foods just outside their grasp serves as an apt visual depiction of the everyday experience of neglected children. What they were deprived of, what they wanted, was so close and yet not attainable to them. Jessie wrote about not wanting her classmates to find out that she lived with her mother in that dilapidated, weird home across the street, as that would mark *her* as undesirable. She went to great lengths to keep this information a secret from everyone else. Liz, too, kept her homelessness a secret from her classmates for fear that it would somehow reflect on her. She developed elaborate routines for keeping the truth hidden.

The children were not only ashamed of their shabbiness and their dirtiness, which they felt marked them as undesirable, but they also were afraid—as bad as their home life was—that if other adults found out how they were living they would be placed into foster care. Kimberly wrote, "I'd always known we were different, but until now I didn't know that different was bad. Until now I hadn't known that there were people who could take me away from my parents. There was something wrong with us, and now that I knew it I couldn't unknow it. I loved my parents and I loved my dogs, and my cats and my panda and my Sheryl, and I didn't want to leave any of them."[5] These children still loved their parents and did not want to be separated from

them and therefore were doubly motivated to keep their home life   t.
What that meant, however, was that they could not really be auth   d
relaxed with other people. They could not have friends over, they   ot
reveal their hunger, they could not discuss or describe what life   ly
like for them. They had to always be on guard, vigilant against   th
leaking out. This resulted in a feeling of not belonging with their friends and
classmates. Even as an adult Jessie felt that other people would be "utterly
revolted" if they realized that she had scabies from her mother's home. "If
they knew that at this very moment, walking right past them is a girl with a
parasite living under her skin. Walking right past them as if she has every
right. She has no right to be among normal people anymore. She knows. It's
something she has known most of her life."[6] The neglect was not something
that happened to her, it was something that she was. "The older I got,"
Kimberly wrote, "The more obsessed I became with maintaining the illusion
that everything in my life was perfect—and as the years passed, I depended
upon it to fly me under the radar with friends."[7] When she was younger she
had fleas. "I could pass the fleabites off as mosquito bites most of the time,
but there was a constant fear that one would jump from my hair or clothes in
school and people would see them. That people would know that I was flea-
infested."[8] The others wrote as well about being lice infested or having the
feeling that the filth and shame of the parental neglect had marked them as
different and undesirable. The neglect began as something externally imposed on them but over time became internalized into an identity as someone
who was different and undesirable. The shame of their home became the
shame of their very self.

In general, school-aged children are amazingly attuned to the social
norms of their classmates, and any violation of those norms is likely to bring
on tremendous shame and discomfort. The neglectful parents, however, did
not seem to care what others had to say. They could not afford to care
because that would require a massive effort on their part to change their
lifestyle (give up drugs, get mental health treatment, stop hoarding). Thus,
they were inclined to minimize the importance of fitting in or seeking approval from others. Liz's father took broken furniture from the curb and
chided Liz to not care what other people thought. That's their problem, he
taught her. Likewise, Jeannette's parents scorned society as materialistic and
shallow as a way to prevent their children from demanding that they do
something about their living conditions. The problem, they were saying, was
with the expectations of the children for wanting more and not with the
parents for giving less. In this way, the neglectful parents who themselves
lived outside of mainstream society passed on that outsider status to their
children through their failure to provide them with the tools and assets to fit
in. For example, Frank's father—having squandered his paycheck on alcohol—fashioned shoes for Frank and his brothers out of used car tires. For the

boys it was agonizingly shameful to walk around with huge pieces of rubber nailed to their shoes, making them the laughingstock at school. The shame was in some ways worse than having no shoes at all. Because there was so much shame associated with their neglect and so much fear of having their secret life revealed, the authors wrote about wanting to disappear, to be invisible—not from their parents in order to avoid abuse as with physically abused children—but invisible to their peers and friends. To disappear would be the ultimate outsider role as it would involve being outside not only the home, the family, and society but also outside the self as well. Liz wrote that there "wasn't room for her full self"[9] in her life.

LOVE FOR THE PARENT

Despite the ongoing discomfort if not outright pain their parents caused them, the authors of the memoirs for the most part loved their parents and wanted nothing more than for their parents to love and take care of them. Kambri, for example, wrote, "While I doubted the practicality of burning the land, I never questioned my father, and I was eager to please him. Ever since I could walk, I'd been at his side helping him on projects, handing him tools, sweeping up, or fetching him a fresh Coors light."[10] She described her father as a "deaf Elvis" who was "cool," and both her parents were so important to her that she would have "swum across the Gulf of Mexico and back to avoid an F"[11] if that is what they wanted. She was thrilled whenever her parents managed—infrequently as it was—to pay attention to her. For example, she described the best day of her life as when her mother took her to a carnival and spent time with her—"everything was as it should be"[12]—and when her father came to watch her play basketball, her "heart fluttered. No one had ever come to see me play."[13] Jessie was flattered when she found out that her mother—once—met with a teacher, because it represented to her "a kind of behind-the-scenes mothering I hadn't known about."[14] Liz's mother would sometimes take a break from shooting up to sing her daughter a single verse of a lullaby and stroke her hair. "The smell of her Winston cigarettes and the faint, sour smell of coke always lingered—scents that lulled me to sleep."[15] The few moments that she and her mother spent in line at the check-cashing center once a month were the highlights of Liz's life. "I was thrilled with her attention."[16] Frank, too, fondly recalled small moments when his father paid attention to him. "Dad nods and puts his hand on mine again. He looks at me, steps away, stops, comes back, kisses me on the forehead for the first time in my life and I'm so happy I feel like floating out of the bed."[17] Kimberly thought her father was brilliant and loved listening to his rambling lectures. "In general I was grateful for whatever nugget of personal insight he could spare."[18] These children received so little by way of parental love, affection, and attention that any crumb of affection thrilled and delighted them.

EPIPHANY

Those crumbs of love sometimes made it so hard for the children to see the neglect for what it was. Because neglect is defined as the absence of something and because it was so pervasive in their lives, it was hard for these children to fully take in the reality that what they were experiencing—the lack of proper food, clothing, shelter—was because of the choices of their parents. An understanding of cause and effect was required for them to see the relationship between a parent's drinking and the grumbling in their stomach. That takes time, especially when the parents—as noted above—were so disinclined for the children to make that connection. What allowed that awareness to finally emerge was observing how other parents behaved toward their children. Even in the poorest neighborhoods that the McCourt family lived in, Frank had the opportunity to observe that other fathers did not drink away the dole or their paycheck (when the father was lucky enough to get a job and sober enough to keep it). Most of the authors had an epiphanal moment in which they realized that, while they were poor as were most of the other families they knew, other families managed not to squander what little they had on alcohol, drugs, and hobbies. They realized that to some extent their parents were choosing to put their needs above the needs of their children. When Frank's brother died, Frank and his father went to town to collect gifts of food for the family. Frank knew that his brothers were home literally starving but still his father stopped to drink and visit at the pub on the way home. "I wonder how long we'll sit here with Malachy and Eugene hungry at home, hours from the porridge, which Eugene didn't eat anyway."[19] For Frank the realization came when he saw that his father not only drank away their food money but also he put his misguided notion of dignity above helping his family. "I wish Dad would come and help us because Mam has to stop every few steps and lean against a wall. She's holding her back and telling us she'll never be able to climb Barrack Hill. Even if Dad came he wouldn't be much use because he never carries anything, parcels, bags, packages. If you carry such things you lose your dignity. That's what he says."[20] Jeannette recalled a humorous moment when she and her brother caught their mother sneaking candy while they were hungry. At first her mother denied eating anything, claiming that she was moving her jaw because her teeth hurt. "Brian yanked the covers back. Lying on the mattress next to Mom was one of those huge family-sized Hershey chocolate bars, the shiny silver wrapper pulled back and torn away. She'd already eaten half of it. Mom started crying. 'I can't help it,' she sobbed. 'I'm a sugar addict, just like your father is an alcoholic.' She told us we should forgive her the same way we always forgive Dad for his drinking."[21] The fact that the candy bar was "family size" and yet not shared with the family was not lost on Jeannette. Another time the children found a valuable ring. "We figured we could sell it and buy food, pay off the house—Mom and Dad kept missing the monthly payments, and there was talk that we were going to be evicted—and maybe still have enough left over for something special, like a new pair of sneakers for each of us."[22] However, their mother insisted on keeping the ring. "It could also improve my self-esteem. And at times like these, self-esteem is even more vital than food."[23] It is notable that when *her* needs were unmet they could be spoken about but not when it was the children's needs. When her father stole her hard-earned money from her piggy bank, she realized that her needs were not a priority for her parents. For Jessie the realization occurred when she was five years old and her mother asked her to tell the teacher that she (Jessie) would be staying late at school and taking the afternoon bus home. Her mother had some thrift store shopping to do. Jessie was too shy to tell the teacher, so she took the regular bus home and waited for her mother. Finally her mother came home with her arms loaded with piles of junk. "I looked around at all of her new acquisitions and thought about how she had chosen these things over me."[24] Jessie may have come to the realization earlier than the others because her other parent (her father) was not colluding in the neglect (her parents were divorced and her father was a competent parent who provided for his children). Jessie, therefore, not only had other children's parents to compare her mother to but she also had another parent to serve as a basis for comparison. That was not the case for the others, and it took them longer to understand that a great deal of their pain and suffering was caused by their parent's choices, the choice to drink or do drugs or refusal to work or change. Liz, for example, found that her father was able to stretch the monthly checks when her mother was in the hospital. "I learned with some degree of relief, as well as hurt, that all three of us could go an entire month eating dinner each night, and usually with something to eat during the day as well, on that same check that I'd spent years watching Ma and Daddy deplete in only days following its arrival. Had it been possible to feed us this well all along?"[25] The emotional pain of understanding that at least part of their physical suffering could have been avoided had the parents been more careful, competent, and loving was a source of tremendous sadness (and some anger) for the authors. When Jessie, as an adult, pampered and nurtured her dog with a sense of love and awe, she wondered about her mother. "Why hadn't she felt the same protectiveness towards me?"[26] Even as an adult the disappointment in that parent's unwillingness or inability to put their child's needs above their own hurt more than any missing meal or missing shoe.

At the same time, the authors also became aware that while some things were in their parents' control, their illness and addictions might not fully be. Liz wrote of being hungry enough to eat a tube of toothpaste because her mother was too delusional to cash her SSI check. She believed based on her experience with her parents that her parents were suffering and used drugs as a way to avoid their psychic pain. She didn't believe that they intended to cause Liz and her sister any harm, they simply couldn't do any better for themselves or their children. It was easier to believe (and certainly true to some extent in some cases) that the pain their parents caused them was not intentional. Liz knew that her sister was angry with their parents, but for Liz it was more emotionally complicated. "Ma said she needed drugs to help her forget the bad memories that haunted her, the thoughts of her mom and dad that caused her to suffer all day long. And even though I wasn't sure what exactly in his past Daddy got high to forget, I knew it must be something very painful, because if Daddy didn't get high, then he would spend days collapsed on the couch in a withdrawal-induced depression."[27] Jessie imagined what it would be like to be inside her mother's brain. "Once I'm in, I try to look around. It's dark, too dark to see. But I can feel what's in there. And there's so much. It's filled with isolation and disregard and abuse. It's filled with uncertainty and self-doubt."[28] Rather than her mother trying to "get inside her head" and understand her daughter, Jessie is trying to understand the world from her mother's point of view, and what she finds fills her with sadness.

This awareness of the limitations of their parents resulted in both empathy for them and a desire to take care of them. Jeannette knew on some level that her father's dream of a glass castle was an empty promise, a lie, but she could never bring herself to confront her father or call him on his delusions. She came to believe that he needed to maintain the illusion more than she needed to speak the truth. She couldn't bear to wound his pride and take away his dreams by pointing out that the glass castle would never be built, that his dreams and his promises were never going to materialize, that she had long ago stopped believing in the castle and in his ability to build it. But she had never stopped loving him. But when Liz's mother got high and shared her childhood stories, Liz felt overwhelmed with love and compassion for her mother. "Ma's pain about her past broke my heart, everything her parents did to her I wished so badly I could take away. I wanted more than anything to take her pain away from her."[29] Liz's mother's pain about her past was more real to Liz than her own pain in the present. Even though she had school in the morning she would stay up all night listening to her mother talk about her childhood. "While Ma spoke I abandoned my needs—sleep, homework, television, and my toys, unused in my darkened bedroom. Her pain blanketed me in its urgency, so that it became difficult to realize that there was any distance—age-wise or responsibility-wise—between us."[30]

This awareness of the suffering that was the foundation of the parent's illness and addiction created a tremendous burden on the children who felt responsible for taking care of their parents. Not only were their parents unwilling or unable to take care of them but also they required (if not demanded) that their children reverse roles and take care of them. Liz wrote, "Drugs were like a wrecking ball tearing through our family, and even though Lisa and I were impacted, I couldn't help but feel that Ma and Daddy were the ones who needed protecting. I felt like it was my job to keep them safe."[31] Jessie became the parent of her mother. "I'm the enforcer of rules, while she retreats into the role of the child. It's the way we've been for as long as I can remember, and I can't imagine us another way. . . . I haven't been able to give up the hope of someday getting her house clean."[32]

Jessie wanted to take care of her mother in part at least so that her mother would then be better able to take care of her. "Even after I told myself I'd walked away, I still clung to a shred of hope that I could change her, that I could unclutter her mind so she could be a normal mother."[33] Jeannette and her siblings banded together to ensure that her mother functioned properly when she accepted a teaching position but then refused to go to work in the mornings. "At least one morning a week, she'd throw a tantrum and refuse to go to work, and Lori, Brian, and I would have to get her collected and down to the street where Lucy Jo waited."[34] In a stunning act of role reversal, they would also grade her student's papers for her, clean up her classroom, and help her prepare lesson plans. Fearing that her commitment to the job was minimal at best, they did what they could to help her not get fired. The family desperately needed the money from the job. Eventually, however, Jeannette's mother would get fired or quit and the family reverted back to its usual state of squalor and neglect.

SUMMARY

The authors of these stories of childhood neglect suffered tremendous physical hardship. They were hungry, dirty, and left to fend for themselves for the better part of their childhood. Yet these children loved their parents and had an attachment bond that could not be extinguished, especially because the children came to believe that the source of their parent's neglect was their own pain and suffering. What these children wanted more than anything was for their parents to put aside their own pain to see that their children were in need of not just food and shelter but also love and attention.

Chapter Eleven

Moving Forward

In the movie *A.I. Artificial Intelligence*, a human woman imprints herself as the mother of a mechanical boy, David. She follows detailed instructions provided by the manufacturer, which involve placing her hand on the nape of the boy's neck and reciting a series of predetermined words: *cirrus, Socrates, particle, decibel, hurricane, dolphin, tulip*[1] (notably, most of the words refer to organic matter). Through this intentional process, David is programmed to love his mother. Once his love has been activated, it is unwavering. It is not possible to turn it off or modify it. David only wants to love and be loved by her. His desire for her love is so strong that he tries to change himself so that he can be more of what he thinks she wants. "If you let me I will be so real for you,"[2] he exclaims in a desperate attempt to win her back and to avoid being abandoned by her. His desire is so strong that after waiting two thousand years in a plastic bubble at the bottom of the ocean, he still has only one thing on his mind: to change himself so that he can finally achieve the state of parental acceptance that he so strongly desires.

The movie heartbreakingly portrays the basic desire most children have—even those abused and neglected—to be accepted and loved by their parents. It depicts a scenario in which—absent any external influence—that desire remains intact, intractable. David cannot imagine a way to go forward except in search of his mother's love. He is stuck. There is no alternate path for his life to take. He is very much like any other maltreated child who is stuck with his unrequited longing and stuck in the belief that it is the parent's love and acceptance that will make the child lovable and worthy of being loved.

The "stuckness" that David represents is a very real part of the maltreatment experience. Like David, the authors of the memoirs were stuck. At least for a portion of their lives they lived with the unquestioned assumption that their only hope for happiness was to win over the heart of the maltreating parent. However, in another sense David is *un*like other maltreated children because he is incapable of the kind of human higher-order functioning that can help maltreatment victims become "unstuck." In his inability to become "unstuck," David represents the outdated idea of the human brain being immutable past a critical period. That is, it was once believed that once a window of opportunity has passed, the human brain was not able to adapt or change. In this view, change and adaptation are highly unlikely. David did not obtain his mother's love and he was, therefore, doomed to fixate on it for the rest of his days. There was no alternate path for David; he was literally trapped in the bubble of his unrequited desire. He is like the therapy client stuck in his life, unable to let go of the pain of the unloving parent and unable to stop searching for that love.

Fortunately, this understanding of the human brain has been revised based on the past two decades of research on brain plasticity.[3] We now know that neural pathways and synapses in the brain are capable of developing alternate routes to accomplish its goals and functions. If one part of the brain is damaged, another part can—with the right support—assume its functioning. New neural connections can be made over the course of a human's life. Humans are not doomed to perpetually reenact a programmed pattern of behavior and maladaptive beliefs. However, absent external influences, it is likely that they will do so. Thus, while change is indeed possible, the human brain is actually hardwired to support continuity and stasis. New information that is encountered is likely to be assimilated into existing beliefs rather than to foster the revision of those beliefs. That is, once ideas about the self and the world are formed (e.g., I am bad, I am stupid, I am unworthy, people are likely to hurt me), new experiences and ideas are likely to be viewed in such a way as to support the existing ideas (e.g., "I didn't get invited to that party because I am stupid and no good"). Thus, once the child has developed the negative beliefs in response to the maltreatment (e.g., "I am bad. I am unlovable"), it is not easy for those beliefs to change. They become woven into the fabric of the person's internal working model of the world, his core schemas about the self and the world. According to Dr. Jeffrey Young, children develop schemas, defined as "patterns of perception, emotion, and physical sensation,"[4] in response to the extent to which their caregiver is able to meet their needs. These schemas then shape the child's interpretations and interactions within subsequent relationships. New information is absorbed in such a way as to confirm those beliefs, and the individual is likely to behave in such a way as to elicit confirming behaviors from others (an adult who was emotionally neglected as a child will develop a schema of emotional deprivation and will behave in such a way as to increase the likelihood that he will remain emotionally deprived).

In thinking about how humans (as opposed to hypothetical mechanical children) can become unstuck and move beyond their childhood experience of abuse and neglect—to stop assimilating new information into the old schemas—the movie illustrates some of the challenges such a journey involves. To begin with, David is trapped literally and figuratively. He is constrained due to circumstances beyond his control. The helicopter he was in crashed and is stranded at the bottom of the ocean. The only thing in his line of sight is the blue fairy whom he believes can turn him into a real boy. He is locked into a belief that the only way to feel good about himself is to become what his mother wants him to be. His "brain" pathways are set. Fortunately, humans are not always as constrained and are able—especially once older and less dependent on their parents—to alter their course, both physically and emotionally.

Thus, one of the tasks of healing from trauma is to modify the belief that the parent must love and accept the child in order for the child to love himself and accept himself as a good and worthy person. In this way, the maltreatment victim is "unbinding" or "unbonding" himself from the maltreating parent, separating himself from that parent and becoming more autonomous. As long as the abuse victim's mind is locked into emotional dependency on the abuser, there is little chance he can move forward away from the pain of the abuse. Like David, the individual would be trapped in a bubble.

A corollary of that task is to help the body heal from the trauma so that it doesn't hold on to the stress, respond to the present as if it were the past, nor seek to reexperience the original trauma over and over again. This kind of "bodywork" represents an emerging field of practice based on brain research that indicates which areas of the brain are affected by trauma.[5] Bodywork can also help abuse victims become "unstuck" and can be done in conjunction with the other tasks outlined in this chapter. Examples of body-oriented treatments include Eye Movement Desensitizing and Reprocessing (EMDR)[6] and Somatic Experiencing.[7]

The central task of decoupling one's self-esteem from one's parents' views can be undertaken by adults alone or in the context of therapy, once they experience themselves as needing to make a change in their life. Children—absent external impetus or intervention—are unlikely to step outside their own bubble of reality to speculate that alternate realities exist, that they will not always be viewed as undesirable and unlovable. Thus, it is critical that they be guided through this process with a safe and trustworthy adult.

There are currently a number of empirically validated therapeutic interventions for adult and child victims of childhood trauma.[8] There are also interventions that are promising but haven't yet been validated.[9] In many of these approaches, there is an important place for the victim to tell his or her story.

STORYTELLING/TRAUMA NARRATIVES

In keeping with the emphasis on the healing art of storytelling reflected by our choice to use memoirs to understand childhood maltreatment, we recommend some form of storytelling, be it formal or informal, oral or written. Storytelling has a long history in the healing of trauma,[10] and deservedly so. The healing power of telling one's story is certainly evident in the memoirs reviewed for this book. The authors painstakingly memorialized their difficult childhood struggle with the hopes and expectations that in doing so they would diminish and manage that pain in a new way. According to trauma expert Bessel van der Kolk, putting a traumatic event into a narrative format moves the memories from the sense memory part of the brain—where the trauma can be activated as presently felt sensations and emotions—into the prefrontal cortex where the trauma can reside as a memory of a past event.[11] Although not everyone is as accomplished a writer as the authors of the memoirs reviewed for this book, thankfully the purpose of telling one's story is not to join the ranks of Pulitzer Prize–winning memoirists but rather to gain the benefits of telling one's story regardless of the objective quality of the product.

Storytelling is such an integral part of healing from abuse and trauma that many evidence-based trauma interventions now use what is referred to as a "trauma narrative" component in their program.[12] The trauma narrative is a written (sometimes based on an audiotaped transcription) account of the chronological story of a trauma experience. This exercise often takes several therapy sessions to complete as the "author" needs to pace himself in the retelling of the story, and he most likely will go back over it several times to add details as he remembers them and is able to process and share them. It is essential that the victim not be revictimized by the storytelling experience. Hence, careful attention to the state of mind and body of the victim is called for during the process. The therapist must encourage the client to tell his or her story only when the client is ready to do so and when the requisite coping skills have been developed. If the therapist attempts to have the child/adult tell the trauma story without being ready or having the necessary coping skills, then the client may be emotionally overwhelmed and resort to avoidant and other defensive postures (although, if the therapist fails to encourage the child/adult to tell his or her story at all, the victims may become stuck and remain avoidant).

When done properly, the intended benefits of the trauma narrative are many. First is the benefit derived from the experience of externalizing the story, taking something that is inside one's head and putting it down on a piece of paper. In doing this, the story (and hence the experience itself) can become less potent and powerful to the trauma victim.

Second, many victims construct their trauma narratives in the safe environment of therapy with a trusted mental health professional. The story is created with the loving kindness and attention of a caring person. Thus, when the story is recalled, the memories may be intertwined with the feeling of having shared it with someone else. When an abuse survivor retells the story with an adult he or she trusts and feels safe with, the power of the trauma experience can be diminished and have less power over the victim.

A third benefit is that once on paper, the victim can share the story with other people (including the abuser, the nonoffending parent, siblings, and friends, among others) and can use the story to spark additional love and support from caring others. Sharing the story can be the springboard for ongoing discussions and for eliciting much-needed empathy and caring. Sharing with others who are supportive may also help the victim to reduce the self-blame and shame associated with the abuse experience.

Fourth, the trauma narrative can be viewed as an exposure procedure whereby the repeated telling of what happened during the traumatic event desensitizes the individual to trauma reminders. Simply the act of telling and retelling the story—if done carefully and sensitively—can allow the victim to feel less overwhelmed by it. This can then decrease the need to avoid reminders of the event, decreasing trauma symptoms and allowing for the resumption of normal functioning. If the child/adult is not overwhelmed by the telling of the story due to having learned appropriate coping skills, the negative emotional impact of the trauma experience can be reduced.

A fifth benefit of storytelling is that adults who write their memoirs to be published can gain satisfaction from knowing that their stories can help others. Authors can imagine future readers drawing upon their story for their own recovery and healing. In this way, their own self-esteem and pride can be bolstered.

Sixth, writing and telling the story provides a platform for examining various thoughts and assumptions about the maltreating parent and one's own role in the maltreatment. During the creation of the trauma narrative the victim can be encouraged to describe his or her thoughts and feelings in order to correct distorted thoughts and beliefs that might underlie ongoing emotional and behavioral difficulties. By telling the facts of the story, it may become clear to the victim that he or she was too young to have warranted the treatment inflicted on him or her. Thus, the process of telling the story may unlock the individual from the false belief that he or she deserved the abuse. In this way the maladaptive cognitions can be corrected. This revision of the thoughts associated with the trauma can unlock the victim from the belief that he or she was bad or unlovable, creating the possibility of improved self-esteem and well-being.

A seventh benefit is that telling the story can also help the maltreatment victim develop empathy for himself or herself. Stating objectively what occurred may make the pain and suffering from the maltreatment more obviously a result of parental actions. Likewise, looking at a picture of oneself at the age the maltreatment began can trigger corrective thoughts about deserving the treatment or that the parents inflicted the pain for the child's "own good." This may be one reason many of the memoirs included pictures of the authors as young children. It is clear from the photographs that they were endearing, innocent children who just wanted to be loved. It would be difficult to look at those pictures and think that any of them deserved to be demeaned, beaten, starved, or molested. Looking at the photographs can also demonstrate how vulnerable they were and how unable they were to question their parents or to protect themselves from the maltreatment. In this way the victims can activate empathy for themselves.

Eighth, telling the story can also allow for a reworking of the beliefs about the perpetrator. It is possible that understanding, if not empathy, for the parent can be elicited and could be part of the healing process (for adults more so than for children). This means not just viewing them as an abusive/neglectful parent, but also seeing them as an individual with his or her own life journey, which most likely included their own experience of suboptimal parenting if not outright abuse/neglect. This search for understanding of the maltreating parent may be what spurred the authors of most of the memoirs to include a biography of their parents. Rather than seeing their parent only as a parent—and a bad one at that—they saw their parents as individuals who suffered their own indignities and pains, who were deeply flawed human beings with a mix of good and bad qualities. This process does not require—nor should it require—excusing the parent for being abusive/neglectful. But there is something to be gained simply in understanding. For example, when the parent is recast as a product of his or own abuse and victim experiences, it becomes clearer that the parent was not so much *choosing* to be abusive/neglectful as unable to overcome his or her own traumatic childhood. This can lead to an understanding—to the extent that it is true—that the parent did not desire to bring pain and suffering to the child, which itself can be healing. In the movie *A.I.*, for example, the mother was a trauma victim who was unable to process her own grief. Her son Martin was in a persistent vegetative state. She longed to be a mother and was unable to realize that desire. Her son was trapped between life and death and she was trapped in her grief, which went "undigested."[13] She, too, was stuck. If the victims can see that the maltreating parent is a victim and that the maltreatment was a result of the parent's personality disorder or other significant limitations, then they can stop blaming themselves for what happened and attribute responsibility for the abuse to the parent.

A ninth potential benefit of storytelling is that the process takes something that most likely was a secret and brings it out into the open. Childhood trauma inflicted by a caregiver is usually inflicted in privacy. As trauma specialist Judith Herman noted, "Secrecy and silence are the perpetrator's first line of defense."[14] The incest is denied, the wounds are hidden, the hurt feelings buried. The child victim dares not name the experience even to himself, let alone speak of it out loud within the family, or disclose it to anyone outside the family. As long as it remains a secret—to the world and even to the self—the victim cannot begin the process of healing and recovery. The abuse must be named, acknowledged, and examined. Telling the story can be a part of that process. The secrecy implies feelings of shame that if expressed may relieve the child of this powerfully destructive feeling. Simply putting it down on paper takes it out of the shadows and thereby promotes healing.

Yet another reason to participate in storytelling is that by promoting resolution of the trauma, it is interrupting the intergenerational cycle of maltreatment. Attachment research has demonstrated that maternal depression interferes with sensitive parenting and is associated with insecure attachments in infants.[15] Research has also demonstrated strong links between unresolved early loss/trauma and maternal depression. That is, when children are maltreated and are unable to work through their loss and grief in a healthy way, they are more likely to suffer the kinds of mental health outcomes that can impair their own parenting, and thereby continue the cycle of maltreatment.[16]

A final benefit of storytelling is that it gives an active voice and presence to the abuse victim who too often was rendered silent and invisible through the maltreatment. In response to most of the maltreatment types explored in this book, the child victims reported as adults that they felt invisible, powerless, and helpless. That is an understandable and normal response to a trauma that was inflicted on them by a caretaker. They were not able to protect themselves or find a way to moderate the behavior of their caregivers. The feeling of helplessness can be internalized both in terms of maladaptive beliefs (i.e., "I am helpless") and in terms of physiological responses (e.g., freezing, shutting down, numbing). The victims felt invisible as a defense and reaction to the abuse and neglect. By authoring one's story, the memoirists were doing something to counter that feeling of muteness and invisibility: They were saying, "I am here," and declaring "this is what happened to me." They made themselves present through the story, present for themselves and present for others. In *1984*, Orwell wrote, "He who controls the present, controls the past. He who controls the past, controls the future,"[17] reflecting the belief that history is written by the victors as a way to maintain control. When maltreatment victims tell their stories, they are reclaiming their past, and by extension, their present and their future.

TRANSFORMATIVE EXPERIENCES

When done properly, storytelling can be a transformative experience for maltreatment victims. It can lead to a reworking of the maladaptive thoughts and feelings associated with abuse and neglect inflicted by a caregiver. It can alter how an abuse victim feels about himself and the world. While storytelling is emphasized here—in keeping with our use of memoirs—there are other opportunities for transformative experiences, such as falling in love, having a child, and entering therapy. Within each lies an opportunity to develop a new understanding of one's value and worth as a person who is capable of love. Forgiveness, as well, can be a transformative experience that can unburden an abuse victim from the pain and trauma of childhood maltreatment. In fact, Tutu and Tutu believe that "without forgiveness, we remain tethered to the person who harmed us. We are bound with chains of bitterness, tied together trapped."[18]

Another kind of transformative experience involves the intentional rewiring of the brain to enhance resilience and coping in the face of future challenges. Integrating Buddhist mindfulness and neuroscience, psychotherapist Linda Graham describes tools and exercises to create more resilient and adaptive coping strategies.[19] Using these exercises may allow individuals (including trauma victims) to rewire their brain, thereby creating their own transformative experience. In that way, each person can be "a resilient hero"[20] in the unfolding story of his life.

SUMMARY

Survivors of childhood maltreatment suffer both physically and psychologically, not just from the experience of the maltreatment but also because of what they believe the maltreatment means about who they are. Through the maltreatment they come to believe that they are unlovable, unworthy, and of no value to themselves or others (although the specific internal message may vary somewhat depending upon the type of maltreatment). Healing from the trauma of maltreatment, therefore, requires a reworking of these thoughts and feelings in order to untether the victim from the perpetrator. The act of storytelling can play a central role in that very important process.

Bibliography

Ainsworth, M. S., Blehar, M., Waters, E., & Wall, S. (1978). *Patterns of attachment: A psychological study of the strange situation.* Hillsdale, NJ: Lawrence Erlbaum.

American Psychiatric Association. (2000). *Diagnostic and statistical manual of mental disorders* (4th ed., text rev.). Washington, DC: APA.

Barrett, H. C. & Behne, T. (2005). Children's understanding of death as the cessation of agency: A test using sleep versus death. *Cognition* 96, no. 2: 1–16.

Bartok, M. (2011). *The memory palace: A memoir.* New York: Free Press.

Baumrind, D. (1969). Authoritarian vs. authoritative parental control. *Adolescence* 3:255–72.

Binggell, N. J., Hart, S., and Brassard, M. (2001). *Psychological maltreatment of children, APSAC study guides.* Thousand Oaks, CA: Sage.

Blackburn, J. (2008). *The three of us: A family story.* New York: Vintage Books, Random House, Inc.

Blizzard, R. A. & Bluhm, A. M. (1994). Attachment to the abuser: Integrating object-relations and trauma theories in treatment of survivors. *Psychotherapy* 31, no. 3: 383–90.

Bowlby, J. (1969). *Attachment.* New York: Basic Books.

Bretherton, I. (1985). Attachment theory: Retrospect and prospect, in *Growing Points of Attachment Theory and Research: Monographs of the Society for Research in Child Development* 209, no. 1–2: 3–35, ed. I Bretherton and E. Waters.

Briere, J. (1992). *Child abuse trauma.* Newbury Park, CA: Sage.

Burden, W. (2010). *Dead end gene pool: A memoir.* New York: Gotham Books.

Burroughs, A. (2003). *Running with scissors: A memoir.* New York: Picador.

Cantor, C. & Price, J. (2007). Traumatic entrapment, appeasement and complex post traumatic stress disorder: Evolutionary perspectives of hostage reactions, domestic abuse, and the Stockholm syndrome. *Royal Australian and New Zealand Journal of Psychiatry* 41, no. 5: 377–84.

CAPTA Reauthorization Act of 2010 (P.L. 111-320). Retrieved from https://www.childwelfare.gov/systemwide/laws_policies/federal/index.cfm?event=federalLegislation.viewLegis&id=142.

Carter, D. (2007). *No momma's boy: A memoir.* New York: iUniverse, Inc.

Children's Bureau of the U.S. Department of Health and Human Services (2012). *Child maltreatment 2012.* Retrieved from http://www.acf.hhs.gov/programs/cb/resource/child-maltreatment-2012.

Chin, S. (2010). *The other side of paradise: A memoir.* New York: Scribner.

Cook, A., Spinazzola, J., Ford, J., Lanktree, C., Blaustein, M., Cloitre, . . . van der Kolk, B. (2005). Complex trauma in children and adolescents. *Psychiatric Annals* 35: 390–98.

Crawford, C. (1978). *Mommie dearest: A true story.* New York: William Morrow and Company.

Crews, K. (2012). *Burn down the ground: A memoir.* New York: Random House Creations.

Darst, J. (2012). *Fiction ruined my family.* New York: Penguin.

de Milly III, W. A. (1999). *In my father's arms: A true story of incest.* Madison, WI: The University of Wisconsin Press.

Deblinger, E. & Heflin, A. H. (1996). *Treating sexually abused children and their nonoffending parents.* Thousand Oaks, CA: Sage.

Doidge, N. (2007). *The brain that changes itself: Stories of personal triumph from the frontiers of brain science.* New York: Penguin.

Dutton, D. G. & Painter, S. (1981). Traumatic bonding: The development of emotional attachments in battered women and other relationships of intermittent abuse. *Victimology: An International Encyclopedia of the Social Sciences* 1: 139–55.

Eisenberger, N. I., Lieberman, M. D., & Williams, K. D. (2003). Does rejection hurt?: An fMRI study of social exclusion. *Science* 302: 290–92.

Etienne, M. (2003). *Storkbites: A memoir.* Walnut Creek, CA: Alluvium Books.

Fairbairn, W. R. D. (1952). *Psychoanalytic studies of the personality.* London: Routledge.

Felitti, V. J., Anda, R. F., Nordenberg, D., Williamson, D. F., Spitz, A. M., Edwards, V., Koss, M. P., & Marks, J. S. (1998). Relationship of childhood abuse and household dysfunction to many of the leading causes of death in adults: The adverse childhood experiences study. *American Journal of Preventive Medicine* 14, no. 4: 245–58.

Ferenczi, S. (1949). Confusion of the tongues between the adults and the child. *International Journal of Psychoanalysis* 30: 225–30.

Flynn, L. M. (2008). *Swallow the ocean: A memoir.* Berkeley, CA: Counterpoint Press.

Ford, J. D., Connor, D. F., & Hawke, J. (2009). Complex trauma among psychiatrically impaired children: A cross-sectional chart-review study. *Journal of Clinical Psychology* 70: 1155–63.

Ford, J. D., Grasso, D., Greene, C., Levine, J., Spinazzola, J., & van der Kolk, B. A. (2013). Clinical significance of a proposed developmental trauma disorder diagnosis: Results of an international survey of clinicians. *Journal of Clinical Psychology* 74: 841–49.

Francis, M. (2012). *Diary of a stage mother's daughter: A memoir.* New York: Weinstein Books.

Frankel, J. (2004). Identification with the aggressor and the "normal traumas": Clinical implications. *International Journal of Psychoanalysis* 13: 78–83.

Goddard, C. R. & Stanley, J. R. (1994). Viewing the abusive parent and the abused child as captor and hostage: The application of hostage theory to the effects of child abuse. *Journal of Interpersonal Violence* 9: 258–69.

Goleman, D. (1985). *Vital lies, simple truths: The psychology of self-deception.* New York: Touchstone.

Gregory, J. (2003). *Sickened: The true story of lost childhood.* New York: Bantam Dell.

Grubb, F. E. (2012). *Cruel harvest: A memoir.* Nashville, TN: Thomas Nelson, Inc.

Harlow, H. F. (1958). The nature of love. *American Psychologist* 13: 673–85.

Harrison, K. (2011). *The kiss: A memoir.* New York: Random House Group.

Hendra, J. & Morrison, B. (2009). *How to cook your daughter: A memoir.* New York: HarperCollins.

Herman, J. (1992). Complex PTSD: A syndrome in survivors of prolonged and repeated trauma. *Journal of Traumatic Stress* 5: 377–91.

Herman, J. (1992). *Trauma and Recovery.* New York: Basic Books.

Herz, R. (2008). *The scent of desire: Discovering our enigmatic sense of smell.* New York: HarperCollins.

Holley, T. E. & Holley, J. (1997). *My mother's keeper: A daughter's memoir of growing up in the shadows of schizophrenia.* New York: William Morrow and Company.

Holloway, M. (2008). *Driving with dead people: A memoir.* New York: Gallery Books.

Howes, P. W., Cicchetti, D., Toth, S. L., & Rogosch, F. A. (2000). Affective, organizational, and relational characteristics of maltreating families: A systems perspective. *Journal of Family Psychology* 14, no. 1: 95–110.

Jones, K. (2009). *Lies my mother never told me: A memoir*. New York: HarperLuxe.

Julich, S. (2005). Stockholm syndrome and child sexual abuse. *Journal of Child Sexual Abuse* 14, no. 3: 107–29.

Kendall, S. B. (1974). Preference of intermittent reinforcement. *Journal of Experimental Analysis of Behavior* 21, no. 3: 463–73.

Kennedy, K., Curtis, B., & Spielberg, S. (2001). *A.I. Artificial intelligence* [Motion picture]. United States: Warner Bros. Pictures.

Kolko, D. J. & Swenson, C. (2002). *Assessing and treating physically abused children and their families*. Thousand Oaks, CA: Sage.

Lawless, W. (2013). *Chanel bonfire: A memoir*. New York: Gallery Books.

Levine, P. (2008). *Healing trauma: A pioneering program for restoring the wisdom of your body*. Boulder, CO: Sounds True.

Love, L. (2004). *You ain't got no Easter clothes: A memoir*. New York: Hyperion.

Maguire, T. (2006). *Don't tell mummy: A true story of ultimate betrayal*. London: HarperCollins.

Mah, A. Y. (1997). *Falling leaves: The memoir of an unwanted Chinese daughter*. New York: Broadway Books.

Main, M., Kaplan, N., & Cassidy, J. (1985). Security in infancy, childhood and adulthood: A move to the level of representation. *Monographs of the Society for Research in Child Development* 50, no. 209: 66–104.

Matthews, K. (2011). *I remember, daddy: The harrowing true story of a daughter haunted by memories too terrible to forget*. London: HarperCollins.

McClain, C. (2014). *Murdering my youth: A memoir*. Create Space Independent Publishing Platform.

McCourt, F. (1991). *Angela's ashes: A memoir*. New York: Touchstone.

Miller, A. (2001). *The truth will set you free: Overcoming emotional blindness and finding your true adult self*. Translated by A. Jenkins. New York: Basic Books. (Original work published in 2001.)

Miller, K. R. (2013). *Coming clean: A memoir*. New York: New Harvest.

Miller, S. J. (2004). Relationships with the punisher. *Psychoanalytic Psychology* 21: 402–16.

Miller-Perrin, C. L. & Perrin, R. D. (2007). *Child maltreatment*. Thousand Oaks, CA: Sage.

Moss, B. R. (1999). *Change Me into Zeus's daughter: A memoir*. New York: Touchstone.

Murray, L. (2010). *Breaking night: A memoir of forgiveness, survival and my journey from homeless to Harvard*. New York: Hyperion.

Myers, A. (2008). *Who do you think you are?: A memoir*. New York: Touchstone.

Orwell, G. (1950). *1984*. New York: Signet.

Patton, S. (2008). *That mean old yesterday: A memoir*. New York: Washington Square Press.

Pelzer, D. (1995). *A child called "it": One child's courage to survive*. Deerfield Beach, FL: Health Communications.

Pennebaker, J. (1997). *Opening up: The healing power of expressing emotions*. New York: Guilford Press.

Perry, B. (2001). Bonding and attachment in maltreated children: Consequences of emotional neglect in childhood. *The Child Trauma Academy* 1, no. 3: 1–10.

Proust, M. (1981). *Remembrance of things past* (Vol. 1). Translated by C. K. Scott Moncrieff and Terence Kilmartin. New York: Vintage.

Rhodes, R. (1990). *A hole in the world: An American boyhood*. New York: Simon & Schuster.

Rhodes-Courter, A. (2008). *Three little words: A memoir*. New York: Atheneum Books for Young Readers.

Roche, P. (2007). *Unloved: The true story of a stolen childhood*. London: Penguin Books.

Rosenblum, L. A. & Harlow, H. F. (1964). Approach-avoidance conflict in mother surrogate situation. *Psychological Review* 12: 84.

Ruta, D. (2013). *With or without you: A memoir*. New York: Random House Group.

Schore, A. N. (2002). Dysregulation of the right brain: A fundamental mechanism of traumatic attachment and the psychopathogenesis of posttraumatic stress disorder. *Australian and New Zealand Journal of Psychiatry* 36: 9–30.

Shapiro, F. (2001). *EMDR*. New York: Guilford Press.

Shaw, D. (2013). *Traumatic narcissism: Relational systems of subjugation.* New York: Routledge.

Sholl, J. (2010). *Dirty secret: A daughter comes clean about her mother's compulsive hoarding.* New York: Gallery Books.

Slaughter, C. (2002). *Before the knife: Memories of an African childhood.* New York: Knopf.

Sonnenberg, S. (2008). *Her last death: A memoir.* New York: Scribner.

Sontag, R. (2008). *House rules: A memoir.* New York: HarperCollins.

Sullivan, F. C. (2008). *The sky isn't visible from here: Scenes from a life.* Chapel Hill, NC: Algonquin Books.

Thomas, S. G. (2011). *In spite of everything: A memoir.* New York: Random House Group.

Toth, S. L., Cicchetti, D., Rogosch, F. A., & Sturge-Apple, M. (2009). Maternal depression, children's attachment security, and representational development: An organizational perspective. *Child Development* 80, no. 1: 192–208.

Tutu, D. & Tutu, M. (2014). *The book of forgiving.* New York: Harper Collins.

van der Kolk, B. A. (1987). The psychological consequences of overwhelming life experience. In *Psychological trauma*, edited by B. A. van der Kolk, 1–30. Washington, DC: American Psychiatric Press.

van der Kolk, B. A. (1989). The compulsion to repeat the trauma. *Psychiatric Clinics of North America* 12, no. 2: 389–411.

van Sleuwen, B. E., Engleberts, A. C., Boere-Boonekamp, M., Kuis, W., Schulpen, T. W. J., & L'Hoir, M. P. (2007). Swaddling: A systematic review. *Pediatrics* 120, no. 4: 2006–83.

Walls, J. (2006). *The glass castle: A memoir.* New York: Scribner.

Winnicott, D. W. (1964). *The child, the family, and the outside world.* London: Pelican Books.

Winterson, J. (2011). *Why be happy when you could be normal?* London: Random House Group.

Woititz, J. (1990). *Adult children of alcoholics.* Deerfield Beach, FL: Health Communications.

Young, J. E. & Klosko, J. S. (1994). *Reinventing your life.* New York: Plume.

Notes

INTRODUCTION

1. CAPTA, The CAPTA Reauthorization Act of 2010, Public Law 111–320 (42 U.S.C. 5106a), retrieved from http://www.acf.hhs.gov/programs/cb/resource/capta2010.

2. Children's Bureau (Administration on Children, Youth and Families, Administration for Children and Families) of the U.S. Department of Health and Human Services, *Child Maltreatment 2012*, retrieved from http://www.acf.hhs.gov/programs/cb/research-data-technology/statistics-research/child-maltreatment.

3. C. L. Miller-Perrin and R. D. Perrin, *Child Maltreatment: An Introduction* (Thousand Oaks, CA: Sage, 2007).

4. V. J. Felitti, R. F. Anda, D. Nordenberg, D. F. Williamson, A. M. Spitz, V. Edwards, M. P. Koss, and J. S. Marks, "Relationship of Childhood Abuse and Household Dysfunction to Many of the Leading Causes of Death in Adults: The Adverse Childhood Experiences (ACE) Study," *American Journal of Preventive Medicine* 14, no. 4 (1998): 245–58.

5. American Psychiatric Association, *Diagnostic and Statistical Manual-IV-TR* (Washington, DC: APA, 2000).

6. J. D. Ford, D. F. Connor, and J. Hawke, "Complex Trauma among Psychiatrically Impaired Children: A Cross-Sectional Chart-Review Study," *Journal of Clinical Psychology* 70, no. 8 (2009): 1155–63.

7. D. A. van der Kolk, "The Psychological Consequences of Overwhelming Life Experiences," in *Psychological Trauma*, ed. B. A. van der Kolk (Washington, DC: American Psychiatric Press, 1987), 1–30.

8. J. D. Ford, D. Grasso, C. Greene, J. Levine, J. Spinazzola, and B. van der Kolk, "Clinical Significance of a Proposed Developmental Trauma Disorder Diagnosis: Results of an International Survey of Clinicians," *Journal of Clinical Psychology* 74, no. 8 (2013): 841–49.

9. Ford, Connor, and Hawke, "Complex Trauma among Psychiatrically Impaired Children."

10. A. N. Schore, "Dysregulation of the Right Brain: A Fundamental Mechanism of Traumatic Attachment and the Psychopathogenesis of Posttraumatic Stress Disorder," *Australian and New Zealand Journal of Psychiatry* 36, no. 1 (2002): 9–30.

1. STORIES OF PHYSICAL ABUSE

1. P. Roche, *Unloved: The True Story of a Stolen Childhood* (London, England: Penguin Books, 2007).
2. Roche, *Unloved*, 4.
3. Roche, *Unloved*, 8.
4. Roche, *Unloved*.
5. Roche, *Unloved*, 6.
6. Roche, *Unloved*, 9.
7. Roche, *Unloved*, 12.
8. Roche, *Unloved*, 21.
9. Roche, *Unloved*, 20.
10. Roche, *Unloved*, 57.
11. Roche, *Unloved*, 10.
12. Roche, *Unloved*, 12.
13. Roche, *Unloved*, 13.
14. Roche, *Unloved*, 61.
15. Roche, *Unloved*.
16. Roche, *Unloved*, 332.
17. Roche, *Unloved*, 335.
18. S. Patton, *That Mean Old Yesterday* (New York: Washington Square Press, 2008).
19. Patton, *That Mean Old Yesterday*, 21.
20. Patton, *That Mean Old Yesterday*, 29.
21. Patton, *That Mean Old Yesterday*, 30.
22. Patton, *That Mean Old Yesterday*, 31.
23. Patton, *That Mean Old Yesterday*.
24. Patton, *That Mean Old Yesterday*.
25. Patton, *That Mean Old Yesterday*, 34.
26. Patton, *That Mean Old Yesterday*.
27. Patton, *That Mean Old Yesterday*, 52.
28. Patton, *That Mean Old Yesterday*, 52–53.
29. Patton, *That Mean Old Yesterday*, 65.
30. Patton, *That Mean Old Yesterday*, 59.
31. Patton, *That Mean Old Yesterday*, 60.
32. Patton, *That Mean Old Yesterday*, 61.
33. Patton, *That Mean Old Yesterday*, 69.
34. Patton, *That Mean Old Yesterday*, 70.
35. Patton, *That Mean Old Yesterday*, 73.
36. Patton, *That Mean Old Yesterday*, 74.
37. Patton, *That Mean Old Yesterday*, 78.
38. Patton, *That Mean Old Yesterday*, 81.
39. Patton, *That Mean Old Yesterday*, 93.
40. Patton, *That Mean Old Yesterday*, 94.
41. Patton, *That Mean Old Yesterday*.
42. Patton, *That Mean Old Yesterday*, 106.
43. Patton, *That Mean Old Yesterday*, 116.
44. Patton, *That Mean Old Yesterday*, 119.
45. Patton, *That Mean Old Yesterday*, 142.
46. Patton, *That Mean Old Yesterday*, 129.
47. Patton, *That Mean Old Yesterday*, 143–44.
48. Patton, *That Mean Old Yesterday*, 229.
49. M. Holloway, *Driving with Dead People* (New York: Gallery Books, 2008).
50. Holloway, *Driving with Dead People*, 16
51. Holloway, *Driving with Dead People*, 47.
52. Holloway, *Driving with Dead People*, 17–18.

53. Holloway, *Driving with Dead People*, 20.
54. Holloway, *Driving with Dead People*, 96.
55. Holloway, *Driving with Dead People*, 97.
56. Holloway, *Driving with Dead People*, 6.
57. Holloway, *Driving with Dead People*, 39.
58. Holloway, *Driving with Dead People*, 7.
59. Holloway, *Driving with Dead People*, 78.
60. Holloway, *Driving with Dead People*, 101.
61. Holloway, *Driving with Dead People*, 111.
62. Holloway, *Driving with Dead People*, 112.
63. Holloway, *Driving with Dead People*.
64. Holloway, *Driving with Dead People*, 132.
65. Holloway, *Driving with Dead People*, 139.
66. Holloway, *Driving with Dead People*, 141.
67. Holloway, *Driving with Dead People*, 166.
68. Holloway, *Driving with Dead People*, 167.
69. Holloway, *Driving with Dead People*, 168.
70. Holloway, *Driving with Dead People*, 169.
71. Holloway, *Driving with Dead People*.
72. Holloway, *Driving with Dead People*, 276.

2. MAKING MEANING OF PHYSICAL ABUSE

1. J. Briere, *Child Abuse Trauma* (Newbury Park, CA: Sage, 1992).
2. J. Herman, *Trauma and Recovery* (New York: Basic Books, 1992).
3. R. A. Blizzard and A. M. Bluhm, "Attachment to the Abuser: Integrating Object-Relations and Trauma Theories in Treatment of Abuse Survivors," *Psychotherapy* 31, no. 3 (1994): 383–90.
4. C. R. Goddard and J. R. Stanley, "Viewing the Abusive Parent and the Abused Child as Captor and Hostage: The Application of Hostage Theory to the Effects of Child Abuse," *Journal of Interpersonal Violence* 9, no. 2 (1994): 258–69.
5. D. G. Dutton and S. Painter, "Traumatic Bonding: The Development of Emotional Attachments in Battered Women and Other Relationships of Intermittent Abuse," *Victimology: An International Encyclopedia of the Social Sciences* 1:139–55.
6. C. Cantor and J. Price, "Traumatic Entrapment, Appeasement and Complex Posttraumatic Stress Disorder: Evolutionary Perspectives of Hostage Reactions, Domestic Abuse, and the Stockholm Syndrome," *The Royal Australian and New Zealand Journal of Psychiatry* 41, no. 5 (2007): 377–84.
7. Other abused children may not search for meaning but rather seek ways to relieve the anxiety and pain of their hopelessness and despair and thereby act out in aggressive ways or dissociate. These children may have stopped or never engaged in a search for the meaning of what happened to them. The victims who wrote their memoirs may be different from other victims who have serious psychiatric disorders or do not have the emotional strength or resiliency to write about their abusive experiences. For some abused children it is not until they are in therapy that they can begin to question why he/she was abused and to reformulate or conceptualize the meaning of what happened to them so that they do not blame themselves and they can begin to understand that it was the caregiver's responsibility, not theirs. However, many children do not receive therapy or receive therapy late when their pathology is entrenched and they have developed personality disorders.
8. S. Patton, *That Mean Old Yesterday* (New York: Washington Square Press, 2008), 30.
9. M. Holloway, *Driving with Dead People* (New York: Gallery Books, 2008), 39.
10. D. Pelzer, *A Child Called "It"* (Deerfield Beach, FL: Health Communications, Inc., 1995), 106.
11. B. R. Moss, *Change Me into Zeus's Daughter* (New York: Touchstone, 1999), 49.

12. R. Rhodes, *A Hole in the World: An American Boyhood* (New York: Simon and Schuster, 1990), 269.

13. F. E. Grubb, *Cruel Harvest* (Nashville, TN: Thomas Nelson Inc., 2012), 191.

14. A. Miller, *The Truth Will Set You Free: Overcoming Emotional Blindness and Finding Your True Adult Self*, trans. A. Jenkins. (New York: Basic Books, 2001), 2.

15. Miller, *The Truth Will Set You Free*, 96.

16. Some adolescents due to their developmental task of becoming independent of their parents combined with their increased cognitive development are better able to see their parent's behavior as cruel and outlandish, but not always and not generally in these stories.

17. D. Kolko and C. Swenson, *Assessing and Treating Physically Abused Children and Their Families* (Thousand Oaks, CA: Sage, 2002).

18. Peter Roche, *Unloved* (London, England: Penguin Books, 2007), 12–13.

19. Roche, *Unloved*, 52.

20. Patton, *That Mean Old Yesterday*, 61.

21. Grubb, *Cruel Harvest*, 235.

22. Pelzer, *A Child Called "It,"* 10.

23. Pelzer, *A Child Called "It,"* 33.

24. Pelzer, *A Child Called "It,"* 136.

25. C. Crawford, *Mommie Dearest* (New York: William Morrow and Company, Inc., 1978), 160.

26. W. R. D. Fairbairn, *Psychoanalytic Studies of the Personality* (London, England: Routledge, 1952), 65.

27. Briere, *Child Abuse Trauma*.

28. B. Perry, "Bonding and Attachment in Maltreated Children: Consequences of Emotional Neglect in Childhood," *The Child Trauma Academy* 1, no. 3: (2001): 1–10.

29. H. F. Harlow, "The Nature of Love," *American Psychologist* 13 (1958): 673–85.

30. L. A. Rosenblum and H. F. Harlow, "Approach-Avoidance Conflict in Mother Surrogate Situation," *Psychological Review* 12 (1964): 84.

31. J. Bowlby, *Attachment* (New York: Basic Books, 1969).

32. M. D. Salter Ainsworth, M. Blehar, E. Waters, and S. Wall, *Patterns of Attachment: A Psychological Study of the Strange Situation* (Hillsdale, NJ: Lawrence Erlbaum, 1978).

33. I. Bretherton, "Attachment Theory: Retrospect and Prospect," in I. *Growing Points of Attachment Theory and Research: Monographs of the Society for Research in Child Development* 209, no. 1–2 (1985): 3–35, ed. I. Bretherton and E. Waters.

34. M. Main, N. Kaplan, and J. Cassidy, "Security in Infancy, Childhood, and Adulthood: A Move to the Level of Representation," in *Monographs of the Society for Research in Child Development* 50, no. 209 (1985): 66–104, ed. I. Bretherton and E. Waters.

35. Bowlby, *Attachment*.

36. Patton, *That Mean Old Yesterday*, 142.

37. Patton, *That Mean Old Yesterday*, 104.

38. Patton, *That Mean Old Yesterday*, 228.

39. Pelzer, *A Child Called "It,"* 132.

40. Pelzer, *A Child Called "It,"* 119.

41. Pelzer, *A Child Called "It,"* 113.

42. Pelzer, *A Child Called "It,"* 67.

43. Crawford, *Mommie Dearest*, 266.

44. Moss, *Change Me into Zeus's Daughter*, 236.

45. Marie Etienne, *Storkbites* (Walnut Creek, CA: Alluvium Books, 2003), 314.

46. D. W. Winnicott, *The Child, the Family, and the Outside World* (London, England: Pelican Books, 1964).

47. Roche, *Unloved*, 61.

48. Patton, *That Mean Old Yesterday*, 94.

49. Patton, *That Mean Old Yesterday*, 70.

50. Pelzer, *A Child Called "It,"* 32.

51. Pelzer, *A Child Called "It,"* 37.

52. Crawford, *Mommie Dearest*, 238.

53. Crawford, *Mommie Dearest*, 266.

54. Crawford, *Mommie Dearest*, 246.

55. Crawford, *Mommie Dearest*, 166.

56. Crawford, *Mommie Dearest*, 260.

57. Crawford, *Mommie Dearest*, 236.

58. Crawford, *Mommie Dearest*, 227–28.

59. Rhodes, *A Hole in the World*, 171.

60. Rhodes, *A Hole in the World*, 46.

61. Moss, *Change Me into Zeus's Daughter*, 26.

62. Moss, *Change Me into Zeus's Daughter*, 71.

63. Moss, *Change Me into Zeus's Daughter*, 81.

64. Etienne, *Storkbites*, 61.

65. P. W. Howes, D. Cicchetti, S. L. Toth, and F. A. Rogosch, "Affective, Organizational, and Relational Characteristics of Maltreating Families: A Systems Perspective," *Journal of Family Psychology* 14, no. 1 (2000): 95–110.

66. As they get older they may also begin to see the world as unjust and unfair and themselves as unfairly treated.

67. Roche, *Unloved*, 10.

68. Patton, *That Mean Old Yesterday*, 34.

69. Holloway, *Driving with Dead People*, 105.

70. Crawford, *Mommie Dearest*, 24.

71. Moss, *Change Me into Zeus's Daughter*, 37.

72. Although it wasn't reflected in these memoirs, some physically abused children become oppositional and disobedient.

73. Holloway, *Driving with Dead People*, 20.

74. Grubb, *Cruel Harvest*, 139.

75. Etienne, *Storkbites*, 82.

76. Etienne, *Storkbites*, 38.

77. Etienne, *Storkbites*, 234.

78. Roche, *Unloved*, 13.

79. Patton, *That Mean Old Yesterday*, 169.

80. Grubb, *Cruel Harvest*, 110.

81. Holloway, *Driving with Dead People*, 139.

82. Crawford, *Mommie Dearest*, 41.

83. Crawford, *Mommie Dearest*, 260.

84. Crawford, *Mommie Dearest*, 14.

85. Etienne, *Storkbites*, 58.

86. Roche, *Unloved*, 52.

87. Holloway, *Driving with Dead People*, 112.

88. Pelzer, *A Child Called "It,"* 54.

89. Crawford, *Mommie Dearest*, 58.

90. Patton, *That Mean Old Yesterday*, 61.

91. Rhodes, *A Hole in the World*, 155.

92. Moss, *Change Me into Zeus's Daughter*, 172.

93. Etienne, *Storkbites*, 166.

94. D. Goleman, *Vital Lies, Simple Truths: The Psychology of Self-Deception* (New York: Touchstone, 1985), 44.

95. Roche, *Unloved*, 21.

96. Roche, *Unloved*, 96.

97. Patton, *That Mean Old Yesterday*, 116.

98. Patton, *That Mean Old Yesterday*, 31.

99. Holloway, *Driving with Dead People*, 96.

100. Moss, *Change Me into Zeus's Daughter*, 192.

101. Pelzer, *A Child Called "It,"* 30.

102. Etienne, *Storkbites*, 58.

103. Crawford, *Mommie Dearest*, 235.

104. Roche, *Unloved*, 21.

105. Kolko and Swenson, *Assessing and Treating Physically Abused Children and Their Families*.

106. Patton, *That Mean Old Yesterday*, 74.

107. Moss, *Change Me into Zeus's Daughter*, 263.

108. Pelzer, *A Child Called "It,"* 37.

109. Crawford, *Mommie Dearest*, 51.

110. Crawford, *Mommie Dearest*, 38.

3. STORIES OF SEXUAL ABUSE

1. J. Hendra and B. Morrison, *How to Cook Your Daughter* (New York: HarperCollins, 2009).

2. Hendra and Morrison, *How to Cook Your Daughter*, 59–60.

3. *National Lampoon* 1, no. 18 (September 1971).

4. Hendra and Morrison, *How to Cook Your Daughter*, 119.

5. Hendra and Morrison, *How to Cook Your Daughter*, 35.

6. Hendra and Morrison, *How to Cook Your Daughter*, 151.

7. Hendra and Morrison, *How to Cook Your Daughter*, 30.

8. Hendra and Morrison, *How to Cook Your Daughter*, 35.

9. Hendra and Morrison, *How to Cook Your Daughter*, 100.

10. Hendra and Morrison, *How to Cook Your Daughter*, 155.

11. Hendra and Morrison, *How to Cook Your Daughter*, 50.

12. Hendra and Morrison, *How to Cook Your Daughter*, 52.

13. Hendra and Morrison, *How to Cook Your Daughter*, 66.

14. Hendra and Morrison, *How to Cook Your Daughter*, 98.

15. Hendra and Morrison, *How to Cook Your Daughter*, 155.

16. Hendra and Morrison, *How to Cook Your Daughter*, 205.

17. Hendra and Morrison, *How to Cook Your Daughter*, 8.

18. Hendra and Morrison, *How to Cook Your Daughter*, 9.

19. Hendra and Morrison, *How to Cook Your Daughter*, 83.

20. Hendra and Morrison, *How to Cook Your Daughter*, 84.

21. Hendra and Morrison, *How to Cook Your Daughter*, 163.

22. Hendra and Morrison, *How to Cook Your Daughter*, 166.

23. Hendra and Morrison, *How to Cook Your Daughter*, 260.

24. D. Carter, *No Momma's Boy* (New York: iUniverse, Inc., 2007).

25. Carter, *No Momma's Boy*, 41.

26. Carter, *No Momma's Boy*.

27. Carter, *No Momma's Boy*, 42.

28. Carter, *No Momma's Boy*, 44.

29. Carter, *No Momma's Boy*, 45–46.

30. Carter, *No Momma's Boy*, 49.

31. Carter, *No Momma's Boy*, 4.

32. Carter, *No Momma's Boy*, 5.

33. Carter, *No Momma's Boy*.

34. Carter, *No Momma's Boy*.

35. Carter, *No Momma's Boy*.

36. Carter, *No Momma's Boy*, 6.

37. Carter, *No Momma's Boy*.

38. Carter, *No Momma's Boy*, 274.

39. Carter, *No Momma's Boy*, 9.

40. Carter, *No Momma's Boy*, 15.

41. W. A. De Milly III, *In My Father's Arms* (Madison, WI: University of Wisconsin Press, 1999).

42. De Milly, *In My Father's Arms*, 10.
43. De Milly, *In My Father's Arms*, 32.
44. De Milly, *In My Father's Arms*, 33.
45. De Milly, *In My Father's Arms*, 34.
46. De Milly, *In My Father's Arms*, 39.
47. De Milly, *In My Father's Arms*, 41.
48. De Milly, *In My Father's Arms*, 43.
49. De Milly, *In My Father's Arms*, 46.
50. De Milly, *In My Father's Arms*, 47.
51. De Milly, *In My Father's Arms*, 48.
52. De Milly, *In My Father's Arms*, 60.
53. De Milly, *In My Father's Arms*, 64.
54. De Milly, *In My Father's Arms*, 91.
55. De Milly, *In My Father's Arms*, 99.
56. De Milly, *In My Father's Arms*, 131.
57. De Milly, *In My Father's Arms*, 132.

4. MAKING MEANING OF SEXUAL ABUSE

1. CAPTA Reauthorization Act of 2010 (P.L. 111-320), retrieved from https://www.childwelfare.gov/systemwide/laws_policies/federal/index.cfm?event=federalLegislation.viewLegis&id=142.
2. J. Hendra and B. Morrison, *How to Cook Your Daughter* (New York: HarperCollins, 2009), 153.
3. Hendra and Morrison, *How to Cook Your Daughter*, 125.
4. Hendra and Morrison, *How to Cook Your Daughter*, 15.
5. C. McClain, *Murdering My Youth* (CreateSpace, 2014), 83.
6. McClain, *Murdering My Youth*, 19.
7. W. A. De Milly III, *In My Father's Arms* (Madison, WI: University of Wisconsin Press, 2012), 3.
8. De Milly, *In My Father's Arms*, 43.
9. De Milly, *In My Father's Arms*, 47.
10. De Milly, *In My Father's Arms*.
11. K. Matthews, *I Remember, Daddy* (London, England: HarperCollins, 2011), 228.
12. Not all sexually abused children feel enthralled by their abusive parent.
13. Hendra and Morrison, *How to Cook Your Daughter*, 101.
14. Hendra and Morrison, *How to Cook Your Daughter*, 9.
15. Hendra and Morrison, *How to Cook Your Daughter*, 151.
16. Hendra and Morrison, *How to Cook Your Daughter*.
17. Hendra and Morrison, *How to Cook Your Daughter*, 119.
18. T. Maguire, *Don't Tell Mummy* (London, England: HarperCollins, 2007), 143.
19. Dominic Carter, *No Momma's Boy* (New York: iUniverse, Inc., 2007), 48.
20. D. Baumrind, "Authoritarian vs. Authoritative Parental Control," *Adolescence* 3 (1969): 255–72
21. De Milly, *In My Father's Arms*, 32.
22. Matthews, *I Remember, Daddy*, 74.
23. Hendra and Morrison, *How to Cook Your Daughter*, 22.
24. Maguire, *Don't Tell Mummy*, 51.
25. Ibid. 71.
26. S. Julich, "Stockholm Syndrome and Child Sexual Abuse," *Journal of Child Sexual Abuse* 14, no. 3 (2005): 107–29
27. Hendra and Morrison, *How To Cook Your Daughter*, 52.
28. Carter, *No Mana's Boy*, 48.
29. De Milly, *In My Father's Arms*, 35.

30. In early writings about sexual abuse, it was believed that in most sexual abuse cases the nonoffending parent colluded with the abuser to allow the abuse to occur. This is no longer believed to be the case. It has been shown that many nonoffending parents have not colluded and truly did not know about the abuse.

31. S. Ferenczi, "Confusion of the Tongues between the Adults and the Child," *International Journal of Psychoanalysis 30* (1949): 225–30.

32. J. Frankel, "Identification with the Aggressor and the 'Normal Traumas': Clinical Implications," *International Forum of Psychoanalysis* 13, no. 1–2 (2004): 78–83.

33. E. Deblinger and A. H. Heflin, *Treating Sexually Abused Children and their Nonoffending Parents* (Thousand Oaks, CA: Sage Publications, 1996).

34. J. Briere, *Child Abuse Trauma* (Newbury Park, CA: Sage, 1992).

35. Ibid.

36. De Milly, *In My Father's Arms*, 23.

37. Ibid., 22.

38. Ibid., 35

39. Ibid., 46.

40. Ibid., 91.

41. Ibid., 32.

42. Briere, *Child Abuse Trauma*.

43. Maguire, *Don't Tell Mommy*, 265.

44. Matthews, *I Remember Daddy*, 51.

45. Ibid., 76.

46. Maguire, *Don't Tell Mommy*, 232.

47. McClain, *Murdering My Youth*, 35.

48. Carter, *No Mama's Boy*, 49.

49. De Milly, *In My Father's Arms*, 117.

50. Ibid., 89

51. Ibid., 35.

52. Carter, *No Mama's Boy*, 48.

53. Matthews, *I Remember, Daddy*, 77.

54. Maguire, *Don't Tell Mummy*, 226.

55. Hendra and Morrison, *How to Cook Your Daughter*, 166.

56. Ibid., 221.

57. De Milly, *In My Father's Arms*, 21.

58. McClain, *Murdering My Youth*, 236.

59. Carter, *No Mama's Boy*, 4.

5. STORIES OF EMOTIONAL ABUSE

1. M. Francis, *Diary of a Stage Mother's Daughter* (New York: Weinstein Books, 2012).

2. Francis, *Diary of a Stage Mother's Daughter*, 37.

3. Francis, *Diary of a Stage Mother's Daughter*, 4.

4. Francis, *Diary of a Stage Mother's Daughter*, 5.

5. Francis, *Diary of a Stage Mother's Daughter*, 3.

6. Francis, *Diary of a Stage Mother's Daughter*, 30.

7. Francis, *Diary of a Stage Mother's Daughter*, 1.

8. Francis, *Diary of a Stage Mother's Daughter*, 20.

9. Francis, *Diary of a Stage Mother's Daughter*, 19.

10. Francis, *Diary of a Stage Mother's Daughter*, 65.

11. Francis, *Diary of a Stage Mother's Daughter*, 25.

12. Francis, *Diary of a Stage Mother's Daughter*, 26–27.

13. Francis, *Diary of a Stage Mother's Daughter*, 29.

14. Francis, *Diary of a Stage Mother's Daughter*, 30.

15. Francis, *Diary of a Stage Mother's Daughter*, 78.

16. Francis, *Diary of a Stage Mother's Daughter*, 79.
17. Francis, *Diary of a Stage Mother's Daughter*, 283.
18. J. Gregory, *Sickened* (New York: Bantam Dell, 2003).
19. Gregory, *Sickened*, 4.
20. Gregory, *Sickened*, 5.
21. Gregory, *Sickened*, 21.
22. Gregory, *Sickened*, 49.
23. Gregory, *Sickened*, 55.
24. Gregory, *Sickened*.
25. Gregory, *Sickened*, 56–57.
26. Gregory, *Sickened*, 61.
27. Gregory, *Sickened*, 63.
28. Gregory, *Sickened*, 70.
29. Gregory, *Sickened*, 68.
30. Gregory, *Sickened*, 141.
31. Gregory, *Sickened*, 81.
32. Gregory, *Sickened*, 82.
33. Gregory, *Sickened*.
34. Gregory, *Sickened*, 84.
35. Gregory, *Sickened*, 84–85.
36. Gregory, *Sickened*, 86.
37. Gregory, *Sickened*, 95–96.
38. Gregory, *Sickened*, 117.
39. Gregory, *Sickened*.
40. Gregory, *Sickened*, 119.
41. Gregory, *Sickened*, 122.
42. Gregory, *Sickened*, 244.
43. Rachel Sontag, *House Rules* (New York: HarperCollins, 2009).
44. Sontag, *House Rules*, 9.
45. Sontag, *House Rules*, 18.
46. Sontag, *House Rules*, 1.
47. Sontag, *House Rules*, 8.
48. Sontag, *House Rules*, 34.
49. Sontag, *House Rules*, 51.
50. Sontag, *House Rules*, 22.
51. Sontag, *House Rules*, 23.
52. Sontag, *House Rules*.
53. Sontag, *House Rules*, 28.
54. Sontag, *House Rules*, 29.
55. Sontag, *House Rules*, 25.
56. Sontag, *House Rules*, 24.
57. . Sontag, *House Rules*, 40.
58. Sontag, *House Rules*, 26.
59. Sontag, *House Rules*.
60. Sontag, *House Rules*, 33.
61. Sontag, *House Rules*.
62. Sontag, *House Rules*, 67.
63. Sontag, *House Rules*, 66.
64. Sontag, *House Rules*, 126.
65. Sontag, *House Rules*, 65.
66. Sontag, *House Rules*, 97.
67. Sontag, *House Rules*.
68. Sontag, *House Rules*, 143.
69. Sontag, *House Rules*, 103.
70. Sontag, *House Rules*, 156.

6. MAKING MEANING OF EMOTIONAL ABUSE

1. N. J. Binggell, S. Hart, and M. Brassard, *Psychological Maltreatment of Children, APSAC Study Guides* (Thousand Oaks, CA: Sage, 2001).

2. Binggell, Hart, and Brassard, *Psychological Maltreatment of Children*, 6.

3. Binggell, Hart, and Brassard, *Psychological Maltreatment of Children*, 6.

4. Binggell, Hart, and Brassard, *Psychological Maltreatment of Children*, 6.

5. Binggell, Hart, and Brassard, *Psychological Maltreatment of Children*, 7.

6. N. I. Eisenberger, M. D. Lieberman, and K. D. Williams, "Does Rejection Hurt? An fMRI Study of Social Exclusion," *Science* 302 (2003): 290–92.

7. Adeline Yen Mah, *Falling Leaves* (New York: Broadway Books, 1997), 36.

8. Mah, *Falling Leaves*, 60.

9. Mah, *Falling Leaves*, 147.

10. Mah, *Falling Leaves*, 210.

11. Rachel Sontag, *House Rules* (New York: HarperCollins, 2009), 83.

12. Mah, *Falling Leaves*.

13. Felicia Sullivan, *The Sky Isn't Visible from Here* (Chapel Hill, NC: Algonquin Books, 2008), 238.

14. Laura Love, *You Ain't Got No Easter Clothes* (New York: Hyperion, 2004), 194.

15. Jeanette Winterson, *Why Be Happy When You Could Be Normal?* (London: Random House, 2011), 7.

16. At some point some abused children stop caring about being loved and approved of and defend themselves by isolating themselves emotionally, mistrusting the world and taking an angry, oppositional stance toward others and having difficulty forming emotionally close/intimate relationships.

17. Mah, *Falling Leaves*, 145.

18. Mah, *Falling Leaves*, 250.

19. Mah, *Falling Leaves*, 267.

20. Sontag, *House Rules*, 214.

21. Sontag, *House Rules*, 212.

22. Winterson, *Why Be Happy When You Could Be Normal?* 4.

23. Winterson, *Why Be Happy When You Could Be Normal?* 22.

24. Sullivan, *The Sky Isn't Visible from Here*, 24.

25. Sullivan, *The Sky Isn't Visible from Here*, 178.

26. Mah, *Falling Leaves*, 55.

27. Winterson, *Why Be Happy When You Could Be Normal?* 76.

28. Sullivan, *The Sky Isn't Visible from Here*, 27.

29. Sontag, *House Rules*, 65.

30. Susanna Sonnenberg, *Her Last Death* (New York: Scribner, 2009), 251.

31. Julie Gregory, *Sickened* (New York: Bantam Dell, 2003), 63.

32. D. Shaw, *Traumatic Narcissism* (New York: Routledge, 2013).

33. Shaw, *Traumatic Narcissism*, 3.

34. Shaw, *Traumatic Narcissism*, 28.

35. Shaw, *Traumatic Narcissism*, 34.

36. Shaw, *Traumatic Narcissism*.

37. Shaw, *Traumatic Narcissism*.

38. Shaw, *Traumatic Narcissism*, 35.

39. Shaw, *Traumatic Narcissism*.

40. Shaw, *Traumatic Narcissism*.

41. Shaw, *Traumatic Narcissism*.

42. Shaw, *Traumatic Narcissism*.

7. STORIES OF EMOTIONAL NEGLECT

1. K. Harrison, *The Kiss* (New York: Random House, 2011).
2. Harrison, *The Kiss*, 5.
3. Harrison, *The Kiss*, 7.
4. Harrison, *The Kiss*.
5. Harrison, *The Kiss*, 9.
6. Harrison, *The Kiss*, 5.
7. Harrison, *The Kiss*, 13.
8. Harrison, *The Kiss*.
9. Harrison, *The Kiss*.
10. Harrison, *The Kiss*, 19.
11. Harrison, *The Kiss*, 20.
12. Harrison, *The Kiss*, 48.
13. Harrison, *The Kiss*, 79.
14. Harrison, *The Kiss*, 89.
15. Harrison, *The Kiss*, 86.
16. Harrison, *The Kiss*, 99.
17. Harrison, *The Kiss*, 193.
18. C. Slaughter, *Before the Knife* (New York: Knopf, 2002).
19. Slaughter, *Before the Knife*, 3.
20. Slaughter, *Before the Knife*, 7.
21. Slaughter, *Before the Knife*, 15.
22. Slaughter, *Before the Knife*, 16.
23. Slaughter, *Before the Knife*, 27.
24. Slaughter, *Before the Knife*.
25. Slaughter, *Before the Knife*, 28.
26. Slaughter, *Before the Knife*, 17.
27. Slaughter, *Before the Knife*, 49.
28. Slaughter, *Before the Knife*, 51.
29. Slaughter, *Before the Knife*, 62.
30. Slaughter, *Before the Knife*, 63.
31. Slaughter, *Before the Knife*, 83.
32. Slaughter, *Before the Knife*.
33. L. M. Flynn, *Swallow the Ocean* (Berkeley, CA: Counterpoint Press, 2008).
34. Flynn, *Swallow the Ocean*, 11.
35. Flynn, *Swallow the Ocean*, 19.
36. Flynn, *Swallow the Ocean*, 84.
37. Flynn, *Swallow the Ocean*, 83–84.
38. Flynn, *Swallow the Ocean*, 88.
39. Flynn, *Swallow the Ocean*, 99.
40. Flynn, *Swallow the Ocean*, 101.
41. Flynn, *Swallow the Ocean*, 132.
42. Flynn, *Swallow the Ocean*, 134.
43. Flynn, *Swallow the Ocean*, 144.
44. Flynn, *Swallow the Ocean*, 205.
45. Flynn, *Swallow the Ocean*, 207.
46. Flynn, *Swallow the Ocean*, 256.
47. Flynn, *Swallow the Ocean*, 264.

8. MAKING MEANING OF EMOTIONAL NEGLECT

1. N. J. Binggell, S. Hart, and M. Brassard, *Psychological Maltreatment of Children, APSAC Study Guides* (Thousand Oaks, CA: Sage, 2001).

2. Binggell, Hart, and Brassard, *Psychological Maltreatment of Children*, 8.

3. K. Kennedy, B. Curtis, and S. Spielberg, *A.I. A.I. Artificial Intelligence* [Motion picture]. United States: Warner Bros. Pictures, 2001.

4. K. Harrison, *The Kiss* (New York: Random House, 2011), 99.

5. T. E. Holley and T. J. Holley, *My Mother's Keeper* (New York: William Morrow, 1997), 40.

6. Holley and Holley, *My Mother's Keeper*, 147.

7. Holley and Holley, *My Mother's Keeper*, 18.

8. A. Rhodes-Courter, *Three Little Words* (New York: Atheneum, 2008), 2.

9. Rhodes-Courter, *Three Little Words*, 288.

10. Rhodes-Courter, *Three Little Words*, 163.

11. S. Chin, *The Other Side of Paradise* (New York: Scribner, 2010), 172.

12. J. Bowlby, *Attachment* (New York: Basic Books, 1969).

13. B. Perry, "Bonding and Attachment in Maltreated Children: Consequences of Emotional Neglect in Childhood," *Child Trauma Academy* 1, no. 3 (2001): 3.

14. M. Bartok, *The Memory Palace* (New York: Free Press, 2011), 241.

15. C. Slaughter, *Before the Knife* (New York: Knopf, 2002), 17.

16. Slaughter, *Before the Knife*, 16.

17. Lawless, *Chanel Bonfire* (New York: Gallery Books, 2013), 13.

18. Holley and Holley, *My Mother's Keeper*, 121.

19. Holley and Holley, *My Mother's Keeper*, 18.

20. Holley and Holley, *My Mother's Keeper*, 328.

21. Rhodes-Courter, *Three Little Words*, 75.

22. Rhodes-Courter, *Three Little Words*, 20.

23. Rhodes-Courter, *Three Little Words*, 1.

24. L. M. Flynn, *Swallow the Ocean* (Berkeley, CA: Counterpoint Press, 2008), 123.

25. Harrison, *The Kiss*, 13–14.

26. Holley and Holley, *My Mother's Keeper*, 328.

27. Chin, *The Other Side of Paradise*, 85.

28. Rhodes-Courter, *Three Little Words*, 240.

29. Rhodes-Courter, *Three Little Words*, 239.

30. W. Burden, *Dead End Gene Pool* (New York: Gotham, 2010), 128.

31. A. Burroughs, *Running with Scissors* (New York: Picador, 2003), 49.

32. Lawless, *Chanel Bonfire*, 39.

33. Bartok, *The Memory Palace*, 31.

34. R. Herz, *The Scent of Desire* (New York: HarperCollins, 2008), 3.

35. Herz, *The Scent of Desire*, 11.

36. Herz, *The Scent of Desire*, 14.

37. M. Proust, *Remembrance of Things Past*, Vol. 1, trans. C. K. Scott Moncrieff and Terence Kilmartin (New York: Vintage, 1981).

38. S. B. Kendall, "Preference for Intermittent Reinforcement," *Journal of Experimental Analysis of Behavior* 21, no. 3 (1974): 463–73.

39. Burden, *Dead End Gene Pool*, 18.

40. Burden, *Dead End Gene Pool*, 109.

41. Chin, *The Other Side of Paradise*, 90.

42. Holley and Holley, *My Mother's Keeper*, 17.

43. Holley and Holley, *My Mother's Keeper*, 118–19.

44. Holley and Holley, *My Mother's Keeper*, 18.

45. W. Lawless, *Chanel Bonfire*, 77.

46. Chin, *The Other Side of Paradise*, 102.

47. Harrison, *The Kiss*, 7–8.

48. Slaughter, *Before the Knife*, 49.
49. J. Darst, *Fiction Ruined My Family* (New York: Penguin, 2012), 59.
50. Chin, *The Other Side of Paradise*, 101.
51. Chin, *The Other Side of Paradise*, 100.
52. Flynn, *Swallow the Ocean*, 149.
53. H. C. Barrett, and T. Behne, "Children's Understanding of Death as the Cessation of Agency: A Test Using Sleep versus Death," *Cognition* 96, no. 2 (2005): 1–16.
54. Bartok, *The Memory Palace*, 66.
55. Harrison, *The Kiss*, 48.
56. Flynn, *Swallow the Ocean*, 222.
57. Lawless, *Chanel Bonfire*, 132.
58. Lawless, *Chanel Bonfire*, 112.
59. Lawless, *Chanel Bonfire*, 110.
60. Harrison, *The Kiss*, 14.
61. Bartok, *The Memory Palace*, 76.
62. Harrison, *The Kiss*, 9.
63. Harrison, *The Kiss*, 8.
64. Harrison, *The Kiss*, 39.
65. Holley and Holley, *My Mother's Keeper*, 161.
66. Holley and Holley, *My Mother's Keeper*, 242.
67. Flynn, *Swallow the Ocean*, 132.
68. Flynn, *Swallow the Ocean*, 188.
69. Burroughs, *Running with Scissors*, 140.
70. Burroughs, *Running with Scissors*, 85.
71. Burroughs, *Running with Scissors*, 66.
72. S. G. Thomas, *In Spite of Everything* (New York: Random House, 2011), 40.
73. Lawless, *Chanel Bonfire*, 68.
74. Lawless, *Chanel Bonfire*, 100.
75. Darst, *Fiction Ruined My Family*, 194.
76. Slaughter, *Before the Knife*, 15.
77. Burroughs, *Running with Scissors*, 125.
78. Burroughs, *Running with Scissors*, 120.
79. Darst, *Fiction Ruined My Family*, 6.
80. Darst, *Fiction Ruined My Family*, 85.
81. J. Woititz, *Adult Children of Alcoholics* (Deerfield Beach, FL: Health Communications, Inc., 1990).
82. Harrison, *The Kiss*, 78.
83. Harrison, *The Kiss*, 103–4.
84. Slaughter, *Before the Knife*, 16.
85. Holley and Holley, *My Mother's Keeper*, 90.
86. Holley and Holley, *My Mother's Keeper*, 164.
87. Lawless, *Chanel Bonfire*, 7.
88. Rhodes-Courter, *Three Little Words*, 1.
89. Darst, *Fiction Ruined My Family*, 204–5.
90. Slaughter, *Before the Knife*, 49–50.
91. Holley and Holley, *My Mother's Keeper*, 165.
92. Holley and Holley, *My Mother's Keeper*, 185.
93. Holley and Holley, *My Mother's Keeper*, 239.
94. Flynn, *Swallow the Ocean*, 229.
95. Rhodes-Courter, *Three Little Words*, 117.
96. Burroughs, *Running with Scissors*, 95.
97. Chin, *The Other Side of Paradise*, 88.

9. STORIES OF PHYSICAL NEGLECT

1. J. Walls, *The Glass Castle* (New York: Scribner, 2006).
2. Walls, *The Glass Castle*, 68.
3. Walls, *The Glass Castle*, 69.
4. Walls, *The Glass Castle*, 3.
5. Walls, *The Glass Castle*, 31.
6. Walls, *The Glass Castle*, 59.
7. Walls, *The Glass Castle*, 23.
8. Walls, *The Glass Castle*, 24.
9. Walls, *The Glass Castle*, 79.
10. Walls, *The Glass Castle*, 210.
11. Walls, *The Glass Castle*, 218.
12. Walls, *The Glass Castle*, 228.
13. Walls, *The Glass Castle*, 237.
14. Walls, *The Glass Castle*, 245.
15. K. Crews, *Burn Down the Ground* (New York: Random House Creations, 2012).
16. Crews, *Burn Down the Ground*, 21.
17. Crews, *Burn Down the Ground*, 7.
18. Crews, *Burn Down the Ground*, 27.
19. Crews, *Burn Down the Ground*, 17.
20. Crews, *Burn Down the Ground*, 34.
21. Crews, *Burn Down the Ground*, 35.
22. Crews, *Burn Down the Ground*, 51.
23. Crews, *Burn Down the Ground*, 63.
24. Crews, *Burn Down the Ground*, 73.
25. Crews, *Burn Down the Ground*, 84.
26. Crews, *Burn Down the Ground*, 101.
27. Crews, *Burn Down the Ground*, 116.
28. Crews, *Burn Down the Ground*, 118.
29. Crews, *Burn Down the Ground*, 150.
30. Crews, *Burn Down the Ground*, 167.
31. Crews, *Burn Down the Ground*, 169.
32. Crews, *Burn Down the Ground*, 183.
33. Crews, *Burn Down the Ground*, 211.
34. Crews, *Burn Down the Ground*, 237.
35. Crews, *Burn Down the Ground*, 251.
36. Crews, *Burn Down the Ground*, 334.
37. L. Murray, *Breaking Night* (New York: Hyperion, 2010).
38. Murray, *Breaking Night*, 5.
39. Murray, *Breaking Night*, 13.
40. Murray, *Breaking Night*, 44.
41. Murray, *Breaking Night*, 48.
42. Murray, *Breaking Night*, 49.
43. Murray, *Breaking Night*, 50.
44. Murray, *Breaking Night*.
45. Murray, *Breaking Night*, 51.
46. Murray, *Breaking Night*, 55.
47. Murray, *Breaking Night*, 56.
48. Murray, *Breaking Night*, 72.
49. Murray, *Breaking Night*, 123.

10. MAKING MEANING OF PHYSICAL NEGLECT

1. CAPTA Reauthorization Act of 2010 (P.L. 111-320), retrieved from https://www.childwelfare.gov/systemwide/laws_policies/federal/index.cfm?event=federalLegislation.viewLegis&id=142.

2. B. E. van Sleuwen, A. C. Engleberts, M. Boere-Boonekamp, W. Kuis, T. W. J. Schulpen, and M. P. L'Hoir, "Swaddling: A Systematic Review," *Pediatrics* 120, no. 4 (2007): 2006–83.

3. J. Walls, *The Glass Castle* (New York: Scribner, 2006), 172.

4. Walls, *The Glass Castle*, 28.

5. K. R. Miller, *Coming Clean* (New York: New Harvest, 2014), 9, 70, 90, 92.

6. J. Sholl, *Dirty Secret* (New York: Gallery Books, 2014), 169.

7. Miller, *Coming Clean*, 90.

8. Miller, *Coming Clean*, 92.

9. L. Murray, *Breaking Night* (New York: Hyperion, 2010), 77

10. K. Crews, *Burn Down the Ground* (New York: Random House Creations, 2012), 27.

11. Crews, *Burn Down the Ground*, 43.

12. Crews, *Burn Down the Ground*, 237.

13. Crews, *Burns Down the Ground*, 118.

14. Sholl, *Dirty Secret*, 41.

15. Murray, *Breaking Night*, 51.

16. Murray, *Breaking Night*, 38.

17. F. McCourt, *Angela's Ashes* (New York: Touchstone, 1991), 193.

18. Miller, *Coming Clean*, 70.

19. McCourt, *Angela's Ashes*, 75.

20. McCourt, *Angela's Ashes*, 98.

21. Walls, *The Glass Castle*, 174.

22. Walls, *The Glass Castle*, 186.

23. Walls, *The Glass Castle*.

24. Sholl, *Dirty Secret*, 90.

25. Murray, *Breaking Night*, 72.

26. Sholl, *Dirty Secret*, 189.

27. Murray, *Breaking Night*, 49.

28. Sholl, *Dirty Secret*, 304.

29. Murray, *Breaking Night*, 55.

30. Murray, *Breaking Night*, 51.

31. Murray, *Breaking Night*, 51.

32. Sholl, *Dirty Secret*, 55.

33. Sholl, *Dirty Secret*, 297.

34. Walls, *The Glass Castle*, 196.

11. MOVING FORWARD

1. K. Kennedy, B. Curtis, and S. Spielberg, *A.I. Artificial Intelligence* [Motion picture]. United States: Warner Brothers, 2001.

2. Kennedy, Curtis, and Spielberg, *A.I. Artificial Intelligence*.

3. N. Doidge, *The Brain That Changes Itself: Stories of Personal Triumph from the Frontiers of Brain Science* (New York: Penguin, 2007).

4. J. E. Young and J. S. Klosko, *Reinventing your Life* (New York: Plume, 1994).

5. B. A. van der Kolk, "The Compulsion to Repeat the Trauma," *Psychiatric Clinics of North America* 12, no. 2 (1989): 389–411.

6. F. Shapiro, *EMDR* (New York: Guilford Press, 2001).

7. P. Levine, *Healing Trauma: A Pioneering Program for Restoring the Wisdom of Your Body* (Boulder, CO: Sounds True, 2008).

8. D. J. Kolko and C. Swenson, *Assessing and Treating Physically Abused Children and Their Families*(Thousand Oaks, CA: Sage, 2002).

9. National Child Traumatic Stress Network, http://www.nctsn.org/resources/topics/treatments-that-work/promising-practices.

10. J. Pennebaker, *Opening Up: The Healing Power of Expressing Emotions* (New York: Guilford Press, 1997).

11. "Bessel van der Kolk Discusses EMDR," https://www.youtube.com/watch?v=Y2cPuv6jKqg.

12. Kolko and Swenson, *Assessing and Treating Physically Abused Children and Their Families*.

13. Kennedy, Curtis, and Spielberg, *A.I. Artificial Intelligence.*

14. J. Herman, *Trauma and Recovery* (New York: Basic Books, 1997), 8.

15. S. L. Toth, D. Cicchetti, F. Rogosch, and M. Sturge-Apple, "Maternal Depression, Children's Attachment Security, and Representational Development: An Organizational Perspective," *Child Development* 80, no 1 (2009): 192–208.

16. M. Main, N. Kaplan, and J. Cassidy, "Security in Infancy, Childhood, and Adulthood: A Move to the Level of Representation," *Monographs of the Society for Research in Child Development* 50, no. 1–2, Serial No. 209) (1985).

17. G. Orwell, *1984* (New York: Signet, 1950).

18. D. Tutu and M. Tutu, *The Book of Forgiving* (New York: Harper Collins, 2014).

19. L. Graham, *Bouncing Back: Rewiring your Brain for Maximum Resilience and Well-Being* (Novato, CA: New World Library, 2013).

20. Graham, *Bouncing Back*.

Index

About the Authors

Dr. Amy J. L. Baker is director of research at the Vincent J. Fontana Center for Child Protection. She is a nationally recognized leader and expert in the field of abused children (especially in the area of parental alienation and loyalty conflicts). She has conducted several original empirical research studies on abused children (including sexual abuse victims, children in residential treatment due to abuse or neglect, children in foster care). She has written eight books on topics related to children's well-being and over seventy peer review publications.

Dr. Mel Schneiderman is senior vice president of Mental Health Services at the New York Foundling and is co-founder and senior advisor and chair of the Research Advisory Committee at the Vincent J. Fontana Center for Child Protection. Dr. Schneiderman founded the first child sexual abuse treatment program located within a child welfare agency in 1986. Dr. Schneiderman has been a leader in the field of child welfare for the past thirty years. He was one of the founders and first chair of the Committee of Mental Health and Healthcare Professionals in New York City. Dr. Schneiderman introduced the first agency-wide universal mental health screening program for children entering foster care in New York City. He is currently the president of the American Professional Society on the Abuse of Children-New York. He has served on several boards and presented at over fifty conferences and workshops; he is the recipient of numerous grants and has published several articles in peer reviewed journals.